TVA

and Black Americans

TVA
and Black Americans

Planning for the Status Quo

Nancy L. Grant

TEMPLE UNIVERSITY PRESS
PHILADELPHIA

Temple University Press,
Philadelphia 19122

Printed in the United States of America

The paper used in this publication meets the
minimum requirements of American National
Standard for Information Sciences—Permanence
of Paper for Printed Library Materials,
ANSI Z39.48-1984

Library of Congress
Cataloging-in-Publication Data

Grant, Nancy, date
TVA and Black Americans : planning for the
status quo / Nancy L. Grant.
p.   cm.
Bibliography: p.
Includes index.
ISBN 0-87722-626-1 (alk. paper)
1. Afro-Americans—Tennessee River Valley—
Relocation—History—20th century.
2. Tennessee Valley Authority.   3. Tennessee
River Valley—Race relations.   4. Afro-
Americans—Employment—Tennessee—
River Valley.   I. Title.
F217.T3G73   1990
976.8′00496073—dc19   88-38515

Frontispiece:
Jackhammer operators,
Douglas Dam, 1942.
(TVA Technical Library)

For my parents,
James Earl and Julia Bee Grant

CONTENTS

ILLUSTRATIONS

FIGURES, TABLE, AND MAP

ACKNOWLEDGMENTS

IN the preparation of this book, I received assistance from many individuals. Constructive criticism and indispensable aid was given by John Hope Franklin and Barry Karl, under whom I had the good fortune to study at the University of Chicago. Many helpful suggestions on the book came from Vincent Franklin, George Fredrickson, Raymond Hall, Richard Lowitt, Sterling Stuckey, Robert Wiebe, and James Wright.

My search for information was made much easier by the library staffs of the Southern Historical Collection at the University of North Carolina; the Trevor Arnett Library at Atlanta University; the Franklin Roosevelt Presidential Library in Hyde Park, New York; the Rockefeller Foundation Archives in Pocantico Hills, New York; and the National Archives and Library of Congress in Washington, D.C.

A special note should be made of the extraordinary cooperation of the TVA. The library staff, particularly Jesse Mills and Willie Mae Howard, facilitated the gathering of difficult-to-find documents and papers and paved the way for numerous interviews with TVA officials and retired employees. The photography staff headed by Robert Kollar found the stark photos of blacks in the Tennessee valley that appear in the book. The Equal Employment Opportunity Office was equally helpful. While in their employment as a summer researcher, I was able to get a better understanding of the TVA bureaucracy. All the individuals whom I asked for interviews were gracious and candid, and J. Max Bond, J. Herman Daves, Walter Goldston, and Guy Johnson in particular gave liberally of their time. Through them, I learned to appreciate the modern application of the term, "southern hospitality."

Some of the analysis presented in Chapter IV is borrowed from my article, "Government Social Planning and Education for Blacks: The TVA Experience, 1933–1945," which appeared in *Education and the Rise of the New South*, ed. Ronald Goodenow and Arthur White (Boston: G. K. Hall, 1981). Used with permission of G. K. Hall and Co., Boston.

Over a period of years I received research support from the National Research Council, the National Fellowships Fund, Northwestern University, and Dartmouth College. I also owe much to the many important suggestions offered by Michael Ames and the rest of the staff of Temple University Press. Finally, my friends and family, particularly my parents and my husband, Harold, gave me the encouragement to get the job done.

THIS is a book about the treatment of blacks by the Tennessee Valley Authority during the New Deal and World War II. It is a study that examines one corner of the New Deal, physically defined by the seven-state watershed of the Tennessee River and its tributaries; economically defined by the marginal farmlands and industry-poor cities; and socially defined by the customs of an Upper South that segregated on the basis of race in education, employment, social services, and politics. The book also examines the promises made by Franklin Roosevelt and the TVA board of directors in 1933 to bring hope and prosperity to all valley inhabitants, both black and white. In the area of race relations, TVA promised a policy of non-discrimination in its hiring and training programs. In this corner, however, definitions remained vague, separations became indistinct, and promises were sometimes broken. Valley residents, though separated by race and class, were linked by economic hardships. The TVA, headquartered in Knoxville with the promise of administrative autonomy, was nevertheless closely linked to Washington, answering to the complaints of Congress, the courts, and the White House. Finally, promises of revitalization and change dissolved into the reality of the racial status quo for blacks living and working in the valley.

TVA and Black Americans is organized along topical rather than strictly chronological lines in order to analyze the breadth of TVA activities in employment and regional development. The treatment of blacks by TVA changed slowly in the years 1933 to 1945. Changes that did occur in the hiring and promotion of black employees, as well as plans for Tennessee valley black communities, were made largely in response to threatened lawsuits or investigations by the National Association for the Advancement of Colored People (NAACP) and the Fair Employment Practices Committee (FEPC). The latter was a government committee established in 1941 by Roosevelt to investigate complaints of racial discrimination in war-related industries and in departments and agencies of the federal government. An aura of unalterable sameness in racial policy pervaded TVA official correspondence, statistical reports, and internal memoranda.

The book is divided into seven chapters. Chapter I examines the promise of the Tennessee Valley Authority as described by New Deal politicians, TVA administrators, publicists, journalists, and other interested parties. This promise is presented within the broad context of social planning as well as within the specific context of race relations. A brief legislative history is presented to place the Tennessee Valley Authority Act of 1933 in a historical context, for this bill was different in scope from any previous river development bill. To understand the multifaceted appeal of the promise, it is necessary to understand the conditions for blacks and whites in the valley on the eve of the passage of the act. Chapter II looks at the reality of TVA and how such factors as the utilization of the planning powers granted under the act, the reliance on "grass-roots democracy," the impact of a decentralized administrative structure, and the racial attitudes of TVA officials affected the formulation and implementation of racial policies. One such policy was the use of racial quotas to ensure a proportionate representation of blacks. The quota system was applied only to unskilled work and was subject to statistical manipulation favorable to TVA. Chapter III evaluates TVA as an employer of blacks. Blacks were offered jobs as janitors, unskilled and semiskilled construction workers, and fertilizer plant operators. In 1933 there was one black supervisor in TVA: the head of Negro training. In 1945 there were two black professionals: the head of Negro training and a chemist. A central dilemma within TVA was finding a hiring and promotional policy acceptable to civil rights activists without alienating local and national political allies or skilled craft unions. TVA's support of local craft unions and the formation of the Tennessee Valley Trades and Labor Council earned the agency respect in liberal and labor circles, but the racially exclusionary policies of these unions further restricted employment opportunities for blacks in all phases of construction.

Chapter IV focuses on the issues of long-range planning for blacks, including vocational training programs, relocation efforts, park development, and model community construction. These efforts to provide supportive services for blacks are placed in the larger context of an entire valley population undergoing the stresses of forced relocations, an influx of "outsiders," and changes in lifestyles and societal expectations. In an effort to avoid controversy and opposition from local white politicians and community leaders, TVA carefully adhered to the valley practices of racial segregation in schools and communities, and restricted economic opportunities for blacks.

Chapter V discusses the reactions of blacks and other interested parties within civil rights organizations and government committees to the plans and programs of TVA. The NAACP and local black organizations were highly critical of TVA's employment policies and long-range plans. The NAACP launched a spirited though largely unsuccessful campaign of political lobbying and threatened lawsuits to force TVA to change its policies. Chapter VI examines the more successful efforts of the FEPC both to investigate complaints brought before it by black TVA employees and to pressure TVA to change its discriminatory policies. Established by Executive Order 8802, the FEPC was authorized to investigate complaints of discrimination on the basis of race, creed, national origin, or religion in private industries under contract with the federal government as well as in government agencies and departments. Always protective of its administrative and personnel autonomy, TVA regarded the antidiscrimination directives from the FEPC not only as regionally insensitive but also as an unwarranted intrusion from an outside governmental force. Chapter VII offers concluding comments and an epilogue on conditions in TVA in the post–World War II period. As the South gradually shed its overt patterns of racial discrimination, so did TVA, although more subtle patterns remained into a more recent time.

The history of blacks during the New Deal and World War II has been the subject of several monographs published in the 1970s and 1980s. Historians of this subject have cast their nets widely, either electing to examine and compare the treatment of blacks in a number of agencies and departments or analyzing the political process and voting behavior of blacks.[1]

This study borrows from government policy analyses, regional and social planning studies, and New Deal political and social histories, as well as studies on southern race relations. I came upon the study of blacks in the TVA through several diverse though connected sources: my general interest in the impact of federal programs on the lives of blacks; my interest in the scope of social and regional planning during the New Deal; my search for southern liberalism during this period. All three channeled into my study of TVA, the southern governmental agency known for its liberalism and experimentation in social and regional planning. Its location in the Upper South also gave it a sizable and diverse black population that questioned and challenged TVA's liberal profile and its social planning powers.

TVA was established by Congress as a permanent agency of the federal government. Indeed, it has survived over fifty years of periodic attempts by Republican administrations to sell the dams and reservoirs to the highest bidder from the private sector. It offers an opportunity to examine race relations in an agency over an extended period, in peace and in war.

As a child of the 1960s, I was always fascinated by the period of American history that I considered to be the closest in scope and impact to the Great Society of Lyndon Johnson. I saw poverty, racial inequality, and an unpopular war as unmet challenges, despite the centralization and apparent commitment of the Johnson administration. I wondered to what extent the challenge of racial inequality had been met or even addressed during an earlier era when government centralization was in a nascent form and the commitment to racial equality absent from all but a few segments of the New Deal.

Moreover, as a member of a black family whose principal provider was a government employee, I had been imbued with the idea that the federal government was a good employer of blacks, certainly offering more security and opportunity for advancement than private employers. The role of the federal government as a good employer of blacks was just one of several Afro-American canons for social and economic advancement. Other canons were the roles of the federal government as a protector of blacks and as a provider of services. These perceived roles predated the Great Society and the New Deal and can be traced to the efforts of the Lincoln administration to abolish slavery and the efforts of Reconstruction Congresses to obtain and preserve the citizenship rights of the newly freed blacks by the passage of the fourteenth and fifteenth amendments.

To protect blacks from violence in the states of the former Confederacy, Congress passed the 1870 Force Acts. Although found unconstitutional in an 1883 Supreme Court decision, these acts for a time provided federal protection for blacks and authorized the use of federal troops against the Ku Klux Klan, a white terrorist organization. The protective and supportive role of the federal government diminished considerably as the United States moved away from the tenets of Reconstruction in the 1870s and toward the ideology of imperialism and the white man's burden by the turn of the twentieth century. Republican presidents from Rutherford B. Hayes through William Howard Taft continued to appoint a few blacks to the traditional "Negro" federal posts. Blacks who were able to vote continued to show allegiance to the party of Lincoln. The nadir of federal support for blacks occurred during the presidency of Woodrow Wilson, who encouraged the efforts of southern congressmen to repeal the fourteenth and fifteenth amendments and sanctioned the segregation of the U.S. Civil Service and federal government worksites in Washington, D.C. The presidencies of Harding, Coolidge, and Hoover did not bring about much improvement.[2]

On the eve of the New Deal, the image of the federal government as protector and employer of blacks had tarnished considerably. Yet blacks and civil rights organizations still considered the federal government to be the best source of legal redress, the best employer, and at times the only protector against riots and lynchings. Indeed, the NAACP throughout the World War I years and the 1920s litigated in the federal court system to end segregation and lobbied in Congress for an antilynching bill.[3]

The Great Depression exacerbated the already precarious position of blacks and made them more vulnerable and in need of protection and relief services from the federal government. During the 1920s blacks had actually lost ground in jobs that had become desirable as a result of technical improvement or the raising of wage scales through unionization. Blacks lost heavily as railroad firemen, as boilermakers, as machinists, and in the building trades generally. In the South, blacks suffered along with other agricultural workers and tenant farmers through the decade-long recession in crop prices and the ravages of the boll weevil and the Mississippi River. After the crash of 1929, unemployed whites took over traditional "Negro" jobs as waiters, bellmen, porters, and truck drivers. The Depression curtailed occupational gains that blacks had made in such industries as iron, steel, meat packing, shipbuilding, and auto manufacturing.[4]

The impact of the federal government on the lives of all Americans, including blacks, increased markedly for better and for worse during the New Deal. Indeed, during the twelve years that this book covers, extraordinary changes in the function and scope of government took place. Although many of the New Deal programs had their roots in earlier reform actions, the New Deal of Franklin Roosevelt was a departure in kind, as well as degree, from its predecessors. Roosevelt issued the call for change in his inaugural address, given 4 March 1933: "I shall ask the Congress for the one remaining instrument to meet the crisis—broad executive power to wage against the emergency, as great as the power that would be given me if we were in fact invaded by a foreign foe."[5]

In the first one hundred days, Roosevelt sent fifteen requests, and Congress returned fifteen pieces of legislation, including acts that took the United States off the gold standard, and created the Agricultural Adjustment Administration (AAA), which channeled money to millions of farmers. In addition, Congress established the National Recovery Administration (NRA), which provided mechanisms for regulating wages, hours, and working conditions in industry, and the Federal Emergency Relief Administration (FERA), which channeled money and relief services to the destitute and unemployed.[6]

During the next seven years, Roosevelt was forced to contend with an increasingly resistant Congress and an uncooperative Supreme Court, which found the NRA and the AAA to be unconstitutional. Nevertheless,

Roosevelt and Congress did create the Rural Electrification Administration, so that American farmers could receive electricity; the National Labor Relations Board, to mediate and investigate worker and employer disputes; the Social Security Administration, to provide unemployment insurance, old age pensions, and relief for dependent children and the handicapped; and the Farm Security Administration (FSA), to provide farmers with loans to avoid bankruptcy and to provide tenants with loans to buy their first farms. By 1940 Roosevelt had greatly expanded the scope and role of the federal government. The federal government became the source of public services and relief for the unemployed and the underemployed, protected the investments and savings of the middle class, and took an interest in the conditions of farmers and industrial workers.[7]

Under Roosevelt, moreover, the federal government expanded in size and became important as an employer as well as a supplier of services. In order to fulfill its expanded role, the government bureaucracy increased the number of civilian federal employees from 580,000 in 1929 to 1,042,000 in 1940. The federal budget increased from 3.0 percent of the gross national product to 9.1 percent.[8]

The number of civilian government employees continued to expand during World War II, from 1 million to over 3.8 million. Although economic emergency programs and public works projects were abandoned during the war, many New Deal agencies remained intact or even expanded, including the Social Security Administration and TVA. New agencies, such as the War Production Board, were established to regulate the conversion of factories to military production. The War Manpower Commission coordinated the labor pool among the military, defense industries, agriculture, and essential civilian production. In 1943 the FEPC was placed under the jurisdiction of the War Manpower Commission. The War Labor Board was created to settle management-labor disputes in war industries and avoid a recurrence of the strikes and labor unrest that had occurred during World War I. Responding to an unwarranted concern for national security, the War Department evacuated more than 110,000 Japanese-Americans and settled them in concentration camps under the control of the new War Relocation Authority. Other new agencies coordinated transportation, prepared propaganda, and censored foreign communications.[9]

The nation's employment picture changed dramatically during World War II. The unemployment rate, which had remained above 20 percent throughout the 1930s, dropped to the point that in 1943 the United States achieved full employment. The civilian labor pool was depleted by the absence of the 16 million men who served in the armed forces during the war. To fill the labor vacuum, industries turned to women. Between 1940 and 1945 the female labor pool jumped by 50 percent as the number of women working outside the home increased from 11,970,000 in 1940 to 18,610,000 in 1945.[10]

Black Americans, men and women, were included in the expansion of governmental services during the New Deal and World War II, although not to the extent of satisfying the contemporary black critics of the New Deal, who sought nothing less than the elimination of the continued economic disparity between the races. Yet black Americans indicated that they considered Roosevelt to be their best chance for economic survival during the Depression. For the first time since the passage of the fourteenth and fifteenth amendments, blacks switched their allegiance from the Republican party to the New Deal Democrats. While support for Roosevelt did not reach its height until the 1936 and 1940 elections, sentiment against the inaction of the Hoover administration was so intense in 1932 that Robert Vann, publisher of the *Pittsburgh Courier*, a black weekly, could suggest that blacks "go home and turn Lincoln's picture to the wall. The debt has been paid in full." [11]

The public image of Franklin Roosevelt as a man who understood suffering and deplored human exploitation also helped make him the most attractive president to blacks since Lincoln. This humane image was strengthened by statements such as one he made to the black president of the North Carolina Mutual Life Insurance Company, promising to "aid the nation toward recovery by providing necessary assistance and regulatory measures for all persons without regard to race." The reputation of Eleanor Roosevelt as a champion of civil rights causes, including an antilynching bill and desegregation statutes, further enhanced her husband's stature in the eyes of blacks.[12]

Roosevelt's commitment to racial equality was tempered by his background and views on race and by what he considered to be political realities. He was a careful, politically astute president whose racial attitudes reflected a patrician's sense of noblesse oblige and whose political behavior was calculated to avoid conflict with powerful southern Democrats who wished to maintain segregation and discrimination in their region as well as existing patterns in agriculture and industry. Majority Leader Joseph Robinson of Arkansas, Finance Committee Chair Byron Harrison of Mississippi, James Byrnes of South Carolina, John Rankin of Mississippi, and John Sparkman of Alabama, among others, were supporters of the New Deal whom Roosevelt did not wish to alienate through significant reforms in race relations.[13]

The lack of such reforms prompted criticism from civil rights organizations. Roosevelt was not its target, although he was the acknowledged leader and decision-maker of his administration; he remained popular in the black press and was praised by the leaders of the NAACP and the National Urban League. Administrators of New Deal agencies and cabinet officers received the brunt of this criticism.

The NRA, created out of the National Industrial Recovery Act (NIRA), was the first to draw the ire of civil rights groups. T. Arnold Hill of the Urban League called Hugh Johnson, the NRA administrator, "a complete failure" for not recognizing the proper position of blacks. The NRA was given broad powers to determine codes of fair practices that would stipulate maximum hours, minimum wages, and collective bargaining. Bowing to southern Democratic pressure, the NRA allowed for a lower southern wage rate based on a perceived lower standard of living in the region. Although the NRA did not officially sanction a "Negro differential," companies used various techniques to evade sanctioned minimum wages, thus excluding some blacks from coverage and misclassifying others. Blacks who worked as domestics, farm laborers, and "yard" workers in various industries were not covered and could therefore be paid below the minimum wage.[14]

In response to discrimination in the NRA, John Preston Davis, a young black lawyer, and Robert Weaver, a black economist, organized the Joint Committee on National Recovery. This organization, which listed forty-two cooperating organizations including the NAACP and the Federal Council of Churches, was actually a two-man advocacy team that filed briefs, made investigative reports, and wrote articles critical of NRA policies. Their efforts led to minor changes in the bituminous coal codes. After the NRA was found unconstitutional in 1935, the Joint Committee turned its energies to other New Deal agencies, including TVA.[15]

The AAA also failed to address the needs of black farmers, particularly black tenant farmers. Many tenant farmers and sharecroppers were forced off their rented land when the AAA began paying farm owners to reduce their crops or plow them under. It was the policy of the AAA to continue the traditional paternalistic relationship between tenant and landowner by paying the owner both his share and his tenants' share of the crop reduction subsidy. The owner was under no obligation to divide the money proportionately among his tenants. Several New Dealers, including Rexford Tugwell, Jerome Frank, and Alger Hiss, wanted the government to pay tenant farmers directly, but they were overruled by the AAA administrator, Chester Davis, and Secretary of Agriculture Henry Wallace. White tenants and sharecroppers suffered under these policies, but blacks suffered a disproportionate hardship by being the first to lose their land. Blacks in all classes of agriculture—owners, tenants, and sharecroppers—suffered declines, while the number of white farm owners actually increased and the number of white tenant farmers declined only slightly.[16]

Other agencies also discriminated against blacks. In the rural South, blacks were frequently denied access to the relief rolls or were harassed in the relief offices when they collected their checks. The FERA also distributed smaller-than-average relief benefits to black families. The average rural white family on relief received $15 in February 1935, while the average black family received only $9. Allowing for regional autonomy, the Civilian Conservation Corps (CCC) sanctioned racially segregated camps in parts of the South and Southwest. Blacks were also discouraged from applying for admission to the camps during harvest season, for fear that too few blacks would be available for work on the farms. In Delaware, where there were too few blacks to form a separate black unit, blacks were excluded from the camps. Robert Fechner, the conservative, southern-born CCC national director, would not allow integration as an option.[17]

The efforts of the Department of the Interior and the FSA were frequently cited as examples of the New Deal's progressive racial policies, yet even they had a mixed record. The FSA has been given high marks by historians who cite the southern liberal credentials of Will Alexander, a former president of the Interracial Cooperation Commission. As agency head, Alexander attempted to ensure that blacks' participation in the FSA's purchase and loan programs was roughly consistent with the percentage of blacks in the southern population. Nonetheless, black sharecroppers who lived on large plantations owned by whites were largely unaffected by the programs, and few blacks were appointed to the local Farm Security boards, which had been given the authority to grant loans.[18]

Harold Ickes, the former president of the Chicago branch of the NAACP and the foremost racial liberal in the New Deal cabinet, initiated desegregation in the Washington, D.C. offices of the Department of the Interior and attempted to hire skilled as well as unskilled black labor on Public Works Administration (PWA) construction projects. Robert Weaver, then an advisor to Ickes, got federal officials to support a policy of hiring a quota of skilled blacks equal to their proportion in the local labor force. He also instituted low-cost housing for blacks. Ickes failed to effect significant change because of conservative political pressures and the recalcitrance of skilled craft unions that refused to accept blacks. Moreover, he supported the construction of segregated housing units in northern as well as southern cities.[19]

Nevertheless, New Deal programs helped blacks to survive the Depression. World War II created opportunities for blacks to make significant advances in the workplace. Nonwhite participation in defense industries rose from less than 3 percent in 1942 to 8.3 percent in 1944. More than a million nonwhite workers were employed in 1944 in war industries. Improvement was also noted in government employment. In 1938 blacks made up 8.4 percent of all persons employed by the federal government in Washington, D.C. By 1944 blacks formed 19.2 percent of the city's federal workforce. The gain was also qualitative. In 1938, 90 percent of all black federal employment was custodial; only 10 percent was clerical, administrative, and professional. By 1944, 40 percent of black workers were custodial, and 60 percent were in higher-paying classifications.[20]

The factors contributing to this advance were the nation's great need for workers and soldiers; the growing militancy of blacks and their insistence on a larger share of industrial and governmental employment; the public hearings and private negotiations of the FEPC, the president's committee on fair employment practices; and the growing political clout of northern urban blacks. By 1940 the urban white labor force had been absorbed by the defense industries, and companies had begun importing whites from outside the industrial centers. Urban black labor was not utilized until other sources were exhausted.[21] Critics of this underutilization of blacks, led by the union organizer A. Philip Randolph, threatened to stage a march on Washington to dramatize the plight of the black worker and to demand an end to segregation in the armed services and racial discrimination in defense industries and government employment. As a result of this threat, Roosevelt issued Executive Order 8802, which banned discrimination in employment by companies filling defense contracts and created the FEPC to investigate complaints. Public hearings helped reveal industry-wide discrimination in the shipbuilding, railroad, automobile, aviation, and copper-mining industries. Unions that excluded blacks or forced them into segregated locals were also targeted by the FEPC. The committee failed, however, to attack the issue of segregation in the workplace and discouraged the use of racial quotas as an employment incentive. Yet despite its limited vision, small budget, attacks by southern Democrats and conservative Republicans, and lack of punitive powers, the FEPC nevertheless served as a foundation for post–World War II antidiscrimination efforts.[22]

During World War II many blacks moved from southern farms to northern cities hoping to find work in factories. Of the one million black workers who were added to the industrial force, over 60 percent were women. A large number of black women had always worked outside the home because of the economic marginality of the black family. After 1942 many black women left their positions as domestics and sought higher-paying jobs in factories. There they found the double barriers of sexual discrimination and racial discrimination. Despite the admonitions of the FEPC, the War Department allowed managers of arsenals, plants, and depots under its supervision to refuse jobs to black women. The U.S. Employment Service continued to accept race-specific job notices and referred black women applicants only to domestic and maintenance jobs.[23]

The barriers that black women and men would face at TVA during the New Deal and World War II were not immediately apparent in 1933 when, just two months after his inauguration, Roosevelt signed an act that gave TVA the mandate to foster an orderly and proper physical and social development of the Tennessee valley. Roosevelt, the first board of directors, the national press, and progressive politicians like Senator George Norris described an agency with uniquely broad powers to change the fundamental causes of poverty and underdevelopment in the valley. TVA would build multipurpose dams that would serve as reservoirs to control floods and at the same time generate cheap hydroelectric power. The power operations were to serve as a "yardstick" to determine reasonable rates for electricity. A public corporation with the powers of government but the flexibility of a private corporation, TVA would manufacture fertilizer, encourage soil conservation and reforestation, and engage in social experiments with the cooperation of state and local agencies. Workers on the dam construction projects were to be housed in all-electric model communities, where they would receive vocational training.[24]

The liberal image of TVA was fostered by its three directors: Arthur Morgan, Harcourt Morgan, and David Lilienthal. A former president of Antioch College, Arthur Morgan was chosen by Roosevelt to be the chairman of the TVA board because of his experience as a flood engineer and his reputation as a visionary planner. Harcourt Morgan (no relation), an agricultural expert, had been president of the University of Tennessee. Although he was born in Canada, he was viewed in the valley as a native. He believed that plans to transform the valley could work only if the population understood and approved of the changes, and opposed what he considered to be Arthur Morgan's autocratic approach to planning. David Lilienthal, the third director, had served on the Wisconsin Public Service Commission. Politically progressive and an advocate of social reform, he sided with Harcourt Morgan on the issue of local cooperation and grass-roots democracy.[25]

The brave new world of TVA was to be achieved through democratic social planning. TVA was the prototypical social planning agency of the New Deal, and the 1930s was the planning decade of the twentieth century. "Planning" became the buzzword for the 1930s, the means by which the survival of the nation state could be secured. The crisis of economic depression, social unrest, and military threat was considered so dangerous that many social scientists, politicians, and military officers, among others, contended that America had to embark on an ambitious program of government and private sector planning in order to remain competitive with the increasingly ordered societies of Germany, Italy, and the Soviet Union. Yet American social planners assured the public that they would distance themselves from the repressive aspects of planning in totalitarian regimes.[26]

Planning in America would be "democratic." Democratic planning based on "the principles of persuasion, consent, and participation" preserved the rights of all the people. Planners had the responsibility of both ensuring the well-being of the majority and protecting the interests of politically and economically marginal groups. Finding an equitable position for marginal groups in a competitive and uncertain economy required a sophisticated understanding of the techniques of the social sciences and a realistic grasp of political and human behavior.[27]

The degree of expertise and sophistication varied greatly among New Deal planners, men with diverse backgrounds and training. By the 1980s planning had evolved into a highly specialized profession legitimized by rigorous training; planning in the 1930s, however, was hardly a profession in a meaningful sense. In fact, practically any individual claiming a long-range vision, and with access to a publisher or government agency, could be a planner. Sociologists, economists, historians, novelists, geographers, geologists, and engineers, among others, made that claim. Indeed, one analyst aptly described New Deal planning as "a mélange of policy making, political improvising, and administrative programming." [28]

Adding to the problems of training and expertise were the different and frequently conflicting backgrounds of New Deal planners. Most planners were found either in academia or in government. William Ogburn taught at the University of Chicago, and Howard Odum at the University of North Carolina. Municipal and city planners were represented by Charles Merriam of Chicago. Planners at the level of the federal government included Rexford Tugwell, a sometime member of Roosevelt's inner circle, and the members of the National Planning Board, an agency established to coordinate the planning and distribution of public works under the NIRA and advise Secretary of the Interior Harold Ickes. The administrators and staff of the TVA were regional-level planners.[29]

Of all the types, regional planning was the most influential and politically important. Proponents of regional planning argued that the country consisted of many culturally, economically, and socially distinct regions and that each region would benefit most from a socioeconomic plan of its own. With a decentralized approach to planning, the regionalists felt, plans for each region would reflect more accurately the needs and wishes of the inhabitants. Although regional planning preceded the 1930s, it fitted very logically into the regionalized administrative structure of the New Deal.[30]

Regional planning, while it had advocates in all parts of the country, was particularly popular in the South. Southern planners were attracted to regionalism because it provided a rationale for preserving the unique characteristics of southern society: namely, an agricultural economy, a rural lifestyle, and racial segregation. Through a decentralized approach to planning, southerners hoped that they, rather than a potentially unsympathetic Roosevelt administration, would control the future direction of the South.

Using the regional model and subscribing to democratic principles, TVA sought to plan for the future of the black and white inhabitants of the valley. TVA officials were constantly confronted by the need to plan for blacks. Unlike regions of the country with small black populations that could be easily ignored, the Tennessee valley had a sizable black population, ranging from 10 percent of the total population in eastern Tennessee to over 40 percent in northern Alabama and western Kentucky. In addition, the strict customs and laws of racial segregation made planning for blacks an imperative throughout the region.

The Tennessee valley comprises parts of seven states—Virginia, North Carolina, Georgia, Alabama, Mississippi, Tennessee, and Kentucky—and covers over 42,000 square miles. During the New Deal period, two million people lived in the watershed area (see map). The majority of the inhabitants of the valley were descendants of English and Scotch-Irish settlers, although 11 percent of the population was black. There were also American Indians living on or near the Cherokee reservation in western North Carolina. The major cities of the valley were Knoxville and Chattanooga, Tennessee.

The valley was one of the poorest regions of the country. Before TVA, the Tennessee River frequently overflowed its banks with disastrous results. Farming methods were unsophisticated, and an enormous amount of soil was annually washed away or blown down the fields. The poor white farmers were frequently described in negative terms. One British observer noted:

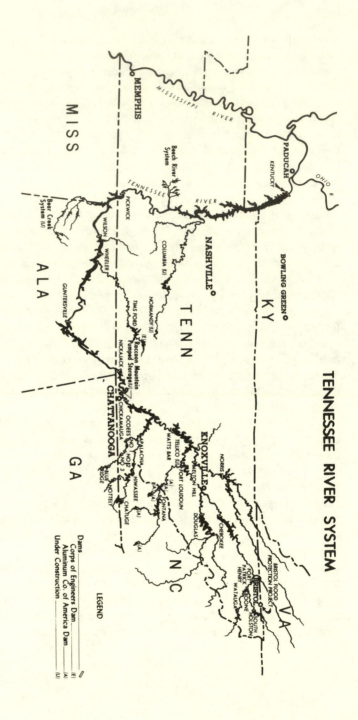

Map of the Tennessee Valley Authority, 1975

Source: TVA Technical Library, Knoxville, Tennessee

> Much of the rural area of the valley was inhabited by peasant farmers,
> who although originally of excellent British stock, had in their mountain
> isolation too often developed into poverty-stricken poor whites. Primitive
> in their reproductive habits as in their farming methods, they multiplied
> rapidly until they presented a typical Malthusian population, pressing hard
> upon its means of subsistence.[31]

The image of the primitive and benighted white Appalachian has been challenged by recent scholarship. Nonetheless, it influenced the relationship
between TVA planners and whites living in the mountainous regions of
eastern Tennessee. Many whites complained that TVA did not respect their
culture, their communities, or the value of their land.[32]

Most blacks who lived in the Tennessee valley experienced the double
edge of racism and poverty. More than 40 percent of the blacks living in
Tennessee were farmers, and many had been left in a weak economic position during the 1920s. By 1930 low prices had forced more and more black
farmers into tenancy. For those rural blacks who left their farms and moved
to Chattanooga or Knoxville or Paducah, Kentucky, the economic situation did not improve. When they could find work, blacks were limited to
unskilled employment in the factories. Their children attended segregated
schools in the cities. The New Deal came to Tennessee in the form of the
AAA, the Works Progress Administration (WPA), the CCC, and the FERA,
but discriminatory patterns of treatment were similar to those in other parts
of the South. Few blacks living in the Tennessee valley were middle-class.
From the small number of black lawyers, professors, bankers, and skilled
artisans in Chattanooga and Knoxville came individuals who criticized and
eventually organized against TVA.[33]

In *TVA and Black Americans*, I contend that TVA did not adequately
address the economic and social problems of blacks. As the subtitle of the
book indicates, TVA officials attempted to solve the racial problem by developing a series of plans that projected a subordinate, segregated position
for blacks, not only for the duration of the New Deal, but for the foreseeable
future as well.

In the process of researching this book, I often asked myself why planning for blacks failed to achieve or aim at equitable results, and why TVA
planners so severely limited their sights where opportunities for significant
changes in race relations were concerned. As democratic planners, were
they too responsive to conservative political and special-interest pressures
purporting to represent the wishes of the regional majority?

I was also aware that the failure to plan adequately for blacks became increasingly a class as well as a racial problem, for a growing body of scholarship supports the contention that TVA planners did little to improve the conditions of the economically marginal regardless of race. Yet for the nonblack poor, planners projected significant economic improvement that would lead eventually to greater social acceptance and economic integration. Race, on the other hand, would always limit economic improvement for blacks and block full acceptance.[34]

Planners who were concerned about the welfare of blacks were not, in fact, in an enviable position during the New Deal. They were frequently caught between, on the one hand, racially intransigent southern whites who kept blacks politically disenfranchised, economically isolated, and physically segregated, and, on the other, civil rights groups and political liberals who fought to end all forms of racial discrimination. In addition, planners had to understand their own developing racial ideologies.

Although this study is certainly not intended to be a comprehensive study of TVA or the Tennessee valley, it does, out of necessity, include references to administrative controversies, bureaucratic changes, and legal and political battles that ostensibly have nothing to do with race. Yet TVA planners did not develop their racial policies in a vacuum; they were influenced by outside political and economic pressures. It is also important to understand the internal agency dynamics out of which emerged important decisions on race. For example, it is useful to know that while TVA chairman Arthur Morgan was struggling to articulate an inoffensive racial policy, he was also battling in the federal courts for the right of TVA to exist, as well as fighting to retain his own job.[35]

In this book I will describe the idealism and sense of mission that pervaded the agency at the outset, and the inevitable changes in scope and commitment over time. TVA planners operated as a "plan-executing agency," emphasizing implementation of plans and the impact on the targeted population. As one later planner has noted, "Planning is not an end in itself. It is a means to an end, the end being action." [36] The charged and highly optimistic atmosphere of the early years raised the hopes of many valley dwellers that a better day was at hand.

On the issue of race, the men of TVA would certainly be judged reactionary in today's terms. By 1930s standards they are harder to characterize. I find useful the New Dealer Aubrey Williams' observation that in the South "we have no liberals, only conservatives and radicals." [37] In the 1930s, among the political, academic, and economic leaders of the South, integration and complete racial equality represented a radical solution. TVA subscribed to a more conservative approach in its search for an "equitable" solution to the race problem. I find little evidence in the personal papers and the government documents of TVA officials of venality or racial hatred. Rather, their expressed concern for the problems of the South makes their limited vision as planners all the more troubling.

TVA

and Black Americans

CHAPTER I

The Promise

DURING the hectic period of the interregnum, President-elect Franklin Roosevelt traveled to Montgomery, Alabama, as part of an inspection tour of the Tennessee valley. Accompanied by congressmen and senators, including Senator George Norris, the chief proponent of valley regional development, Roosevelt expounded on the possibility of using the World War I–era dam facilities at Muscle Shoals as the cornerstone for the development of the region. After paying homage to the ghosts of the capital of the Confederacy, Roosevelt extemporaneously painted a glowing if vague picture of the future role of Muscle Shoals.

> Muscle Shoals is more today than a mere opportunity for the federal government to do a kind turn for the people in one small section of a couple of states. Muscle Shoals gives us the opportunity to accomplish a great purpose for the people of many states and indeed for the whole Union. Because there we have an opportunity of setting an example of planning not just for ourselves, but for the generations to come, tying in industry and agriculture, and forestry and flood prevention, tying them all into a unified whole over a distance of a thousand miles so that we can offer better opportunities and better places for living for millions of yet unborn in the days to come.[1]

Less than three months after his swing through the Tennessee valley, Roosevelt, now the president, sought to transform rhetoric into legislative reality. On 10 April 1933 Roosevelt sent a message to Congress requesting the creation of the Tennessee Valley Authority. Using the terminology of regional planning, Roosevelt outlined a plan for the utilization of the land and waters of forty-two thousand square miles of the Tennessee valley. He included the dam and nitrate plants at Muscle Shoals, unused since World War I, stating, "The continued idleness of a great national investment in

3

the Tennessee Valley leads me to ask Congress for legislation necessary to enlist this project in the service of the people."[2]

Roosevelt chose to emphasize the broad impact of the projected social and economic programs:

> It is clear that the Muscle Shoals development is but a small part of the potential public usefulness of the entire Tennessee River. Such use, if envisioned in its entirety, transcends mere power development; it enters the wide field of flood control, soil erosion, afforestation, elimination from agricultural use of marginal lands, and distribution and diversification of industry. In short, this power development of war days leads logically to national planning for a complete river watershed involving many states and the future lives and welfare of millions. It touches and gives life to all forms of human concerns.[3]

He also stressed the unique regional planning aspect of the agency. TVA was to be given broad planning functions—functions that had never been granted except in time of war:

> I, therefore, suggest to the Congress legislation to create a Tennessee Valley Authority—a corporation clothed with the power of government but possessed with the flexibility and initiative of a private enterprise. It should be charged with the broadest duty of planning for the proper use, conservation, and development of the natural resources of the Tennessee River drainage basin and its adjoining territory for the general social and economic welfare of the nation. This authority should also be clothed with the necessary power to carry these plans into effect. Its duty should be the rehabilitation of the Muscle Shoals development and the coordination of it with the wider plans.
>
> . . . Many hard lessons have taught us the human waste that results from lack of planning. Here and there a few wise cities and counties have looked ahead and planned. But our Nation has "just grown." It is time to extend planning to a wider field, in this instance comprehending in one great project many States directly concerned with the basin of one of our great rivers.[4]

Having warned of the dangers of growth without direction and control, Roosevelt intimated in a later speech that Tennessee river development was the first of many similar projects throughout the country:

4

This in a true sense is a return to the spirit and vision of the pioneer. If we are successful here, we can march on, step by step in a like development of other great national territorial units within our borders.[5]

During the month of April, Roosevelt continued to meet with congressmen, urging them to "draw the bills that you think represent our collective views that we have been expressing here." George Norris took the leadership role in sponsoring the TVA bill in the Senate, and Representative Lister Hill took a similar role in the House. Both men had been vocal advocates for development of the Tennessee valley since the 1920s.[6]

Efforts to harness the potential and control the ravages of the Tennessee River and its tributaries actually began a century before Norris and Hill became involved. In 1824 Secretary of War John C. Calhoun sent a report to President Monroe that recommended improvements on the Tennessee as part of a national program to connect the various parts of the country by roads, canals, and river channels. From 1824 on, one goal was to control the flow of the river so that it would be navigable from Knoxville to Paducah, Kentucky, where it merged with the Ohio shortly before the latter flowed into the Mississippi. Several attempts were made during the nineteenth century to create channels for navigation. A major barrier was a section of turbulent rapids and uneven falls in northern Alabama called Muscle Shoals.

By 1900 two other elements had been added: hydroelectric power and conservation. The new electric power industry began searching for new and more profitable plant locations on major rivers in order to harness the power generated by newly constructed dams. Several power companies sought to build along the Tennessee at Muscle Shoals, only to be thwarted by public opposition and antitrust laws.

The conservation movement, introduced during the administration of Theodore Roosevelt, was to have an important impact on the fortunes of TVA. It promoted the view that only government had the power, scope, and vision to protect and manage the nation's water supply and ensure orderly and acceptable growth.[7] In an action consistent with his belief in government control of natural resources, Theodore Roosevelt in 1903 vetoed a bill that would have permitted the construction of a dam at Muscle Shoals by a private company:

Wherever the government constructs a dam and lock for the purpose of navigation there is a waterfall of great value. It does not seem right or just that this element of local value should be given away to private individuals of the vicinage, and at the same time the people of the whole country should be taxed for the local improvement. . . . It seems clear that justice to taxpayers of the country demands that when the government is or may be called upon to improve a strain the improvement should be made to pay for itself, so far as practical.[8]

This pay-as-you-go principle was a precedent that his distant cousin Franklin sought to maintain twenty-eight years later in creating competitive rates for the electricity generated by TVA dams.

In 1916 the National Defense Act authorized the government to develop domestic sources of the nitrates needed for the manufacture of explosives. Subsequently two nitrate plants and a dam to supply hydroelectric power to them were built at Muscle Shoals. The war ended before the plants were operational or the dam completed. No longer needed for munitions, the nitrate plants as well as the incomplete dam were the subjects of controversy throughout the 1920s. The Democrats, led by representatives from Tennessee and Alabama, called for a four-point plan involving the development of the valley, nitrates for national defense, fertilizer for agriculture, and dams for navigation and power. The Republicans, citing waste and the possibility of mismanagement, called for either the leasing or the sale of the federal property to private companies. Reed Smoot of Utah suggested that Wilson Dam be sold for scrap and described the Democratic plan as a conspiracy by southern congressmen to put private utilities out of business. The Republican-controlled Congress defeated appropriations for the completion of Wilson Dam.[9]

In 1921 the Harding administration, tiring of the white elephant, decided to sell the Muscle Shoals complex to the highest bidder. Henry Ford, the automobile magnate, offered to lease the dam and buy the nitrate plants. Several southern congressmen, including Lister Hill of Alabama, supported the Ford bid in fear that the government might never develop the area. Hill called Ford's bid "the greatest offer ever made by a citizen to his government." [10]

Not all welcomed Ford's offer. Conservationists were concerned that a national resource might be turned over to a private company in violation of the federal Water Powers Act, passed in 1920 to prevent just such an arrangement. Others questioned the low price that the government placed on the facility. The most vocal critic of Ford's bid was the progressive Republican senator from Nebraska, George Norris. Norris was concerned that although Ford promised river development, he was only interested in using cheap power generated by government-built plants to produce auto parts and other industrial products. Thwarted by Norris and other progressives, Ford withdrew his offer in 1924. Other companies, including Alabama Power Company and American Cyanamid, also unsuccessfully bid for the dam and nitrate plants.[11]

Throughout the 1920s Senator Norris sponsored several bills for the federal maintenance and development of the Tennessee River, including the existing facilities, and the construction of new dams for flood control. His bills passed both houses, only to be vetoed by Presidents Coolidge and Hoover. In vetoing the Muscle Shoals bill of 1931, Hoover expressed his political and economic philosophy while attempting to address the call for more extensive support of public utilities in the wake of the private utilities scandal of the early 1930s:

> This bill raises one of the most important issues confronting our people. That is squarely the issue of Federal Government ownership and operation of power and manufacturing business not as a minor by-product but as a major purpose. Involved in this question is the agitation against the conduct of the power industry. The power problem is not to be solved by the Federal Government going into the power business. . . . the remedy for abuses in the conduct of that industry lies in regulation. . . . I hesitate to contemplate the future of our institutions, of our government and of our country if the preoccupation of its officials is to be no longer the promotion of justice and equal opportunity but is to be devoted to barter in the markets. This is not liberalism, it is degeneration.[12]

If the relatively narrowly defined bill of 1931 elicited a label of degeneration, the more broadly conceived 1933 bill would surely have been vetoed with even greater emotion and condemnation. But in 1933 Franklin Roosevelt, a supporter of regional planning and development, was in the White House.

Senator Norris introduced the Senate bill, while Edward Almond and Lister Hill of Alabama and John McSwain of South Carolina presented the House bill. Hill had in the intervening decade elected to support the concept of government river development over the private sector and became an articulate defender of the House bill in debate. Between 11 April and 17 May, the House and Senate conducted hearings on the two bills. Conservative Republicans raised the specter of socialism. Henry Ransley, Republican representative from Philadelphia, observed: "Government is to expend millions but like every Government operation, it will not pay for

7

itself. . . . Is this sum to be spent on an experiment which is socialistic? . . . Are business and income to be taxed until income is destroyed?" Opponents of TVA were outvoted, and southern Democrats were placated by the inclusion of a 5 percent payment to state governments for the injury to the tax base incurred as a result of the permanent flooding of lands by TVA dams.[13]

The statute that finally emerged on 17 May was, like most legislation, the product of a compromise between the executive branch and Congress. From congressional initiative came the authorization to take over the Muscle Shoals properties, to utilize the nitrate plants in a fertilizer program, and to use Wilson Dam to generate electric power. Such powers were present in Section 4, which provided authorization to acquire real estate for the construction of dams, reservoirs, transmission lines, powerhouses, and other structures, and in Section 5, which authorized TVA to contract for production of fertilizers and to produce, sell, and distribute electric power. Two other provisions reflected Roosevelt's expanded vision of TVA. Section 22 gave TVA the power to construct dams, powerhouses, and navigation projects on the Tennessee River and its tributaries; Section 23 established a basis for the program of regional planning and development. Its six objectives were: (1) the maximum amount of flood control; (2) the maximum development of the Tennessee River for navigational purposes; (3) the maximum generation of electric power consistent with flood control and navigation; (4) the proper use of marginal lands; (5) a proper method of reforestation; and (6) the economic and social well-being of the people living in the river basins.[14]

Section 23 had the widest implications for social and economic planning. Congress, perhaps sensing this, elected to make the president directly responsible for TVA's planning activities. Only the president was authorized to make surveys and general plans for the area. Roosevelt, annoyed at this attempt to split the powers of TVA, delegated these powers to its board of directors by an executive order.[15]

Norris argued that an expansion of the facilities at Muscle Shoals, particularly a system of dams along the unpredictable and flood-prone Tennessee River, would not only improve the farmlands in the valley through the use of nitrate fertilizer, but would also provide hydroelectric power and electricity for the valley. In addition, it would involve the government in public utilities management and regulation. In Roosevelt, the Muscle Shoals project found a cautious supporter who felt that a program of limited government ownership of public utilities, and their use as a yardstick for regulation, was a potentially important innovation. Roosevelt also saw the politically beneficial implications of advocating conservation and the improvement of rural life.[16]

TVA represented not only the fruition of a progressive program, but also the incorporation into public policy of the regional planning tenet that held that governmental social planning could best be implemented within "geographically unified regions." Rejecting a monolithic approach to social planning wherein economic and social welfare programs would be centrally administered in Washington, regional planners believed that governmental planning would be more effective and humane if plans and programs could be tailored to meet a region's specific needs and customs.[17]

The Tennessee valley region fitted the definition of a geographically unified district very well. Containing parts of seven southern states (Alabama, Georgia, Kentucky, Mississippi, North Carolina, Tennessee, and Virginia), the valley's inhabitants indeed shared similar historical, cultural, social, and economic characteristics. The depressed state of the valley's economy, its inadequate educational system, its cultural isolation, and subsistence farming made the Tennessee valley an attractive area for regional planners interested in reshaping and revitalization.[18]

Of all the New Deal government agencies, TVA showed the greatest promise of bringing about a rational and effective form of government planning. It enjoyed strong presidential and congressional support and a large operational appropriation.[19] Yet Congress, despite its willingness to approve Sections 22 and 23, for the most part continued to think of TVA along the old lines of power and flood control. Even Senator Norris saw TVA only as a source of hydroelectric power. For the majority of Congress, TVA was merely the Muscle Shoals corporation of previous years with some additional, ill-defined, powers and functions. In the congressional debate, little interest was taken in Sections 22 and 23; the focus was on the question of power generation and public utilities.[20]

The rest of American society was much more interested in TVA's social planning features. The public, in both the North and South, received large doses of favorable information about TVA from local and national newspapers. The *New York Times* followed the early days of TVA more intently than any other northern newspaper. Between 1933 and 1939, it ran no fewer than twelve feature articles. Both in feature-length, front-page articles and on its editorial page, the *Times* praised the concept of a regional development project. The themes that appeared most frequently had to do with regional planning and the reactions of the valley inhabitants.

Because of his high profile in TVA as well as his penchant for dramatic statements, Arthur Morgan, the Roosevelt-appointed chairman, was the TVA official most often quoted. Morgan used this attention to enhance TVA's image as a social planning agency. "The TVA is not primarily an emergency unemployment relief measure," he wrote. "The main . . . purpose is to build up the permanent social and economic prosperity of the Tennessee Valley." In another article he stated: "The President sees the Valley Authority as a means for displacing haphazard and unplanned and unintegrated social and industrial development by introducing elements of order, design, and forethought." Emphasizing the agency's experimental nature, he continued: "If the TVA is successful in achieving rehabilitation within the limited region of the TVA, methods and results developed could be of great value for the rest of the United States."[21]

While emphasizing the innovative aspects of TVA regional planning, Morgan was careful to point out that it would be of a benign nature and would incorporate the wishes of the inhabitants. Perhaps anticipating the criticism of the business community and right-wing political opponents, Morgan stressed TVA's opposition to a Soviet model of broad-scale social and economic planning. He insisted that TVA had no five-year or ten-year plan. It was not a government scheme that would be imposed on the population. TVA would adopt a pragmatic and experimental attitude and would be willing and able to discard plans or programs that did not work or were viewed by the local population as objectionable. "Taking any issue that may require attention, there is an effort to meet that particular issue so as to achieve good and enduring results by whatever methods will work best in that case."[22] He stressed that the social programs were not an attempt to restructure the Tennessee valley totally, but rather a gentle prod to bring the valley into the twentieth century. It was no coincidence that directly opposite Morgan's 25 March 1933 *New York Times* article was an article on Mussolini's corporate system and its "disturbing" effect on individual liberties.[23]

Articles written by *Times* reporters were also enthusiastic about TVA's social programs: "Laboratory for Advanced Ideas," "TVA Plans Change in Life of District," "Ramparts of the Tennessee Valley: A Powerhouse Source," "A Dream Takes Place on the Tennessee."[24] One reporter wrote, "When the TVA Act was passed three years ago, most people even in Washington were thinking of the valley in terms of electric power. Those terms are still valid, but the objective has broadened until it has become the revivification of the life of a people."[25]

TVA, through its Information Division, augmented the predominantly favorable local and national coverage by advertising its program and distributing thousands of booklets setting forth its advantages. Through its subsidiary, the Electric Home and Farm Authority, Inc., TVA engaged in extensive mailings. Booklets went to newspapers, publicity agencies, civic clubs, chambers of commerce, magazines, and municipalities. In addition, public relations pamphlets were handed out to tourists who visited the various dam construction sites.[26] TVA was also responsible for much of the publicity generated by the parade and festivities held in Tupelo, Mississippi, to celebrate its vote to buy TVA electricity. The policy of widespread publicity was finally called into question by members of the Southern Newspaper Publishers' Association, who complained that TVA was given free publicity and free postage, while private utilities had to pay thousands of dollars to advertise themselves.[27]

TVA counteracted negative publicity in its first two years by holding frequent press conferences and by sending its administrative officials all around the country. An attempt was made to equate public approval of TVA with patriotism. In a Chicago speech in 1934, Arthur Morgan attacked the newspaper criticism that the agency had been receiving, primarily from areas that were coal or petroleum suppliers and saw cheap TVA electricity as unfair or potentially destructive competition.[28] He stated that when a newspaper went out of its way to criticize the administration program, "its attitude borders on treason."[29] This attempt to put critics on the defensive merely served to anger some members of the press, who proceeded to increase their negative coverage of the agency and, particularly, its chairman.

Although late 1934 signaled the end of the honeymoon between TVA and the press, the favorable media blitz of the first two years had raised expectations in the minds of most private citizens. Particularly attractive to those living outside the Tennessee valley was the prospect of similar projects throughout the country: all Americans would eventually share the benefits they read and heard about. For those living in the valley, TVA appeared to promise a new life, a way out of poverty, a chance to share the American Dream.

Both national and local papers predicted that TVA would have a profound effect on the residents of the Tennessee valley. Reporters were sent down to interview private citizens, politicians, and TVA officials. They came away with a semiromanticized idea of the impact of TVA. "In the heart of the old Confederacy—Shiloh, Corinth, Lookout Mountain—battles trampling down crops that in one sense never grew again. The silence fell and not until recently over large areas was it broken." The Tennessee valley was described as a depressed area lacking a modern economy. Reporters contrasted the "happy farms of the Tennessee Blue Grass" with the "breezeway" and "dogtrot" cabins of the Tennessee valley. TVA's social programs would bring the people into the twentieth century. The inhabitants would be taught basic vocational skills, for "more important than the power 'yardstick' is the teacher's 'yardstick.'" While employed temporarily in reservoir clearance, residents would be taught proper hygiene and sanitation as well as home management. Local skills in furniture making and ceramics were to be encouraged to the extent that home industries and small artisan cooperatives could become self-sufficient and profitable.[30]

Newspapers of the Tennessee valley tended to concentrate on the economic benefits for the area, elevating TVA to something close to a godsend. According to these papers, TVA would provide short-range help by creating jobs and improving housing, health care, and schools, and long-range help by modernizing vocational skills, improving area farming, and creating tourist attractions through residential parks.[31] Indeed, the *Knoxville News-Sentinel* ran an article entitled "More Time for Flowers": Tennessee valley housewives would have more time to tend their flowers because TVA-sponsored electricity would "wash the dishes, heat the water, cook the meals, sweep the floors, and launder the clothes."[32]

The editor of the *Chattanooga News*, George Fort Milton, had been an early supporter of Roosevelt and had expressed hope that the Tennessee valley might be turned into an American Ruhr valley. Milton, an accomplished historian and newspaperman, also fancied himself to be a regional planner and welcomed TVA as a social planning agency as well as a conduit for industrial development. He acknowledged that the Tennessee valley was in desperate need of assistance but warned "outsiders" that it would take considerable energy and patience to educate inhabitants away from the "old ways," for the "East Tennessean is stubborn and resists being improved upon." Yet in the early years of TVA, he remarked, the agency was regarded by many residents as "our special Federal Santa Claus."[33]

The promise of TVA was perhaps exaggerated by the press to increase interest and readership and by politicians (from Roosevelt down to local officials) to increase enthusiasm and loyalty at the voting booth. The promise was also exaggerated by politicians, academics, and the press to help fill a void created by the lack of hope in the lives of valley residents in particular and in the nation as a whole. The reality of TVA fell somewhat short of a visit from a "Federal Santa Claus," but the promise and hope of the early years were needed to temper the very real poverty in the valley.

Regional planners described the valley as a unified geographic region consisting of the seven-state watershed area of the Tennessee River and its tributaries. Within the watershed area were two medium-sized cities, Knoxville and Chattanooga (both in Tennessee), and hundreds of small towns and crossroaded villages as well as isolated farms located in the hollow and on the mountainsides. There were many cultural and economic linkages and similarities throughout the valley. Most of the white inhabitants of the valley were descendants of Scotch-Irish who had migrated from the southeastern states in the early nineteenth century. Foreign-born people made up less than 0.5 percent of the total population, and whites of foreign or mixed heritage numbered only 1 percent. Homogeneity also characterized religious affiliation. Over 98 percent of all valley church members belonged to Protestant denominations, mostly Baptist and Methodist. Fundamentalism was strong, and antievolutionary zeal was celebrated. To paraphrase H. L. Mencken, a Catholic was almost as rare as an oboe player in the Tennessee valley.[34]

The valley as a whole was by 1930 below the national average in per capita income, agricultural production, education, and health benefits. Most experts worried about soil erosion and the sporadic flooding of the Tennessee River, caused by one of the highest average rainfalls in the continental United States. Indeed, the valley's average annual net farm income of $639 was just over a third of the estimated national average of $1,835 per year. Only South Carolina posted a lower per capita income than the average for the seven valley states. Soil erosion was so severe that by 1930 about 85 percent of the valley's 13 million acres of cultivated land had been damaged.[35]

Photographs of the valley popular with the national press showed a deeply gullied moonscape, barren of trees and ground cover. The continuous planting of corn, tobacco, and cotton had reduced the fertility of the soil to such a degree that fertilizer could not replenish the nutrients. Many farmers were caught in a cycle of ever-increasing poverty. Those who lost their farms did not have many options: the once thriving timber industry had disappeared by the 1930s, leaving the local economy of western North Carolina in disarray. Many local industries had been in a general decline since the turn of the century, and the crash of 1929 only sent more coal and iron ore mines into bankruptcy. Foundries and mills in the cities continued to lay off workers, so that a move to the city did not ensure prosperity or even a job, although both Chattanooga and Knoxville experienced an increase in size during the 1930s.[36]

For those who remained on the farm, life was hard, and many had to do without conveniences that more prosperous regions of the country had learned to expect. Only 0.2 percent of the farms in the Tennessee valley had electricity, compared with 13.5 percent throughout the United States. Only 3 percent had running water. Diseases such as tuberculosis, typhoid, and malaria were much more common than in the nation as a whole. While fertility rates were higher, so were the infant mortality rates. Fewer doctors, dentists, and hospital beds were available. The seven valley states ranked among the nation's ten lowest in educational quality. School systems in the valley spent $23.35 per child a year, compared with the national average of $68.02. Not surprisingly, the illiteracy rate for white adults was 6.8 percent, compared with a national average of 1.5 percent.[37]

Although planners emphasized the homogeneity of the valley population, significant differences in political history, culture, class, and race existed. The Tennessee River may have connected the East Tennessee hills with the rest of the south-central states, but the Civil War had created a political schism between east and west that had not resolved by the 1930s. During the Civil War, East Tennessee, along with portions of northwestern Alabama, had not heeded the confederate call to arms and had sided with Lincoln and the Union. East Tennessee continued to send Republicans to Congress during the 1930s, while the rest of the valley sent Democrats, including John Rankin of Mississippi (whom Roosevelt referred to as "my good friend"), Lister Hill, and Kenneth McKellar, senator from Tennessee and a sometime opponent of Roosevelt, the New Deal, and TVA.[38]

Reporters who traveled throughout the valley noted its diverse cultural dimensions. The hills of western North Carolina and eastern Tennessee were filled with the sounds of Scottish folk ballads, Irish jigs, and Protestant hymns, while western Kentucky and Tennessee and northern Alabama and Mississippi reflected the influence of the Mississippi Delta region: here, blues and jazz were heard.

A related factor in the region was the sizable presence, and uneven distribution, of blacks. The most marginal people in a marginal region, blacks constituted only 10 percent of the valley population, but most blacks lived in the cotton-producing subregion of northern Alabama, where in several counties they numbered more than 50 percent of the population. Blacks living near Florence and Muscle Shoals, Alabama, were employed primarily as sharecroppers or tenant farmers. Those who owned farms had an average holding of only 45 acres, while whites owned an average of 100 acres. Sharecroppers and tenant farmers were encouraged to plant crops up to the door of the house and consequently were unable to spare space to plant a garden to grow food for a proper diet. Religion was the most significant form of cultural expression in the black communities, rural as well as urban. Segregated and combining African and Protestant religious traditions, the black churches in the valley were, like their white counterparts, predominantly Baptist and Methodist, with a sizable representation of Holiness and sanctified churches.[39]

Life on the margins of a poor society required circumspection and docility for many blacks. Protest and organizing against class and race oppression did not enhance a person's chances for survival. Having lost ground after a brief period of World War I–induced prosperity, black farmers in the Tennessee valley by 1933 were looking for and hoping for a revitalization program like TVA, which promised better treatment and living conditions for everyone in the valley.[40]

Urban blacks living in Knoxville and Chattanooga also eagerly awaited the arrival of TVA. Blacks had lived in Knoxville from its inception in the 1760s as a center for trading between Anglo-Americans and the Cherokee, Choctaw, and Chickasaw Indian nations already present in the valley. Most blacks in Knoxville before the Civil War were "free persons of color." After the passage of the fourteenth and fifteenth amendments, blacks voted in local, state, and national elections. Although they continued to vote in state and national elections into the twentieth century, their numbers were greatly reduced by a poll tax, passed ostensibly as a reform measure in 1890. The poll tax of one dollar was equivalent to one or two days' wages for an average black worker. Blacks voted in large numbers in city elections and regularly elected aldermen from all-black wards to the Knoxville city council. In 1912 another reform measure instituted a commission form of government with at-large elections, a change that nullified black voting strength and made it almost impossible to elect blacks to city-wide office.[41]

Most blacks worked as common laborers and domestic servants. Knoxville was not highly industrialized, and most of the unskilled work was in construction. There was a black middle class comprising schoolteachers, college professors, doctors, lawyers, and skilled tradesmen. A dominant force in the black community was Knoxville College, founded in 1875 by the United Presbyterian Church. College professors and doctors associated with the college hospital played an important role in petitioning for improvements in housing, health care, and education. Many projects, although initiated by the black community, relied on white cooperation for guidance and support. Through the cooperation of whites, black Knoxvillians were able to get black branches of the Young Men's Christian Association and the Young Women's Christian Association, as well as two segregated public parks and a Carnegie-funded library.[42]

Race relations in Knoxville were sorely tested by a 1919 race riot that resulted in property destruction and one death in the black community. The riot was started by a white mob, frustrated at being unable to lynch a black man accused of killing a white woman. The traumatic events of that summer created a sense of fear and vulnerability among blacks. Institutions like the Colored Board of Trade and the black *East Tennessee News* recommended perseverance and cooperation with the "better" elements of the white intellectual and business communities. Others reacted by organizing a chapter of the NAACP, which led an unsuccessful effort to defend the accused black murderer.[43]

The spirit of protest was not sustained into the 1920s. By 1923 the local NAACP was dormant. Accusations of criminal activity and cowardice among the leaders created considerable disharmony in the community. Moreover, living conditions and economic opportunities were considered good in comparison with other parts of the region, although such opportunities were restricted to nonindustrial and unskilled occupations. Blacks in Knoxville, perhaps because they made up only 15 percent of the population, were able to patronize most white businesses and could sit anywhere on public transportation. Blacks and whites worked together in integrated work crews on road and building construction. Still, living conditions were not equal. Blacks were excluded from certain restaurants, hotels, and store lunch counters. Many of the streets in black neighborhoods were unpaved, making transportation impossible when it rained. Although conditions were better than in the rural areas, urban blacks also suffered disproportionately from diseases like tuberculosis. Over 34 percent of their homes were without indoor plumbing, and 60 percent were without electricity. Four out of five black workers were unskilled. The educational facilities were overcrowded, the one black high school having an enrollment of 1,060 despite a listed capacity of only 560. By the beginning of the Depression, morale was at an all-time low. Unable to start a new NAACP chapter in Knoxville, William Pickens, the national branch secretary, wrote, "It seemed more profitable to please the white population, it seemed more profitable to cater to the prejudices of whites." Consequently, many blacks both nationally and in the valley hoped that the coming of TVA would bring not only jobs, but a rebirth in spirit.[44]

Chattanooga also looked forward to the coming of TVA. Blacks made up 30 percent of the population during the 1930s, down from 50 percent during the Civil War period. Migration to the North and the annexation of predominantly white suburbs contributed to this proportionate decline, although there remained over 400,000 blacks in Chattanooga and the surrounding counties. Blacks in Chattanooga could vote in local, state, and national elections, although they were also limited by the poll tax and lost some political power in 1912 when the city switched to the commission form of government. Yet because of their greater population and better organization in the wards, blacks continued to hold the balance of power in city elections, and black political bosses were openly courted by white politicians.[45]

Unlike Knoxville, Chattanooga was a highly industrialized town with a long history of strong unions. Many blacks who worked in the foundries, on the railroads, and in the construction trades were members of segregated locals in the American Federation of Labor. Skilled workers and union officials were part of the black middle class of Chattanooga and served as leaders in the community along with a few ministers and lawyers. Chattanooga had a smaller black middle class than Knoxville, primarily because of the absence of an accredited black college. Black schoolteachers, although influential in the community, were in such a financially precarious position that few could afford to take leadership roles. Racial segregation was more pronounced in Chattanooga, and blacks lived and worked in a more separate environment. The larger population permitted the development of black clubs, theaters, schools, banks, and other social and economic institutions. Racial tensions remained high during World War I and the 1920s, with instances of racially motivated violence, but no riots. A Chattanooga branch of the NAACP was started, and it suffered a fate similar to that of the Knoxville branch. Economic pressures from unsympathetic whites caused many of the officers to resign in 1923. By May 1933 Chattanooga blacks, like their Knoxville counterparts, were apathetic. Both groups desperately needed not only economic opportunities, but also a renewed belief in their own ability to change their environment.[46]

Politicians from senators to ward bosses, businessmen from corporate heads to shopowners, large and small farmers, college presidents, and ordinary citizens awaited the promised transformation of the valley, some with eagerness, some with trepidation. No group had more to gain than blacks living in the valley. Over the next twelve years, TVA, through its official policies and informal practices, showed the extent to which blacks were to be included in that transformation.

CHAPTER II

The Reality

THE very nature of bureaucratic governance routinely leads to a discrepancy between promise and reality in both legislation and the administration of government agencies. In the best of circumstances, political and administrative compromises frequently change the scope and direction of plans. The first twelve years of TVA were rife with controversy, policy disputes, political compromises, and administrative changes, all of which greatly affected the Authority's impact on the nation and the valley. That there was a discrepancy between TVA's promise and its reality is not in itself surprising, yet the degree to which it fell short of its prescribed goals for successful transformation is significant, particularly in the area of race relations.

In addition to bringing renewed life to the Tennessee valley, TVA promised to treat all the valley inhabitants fairly regardless of race, giving each equal consideration for jobs and benefits. This promise of equality of opportunity—given by the chairman and high administrative officials—was viewed as very important by civil rights advocates, particularly because of TVA's location in states that practiced, during the 1930s, many forms of racial discrimination. The promise, if kept, could have signaled the end of federal sponsorship of racial inequality. Unfortunately, the promise of nondiscrimination in job opportunities, housing, and community development was translated into a reality that, at best, maintained existing patterns of discrimination and, at worst, brought about racial exclusion and heightened racial tensions.[1]

The promise of nondiscrimination in TVA first appeared in written form in 1934, with the publication of the Authority's *Employee Relationship Policy*. The TVA board of directors issued this document principally to clarify and augment its stand against political appointments and patronage. Advocates of civil rights, however, such as the NAACP, the National Urban League, and local Tennessee valley black organizations read a message of broadened opportunities in the statement that "appointments . . . will be made solely on the basis of merit and efficiency. . . . Promotion, demotion, transfer, retention in or termination of, service with TVA will be made on the basis of merit and efficiency." Most importantly, TVA issued a statement that "no discrimination in occupational classification or in rates of pay shall be made on the basis of sex or race." This latter statement was seen as a progressive step toward a color-blind employment policy and away from government discrimination. If blacks were qualified for employment or promotion, they would be given an equal chance to compete.[2]

NRA officials had discussed establishing a "Negro differential"—the practice of paying blacks less than whites for the same jobs. Southerners argued that this differential had been built into the South's private business economy, which would be destroyed by an immediate equalization. Advocates of the "differential" further argued that equalization would create greater unemployment for blacks. Indeed, early investigations of the NRA and the AAA showed that when equal wages were enforced for blacks and whites, employers hired a disproportionate number of whites and virtually excluded blacks from jobs they had previously held.[3]

Nevertheless, TVA stated that it would not use a "Negro differential," officially or unofficially. In addition, at the suggestion of Floyd Reeves, the first director of personnel, and with the support of Arthur Morgan, TVA initiated a quota system to ensure an adequate number of black employees. Throughout its initial construction period (1933–1945), TVA made an effort "to maintain the same proportion of Negroes to whites in its employment as their proportion in the total population of the area." About 11 percent of the Tennessee valley population was black, and TVA managed to keep its overall percentage of black workers at approximately 11 percent in most of those years. The quota was maintained through careful attention to the racial background of each TVA worker. Where the black population in the area was large, as in the area around Wheeler Dam in northern Alabama, the quota for black workers was kept as high as 40 percent of the total workforce. Where the black population was small, as in eastern Tennessee, the percentage of blacks in the workforce was also small. TVA justified the use of the quota system by saying that it was intended "to minimize the tendency to give employment to white workers rather than Negro workers during a period of unemployment and increased competition for jobs."[4]

Unfortunately, the promise of the TVA quota system remained unfulfilled (Figures 1 and 2). Indeed, the Authority's nondiscriminatory racial policy as well as its general program of major social reform and change in the valley remained far more impressive in speeches and newsprint than in practice. In reality, TVA was a government agency unable or unwilling

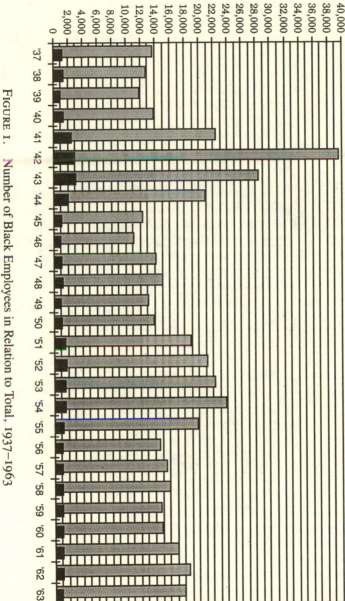

Number of Employees

Total Employees

Black Employees

FIGURE 1. Number of Black Employees in Relation to Total, 1937–1963

Source: TVA Technical Library, Knoxville, Tennessee

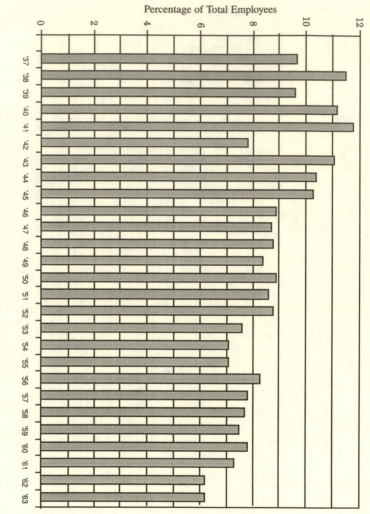

FIGURE 2. Percentage of Black Employees, 1937–1963

Source: TVA Technical Library, Knoxville, Tennessee

to live up to its self-generated publicity. In the area of race relations, TVA promised that its quota policy would ensure fair treatment of blacks. In fact, the quota system ensured that blacks would be hired only in the lowest, most temporary positions.[5]

TVA stated that its quota was maintained for the benefit of blacks, but not at the expense of whites. It assured its white employees that their ranks would not be diminished by the inclusion of a representative proportion of blacks. It also stated that it would continue to adhere to its policy of "merit and efficiency" as its sole requirement for employment. Given these promises, TVA decided that it could meet its percentage objectives with the minimum of disturbance to local custom or governmental policy by confining its racial quota system to blacks employed in the construction section. Through the employment of blacks in reservoir clearance work, TVA claimed that it had been able to meet two of its stated objectives: the employment of blacks in proportion to their population percentage in the valley, and adherence to the merit principle of employment.[6]

Reservoir clearance work was unskilled and temporary in nature—the average employment lasted only six months. This allowed TVA to establish simple sign-up procedures that ensured large numbers of blacks in the desired locales, while the unskilled nature of the work allowed it to hire without using any qualification tests. The agency used the quota only for unskilled or semiskilled positions, stating that it was possible to use quotas without violating the merit and efficiency principle only as long as these fixed proportions were not applied to each specific occupation.[7]

TVA would therefore not use racial quotas to fill skilled positions, insisting that "in most of the skilled occupations relatively few applicants of the Negro race have competed successfully with white applicants in training, experience, and examination requirements." TVA assumed that the majority of black applicants would be unsuitable for skilled work. Yet there is evidence that it would not hire blacks for skilled positions even when they were qualified. In 1938 it hired Francis Steele, a highly trained electrician, under the assumption that he was white. Steele reported for the job, announced that he was a Negro, and was promptly fired. The reason given was that white employees would not work with him.[8] The limited number of blacks in administrative positions were employed as interviewers, labor relations counselors, and supervisors of Negro training. They were given duties only in race relations and held no positions of authority. By easily filling the quota through unskilled and temporary positions, TVA avoided having to concern itself with proportionate representation if and when skilled black applicants appeared. In fact, the personnel department had no incentive to hire black skilled workers or to break down job barriers. Thus, the TVA quota system did not significantly help the employment situation among blacks in the Tennessee valley. The vast majority of its black employees were hired at the minimum wage and for the shortest period of time.[9]

Paradoxically, although TVA acknowledged having a racial quota for unskilled employment, it denied having an overall racial policy and insisted that it followed a policy of nondiscrimination in regard to race. In TVA's definition, a nondiscrimination policy meant no official barriers to the employment of blacks, no official discrimination in social programs and extension services, and at the same time, no special efforts to ensure equal treatment of minorities in TVA or the surrounding valley. It hoped to effect in one sense a policy of no policy in regard to race. Its officials stated that any effort to ensure an advantageous position for blacks would, in effect, show an awareness of racial groups and would contradict TVA's policy of impartiality.[10]

Perhaps the clearest and most revealing statement concerning the reality of the Authority's racial policies was made by the TVA official who stated:

> The Authority has no special mandate or suggestion in its act that would suggest a direct or separate approach to the solution of the economic problem of the Negro population in the Valley. It is believed, however, that the record of the Authority shows that whenever its program has touched upon the problem of the Negro, it has made every effort to discharge its responsibility as a governmental agency serving the public of the Valley as a whole.[11]

The self-limitation of the TVA policy served to reduce the scope and energy of the social and economic programs that could have helped minorities. Yet this self-limitation was not just confined to minority policy, but rather was characteristic of an approach to policy implementation that reduced the impact of *all* social and economic revitalization programs. TVA operated in a reality much more complicated and far less clear-cut than either the romantic views of the publicists and journalists or the careful, rational projections of New Deal planners. As one social scientist observed:

> Leaders of an operating organization have problems separate from those who function primarily in the realm of symbols. . . . Doctrine, being abstract, is judiciously selective and may be qualified at will in discourse, subject only to the restrictions of sense and logic. But action is concrete,

generating consequences which define a sphere of interest and responsibility, together with a corresponding chain of commitments.[12]

In formulating its programs, TVA was restricted by such factors as vague planning powers, congressional scrutiny, national and local special-interest pressure, organizational weaknesses, and conflicting personal philosophies on the board of directors, all of which had an impact on racial policies and their implementation within TVA.

The Tennessee Valley Authority Act, as stated above, essentially produced a hybrid of the broad social planning agency outlined by the president and the agency with a more limited function of power production and flood control outlined by Congress. As is in the nature of compromises, the essential thrust of the original proposals was modified significantly. The original presidential concept was weakened, since the act provided, in reality, a rather circumscribed authorization for regional planning. TVA's power to conduct surveys and make general plans for the area came from an indirect delegation of power from the president. Congress did not give the board of directors of TVA a clear mandate to effect social plans for the area. In an area as potentially controversial as governmental social planning, the fact that TVA did not have clear authority from Congress significantly handicapped its planning program.[13]

TVA was reluctant to rely on the TVA act for its powers of social planning, preferring to justify developmental activity through its "action program." The "action program" consisted of whatever support activity was necessary to construct and maintain TVA's large power production, flood control, and fertilizer production plans; both regional and social planning were initiated to promote the rationality and efficiency of TVA's production programs. TVA could not, however, initiate broad plans with much flexibility or creativity, and was forced to look first at its immediate needs and formulate limited plans to meet them.[14]

The Division of Regional Planning reflected the hesitancy and self-limited scope of TVA planning. Initially a focal point of interest for academic regional planners and liberal New Dealers, this division was originally designed to make a vital contribution to the overall TVA program. Yet as a result of increased conservative criticism from Congress and the courts of other aspects of its programs—along with the 1938 dismissal of Arthur Morgan, who was the strongest supporter of regional and social planning on the original board—TVA decided to reduce the division's size and responsibility. Finally, in 1938, TVA was reorganized and the Division of Regional Planning was reduced, its staff and responsibilities divided among the departments of Regional Planning Studies, Public Health and Safety, Commerce, Agricultural Industries, and Reservoir Property Management (Figures 3 and 4). Morale suffered greatly, and there was a large turnover of staff and management.[15] Several social scientists contend that 1938 marked the end of regional planning initiatives within TVA. One observed in the 1950s that "TVA has not done comprehensive and systematic social and economic planning since 1938 nor has it sought to undertake such activities, although it has never formally rejected the idea that it is a planning agency for the region."[16]

From its inception, TVA was embroiled in legal battles over its constitutionality. Private utilities challenged its power program three times. The first and most significant challenge was a suit brought by George Ashwander and thirteen other holders of Alabama Power Company's preferred stock, claiming that the government lacked the constitutional power to engage in the electric utility business. The ideological battle over private versus public utilities, which had surfaced in congressional debate over the TVA act, was now in the courts. In 1936 the Supreme Court ruled that TVA could sell electricity generated from Wilson Dam to whomever it wished. The Court ruled narrowly, confining its decision to Wilson Dam and opening the way for further challenges to other dam sites. Two other challenges by private utilities were also settled in TVA's favor. These court challenges, however, placed parts of the TVA program under a cloud and, in the case of the Ashwander suit, under a court injunction that restricted TVA's power business for two years.

A suit brought by George Berry, a Tennessee Democratic leader and strong supporter of Roosevelt, created political embarrassment for TVA. Berry had purchased an old quarry that was in line to be flooded by Norris Dam, the first TVA-constructed dam. Arthur Morgan, the board chairman, refused to recognize Berry's claim, revealing his suspicion that Berry had had no intention of ever operating the quarry and had purchased it merely to collect a condemnation settlement from the government. In this politically sensitive matter, Arthur Morgan, acting on behalf of TVA, incurred not only the wrath of Berry and other local politicians, but also the public criticism of the two other members of the TVA board, who were much more pragmatic in their approach to local political and business interests. It is not surprising that TVA officials under siege by power companies and others were reluctant to engage in broad-reaching plans and surveys certain to attract new lawsuits and the loss of politically powerful friends.

The Berry case illustrated the dissension among the three directors during the crucial period between 1933 and 1938. This dissension was another

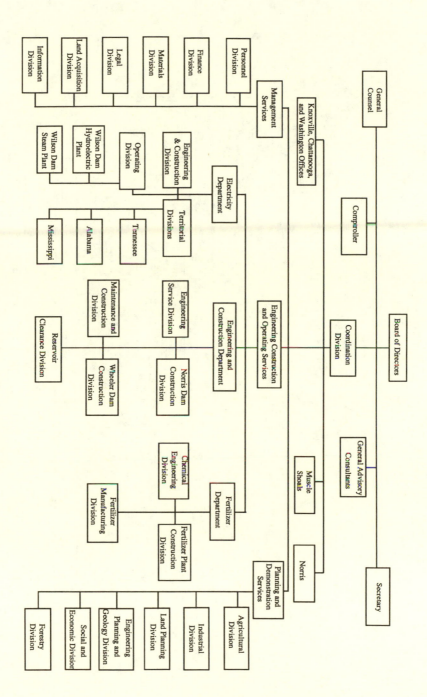

FIGURE 3.   Organizational Chart of TVA, 1934

Source: TVA Technical Library, Knoxville, Tennessee

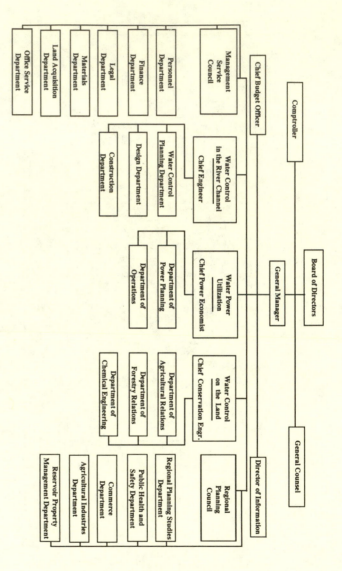

FIGURE 4.   Organizational Chart of TVA, 1938

Source: TVA Technical Library, Knoxville, Tennessee

factor decreasing the scope and effectiveness of the social planning component within TVA, the component responsible for some racial policies. Arthur Morgan was to become increasingly disenchanted with his fellow board members, Harcourt Morgan and David Lilienthal, as they began to outvote him on major policy decisions two to one.[17]

Arthur Morgan was the epitome of the self-made man. With little more than a high school education, Morgan apprenticed under his father and became a successful engineer. He soon made the construction of dams for flood control his specialty. Described by his biographer as a utopian who was fascinated by Edward Bellamy, Morgan described himself as a progressive social engineer who believed that since business could be well managed and science operated under universal laws, then society, with the aid of technology, the social sciences, and moral ethics, could be transformed for the better. During the 1920s Morgan had served as the president of Antioch College, transforming it from a traditional liberal arts college operating under a deficit into a solvent work-study college with an emphasis on practical experience and community service. Selected by Roosevelt because of his engineering and administrative experience, Morgan was consulted on the appointment of the other two directors and believed himself to be the first among equals. He embarked on a broad-based publicity campaign to sell TVA to the public, expressed his opposition to political patronage, and showed an aversion to politicians and local business interests, while extolling the virtues of the local folk culture and acknowledging the need to arrive at a compromise with private utilities.[18]

Morgan soon encountered difficulties with his opposite in ideology and personality, David Lilienthal. Lilienthal was a thirty-three-year-old wunderkind, a Harvard-trained lawyer, a "Wisconsin progressive," a protégé of Felix Frankfurter, and an advocate of public utilities. Far more pragmatic and politically astute than his much older colleague, Lilienthal made an effort to ingratiate himself with those in important positions, including Roosevelt. Morgan clashed with Lilienthal over the latter's willingness to wink at patronage and political appointments within TVA and his unwillingness to reach an amicable consensus with private utilities. The clash culminated in 1938, when Arthur Morgan took his conflict with Lilienthal to the press and accused the majority on the board of malfeasance in the Berry case. This airing of dirty laundry created bad publicity for a beleaguered agency and provided Republicans and a few conservative Democrats with an excuse to call for a congressional investigation of its activities. The Joint Committee to Investigate the Tennessee Valley Authority was convened in the spring and summer of 1938 to investigate Morgan's allegations.

In addition, the committee heard from power companies, organizations, and private citizens who testified that TVA had treated them unfairly. The NAACP used this opportunity to present evidence that TVA had violated its employment policy and had discriminated against blacks. After hearing much diverse testimony, the committee, which was controlled by Democrats, absolved TVA of any wrongdoing in the Berry case and dismissed the complaints by the private utilities. It did, however, order TVA to investigate the NAACP's complaints.[19]

Although the hearings afforded the NAACP a forum, the chaos that precipitated the hearings did much to divert TVA from its initial plans for valley revitalization, under which changes in race relations might have occurred. Arthur Morgan, under siege from within TVA, was also unpopular with the local population, who relied on TVA's jobs, training programs, and model housing, but resented the paternalistic tone of his call for a new society, a better civilization. Senator Bachman of Tennessee, an early TVA supporter, sent Morgan an angry letter that concluded:

> Finally I do resent, on behalf of my people, and for myself, the suggestion that we are in need of a new cultural civilization, which you continuously advocate in your addresses. . . . A people whose forbears went with Sevier to Kings Mountain, destroyed Ferguson and forever broke the hope of British domination in this country . . . are surely in no need of intellectual or sociological admonitions in the pursuance of their welfare.[20]

The TVA social planning agenda lost its chief proponent when Morgan was fired by Roosevelt in March 1938. TVA also lost its potential to make significant changes in the societal structure from above, although even Morgan's list did not include race relations.

Another factor that limited the scope of TVA social planning and had a direct impact on race relations was TVA's avowed commitment to "grassroots" democracy. Although the autocratic Arthur Morgan was less sympathetic, both Lilienthal and Harcourt Morgan were advocates of planning government programs around the wishes and needs of the local inhabitants, particularly the politically and economically powerful, as much as possible.

This philosophy affected planning in areas that impinged upon the cherished beliefs and customs of the local inhabitants. T. Levron Howard articulated the attitude of his fellow TVA regional planners when he stated: "The TVA is not attempting to impose a new way of living upon the people of the valley. Rather, we are attempting to blend modern form with the long-existing habits and social customs of the locality."[21] Two of the longstanding customs of the valley were racial separation and the inferior economic and political status of blacks. A reliance on "grass-roots democracy" provided TVA with a ready excuse for not forcing social and economic change on a white majority committed to maintaining the racial status quo.

The policy of attempting to blend its own practice into the racial habits of the region was not, of course, limited to TVA: it was part of an overall conservative strain within New Deal recovery agencies. It was the policy of such agencies as the Federal Housing Administration, the AAA, and even the Ickes-led PWA to maintain segregated facilities in areas that customarily practiced racial segregation. Unlike the above agencies, however, TVA was an agency committed to planning for a future society, and its hesitancy to break existing habits was most significant.

TVA relied on local political organizations as well as civic groups and state planning commissions to help administer its social and economic programs, preferring to work through existing organizations rather than establish new ones. In this way, local agencies could be assured of a hearing for their suggestions and wishes. In most instances the wish of these local organizations was to preserve the status quo as much as possible. The relationship between TVA and the regional land grant colleges illustrates this tendency. TVA provided consultants and research tools for a "joint program of agricultural development and watershed protection through improved fertilization" in the white land grant colleges. (The program consisted of testing food products developed by the Authority.) TVA also tested phosphate fertilizers on local farms. The farms were picked primarily by the university or the state agricultural extension service, with TVA's approval. To be picked as a demonstration farm was to be assured the use of the most modern equipment, a supply of fertilizer, and advice from trained consultants. The farmer chosen by the university tended already to be the most efficient and prosperous in the area. Thus, TVA was indirectly involved in furthering the power and wealth of the leading farms of the area, which in turn served to bolster the region's entrenched farm interests.[22]

The land grant program also helped to preserve the status quo in the area of race relations. Money, research tools, and agricultural consultants were provided only to white universities in this totally segregated system, thus excluding all blacks from participating in or contributing to the program. The black agricultural colleges had no place in the TVA fertilizer program and did not benefit from the TVA-inspired academic and financial improvement of their white counterparts. While the position of the black agricultural colleges remained static, the white land grant colleges improved with TVA's help.[23]

The adherence to local control perpetuated old inequalities not only on a broad regional level, but also on a very local level. In 1933 blacks were discouraged and prevented from taking the examination to work at Wheeler Dam, not because of any official policy of TVA, but because of the personal prejudices of local postal employees who were given the responsibility to hand out applications on request. When these non-TVA workers refused to give applications to blacks, TVA elected to waive the examination requirement for blacks rather than supersede or disrupt local control over the distribution process.[24]

Commitment to democratic planning left TVA susceptible to local and national special-interest groups that sought to influence and direct its social planning programs. TVA attempted to accede to the demands of such groups in proportion to their power and potential for damage to the agency. The more successful groups tended to be economically or politically powerful in the valley.

Among the most powerful were the large agricultural owners of the region. They, along with influential conservative members of the AAA, sought to influence TVA's policy of compensation for agricultural lands flooded by TVA reservoirs. The large landowners wished to receive all the money from the government. They in turn would distribute funds for the relocation of the tenant farmers and sharecroppers who had lived on their land. By seeking to control the distribution process, the large landholders also sought to perpetuate the owner–tenant farmer relationship. Progressive reformers in the New Deal administration, including Will Alexander and Rexford Tugwell, wanted to change the social and economic relationship between tenant and owner by having TVA pay tenants directly. Within TVA, many regional planning field workers also hoped that TVA would be instrumental in breaking the tenants' dependency on the owners. Instead, TVA chose to support the status quo and paid compensation only to the owners.[25]

Several southern politicians formed a powerful pressure group whose energies were directed at preserving the racial status quo. Not only were John Sparkman, Lister Hill, and John Rankin staunch TVA supporters in Congress, but all were also committed to the maintenance of racial segregation and unequal employment opportunities. Hill provides an interesting illustration of Aubrey Williams' dictum that "there are no southern liberals, only conservatives or radicals," at least regarding race. A supporter of "liberal" positions on health care and other social programs, a prototypical New Deal Democrat, Hill remained opposed to civil rights legislation throughout his career, to the point of signing the 1954 "Southern

Manifesto" in opposition to court-ordered desegregation.[26] During the New Deal, Congressmen Sparkman of Alabama (elected in 1937) and Rankin of Mississippi complained that TVA was breaking too many racial barriers. In 1943 both congressmen wrote to David Lilienthal concerning TVA's hiring of three black security guards. Rankin emphasized the severe risk that TVA was taking in pursuing its "liberal" racial policy. Part of the risk was due to the potential for racial violence throughout the South:

> Let me suggest . . . that with the growing tension throughout the South, the TVA is taking too great a risk in placing negroes [*sic*] as guards of these dams. If you are aware of what is happening at Mobile, Vicksburg, Laurel, Tupelo and Corinth, and understand the feelings of the white people of the South, you can appreciate the fact that this issue is charged with dynamite.[27]

Sparkman warned that "a group of iron workers have stated that they are going to throw the negroes in the river." [28]

The risk was also political. Rankin stressed that by hiring the three black guards, TVA would "engender more bitterness among southern representatives and southern senators than anything else I could mention, and I do not want to see you injured by it." Rankin went on to proclaim his allegiance to TVA and describe himself as a true friend of the Authority. "As you know, the TVA is near and dear to my heart. I went through the battle of my life for its creation, and I have carried on its fight in the House from that day to this." Rankin noted that TVA had many enemies and implied that it could not risk alienating otherwise staunch supporters. He closed by suggesting that Lilienthal "quietly remove these negroes as guards and, if necessary, assign them to manual employment, and eliminate this source of irritation and friction. Believe me it is the better part of wisdom that you do this." [29]

Lilienthal replied that the TVA was very conscious of "the community relations aspect of employment practices." Citing the many meetings with Wilson Dam employees and their supervisors, as well as the interested and concerned members of the local community, Lilienthal assured Rankin and Sparkman that hostility and serious discontent had been defused. He also assured the congressmen that the blacks were hired to fill newly created positions and would not replace white guards. In addition, the congressmen were told that no new precedent for the area was being established. Black public safety officers and black police officers and building guards were frequently employed in southern cities.[30] TVA intended to hire these three guards to function as watchmen (that is, they would not be giving directions to whites). By this time TVA had departed from its previous practice of meeting its black employment quota through large-scale hiring in construction work. In 1943 it was attempting to expand its hiring "in the occupations in which qualified Negroes are available and accustomed to working in this area." [31]

In this case, TVA did not bow to considerable pressure. The three black building guards were hired, and no difficulties were reported after they were placed on active duty. Yet this type of pressure fostered hesitation and caution, and additional pressure and protest from Rankin caused a slight change in employment practices. In 1944 the Personnel Department permitted a black woman to take an examination for a clerical position (file clerk). This action, unlike the episode of the three security guards, was a departure from customary job classifications for blacks. Although clearly annoyed by Rankin, whom he called one of the most reactionary forces in the House, Lilienthal was concerned about the personnel decision and complained, "This action is untimely as hell." The black woman was not given the clerical position.[32]

Civil rights organizations, particularly the NAACP, also made up a very concerned special-interest group. Unlike many pressure groups that TVA had to contend with, they were concerned that TVA's regional planning program was too limited in its goals to create a climate and a basis for social change. The NAACP criticized TVA's employment practices, its lack of interest in including blacks in experimental model communities and training programs, and the general lack of desire to break down racial barriers within TVA itself and in the valley region.

Three investigations of TVA sponsored by the NAACP, and one investigation by Robert Weaver, assistant to the secretary of the interior, produced documented evidence that racial discrimination occurred in all departments and at all administrative levels of TVA. These investigations also concluded that TVA was not making a significant effort to change its practice during the New Deal era.[33]

TVA responded to these specific allegations by sponsoring an investigation of race relations by its own staff. To the dismay of the board of directors and the general manager, most of the allegations of the NAACP investigators were supported by the TVA-sponsored reports.[34] Authority officials responded to the direct criticism contained in Weaver's report by establishing a racially mixed Race Relations Committee in the Personnel Department to investigate allegations of discrimination. Yet the committee had no police powers and could only investigate complaints and offer suggestions for change. In practice, it frequently attempted to diffuse criticism of TVA by both black TVA employees and civil rights organizations.[35]

In 1938 the NAACP bitterly observed that TVA, after five years of operation, had evolved no integrated policy for dealing with questions affecting Negroes: TVA still "regards Negroes as a labor commodity rather than as citizens."[36] In 1942, after nine years of exposing discrimination in TVA, a Tennessee NAACP official wrote: "To summarize, the whole TVA situation is rotten as far as Negroes are concerned."[37]

While philosophical adherence to democratic planning on a regional basis made TVA susceptible to pressure from special-interest groups, other factors caused it to support the wishes of some special-interest groups over others. Among these factors were the personal views and beliefs of the top administrative personnel, especially the three directors of the board.

A decentralized administrative structure made administrators' personal views and beliefs particularly important in shaping policy and directives in TVA. Large private corporations tend to have a large board of directors and to delegate administrative control to a president or general manager. TVA in its early period entrusted control to its three full-time directors, Arthur Morgan, Harcourt A. Morgan (no relation), and David Lilienthal; the director of personnel, Gordon Clapp; and after 1936 the general manager, John Blandford.[38]

The chairman of the board, Arthur Morgan, held a good deal of power during the formative period between 1933 and 1938. He was responsible for the appointment of key TVA officials, including the director of personnel. Until 1936 he also served as the general manager, whose functions and duties were "to be those customary to the General Manager of a private corporation, and to include the coordination and general administration of the various activities of the corporation." In addition to these duties, the chairman was given the ultimate responsibility for regional and social planning, housing, training (other than agricultural), flood control, and soil conservation—in short, the majority of TVA's social programs.[39]

The responsibility for all matters relating to agriculture, from experimental farms to the maintenance of the Muscle Shoals nitrate-fertilizer plants, was given to Harcourt A. Morgan. The third director, David Lilienthal, whose expertise was in utility regulation, was given responsibility for legal problems, land appraisal, purchase, condemnation, and power distribution. The board members, while functioning as a unit on questions of general policy, functioned as individuals in the administration of their specific designated areas.[40]

The positions of director of personnel and general manager were also important in the administrative structure of TVA. TVA was autonomous from the Civil Service; consequently, the director of personnel could initiate and formulate independent hiring policies. One of his responsibilities was to construct examinations for skilled and semiskilled positions. He also acted on requests from department supervisors for replacement personnel and ruled on promotion recommendations. The first director of personnel was Floyd Reeves, whom Arthur Morgan hired away from the University of Chicago.[41]

The position of general manager became part of the administrative structure in 1936. TVA had suffered from administrative inefficiency when it operated under the leadership of a chairman–general manager. Over the objections of Chairman Arthur Morgan, the other board members voted to establish the office of general manager as the chief administrator to whom all department heads reported. He was responsible for the execution of the board's decisions and policies and for the preparation of the budget. During the New Deal period, however, the general manager remained subordinate to the three active board members.[42]

The first general manager was John Blandford, a former director of public safety in Cincinnati, who served until 1939. In 1939 Blandford resigned, and Gordon Clapp, the director of personnel, replaced him. Clapp, who later became the chairman of the board, was a native of Wisconsin and had received a master's degree from the University of Chicago.[43]

Throughout the period of administrative restructuring, the three directors retained much control over the shaping of TVA policies and future plans. Lobbyists who wished to influence decisions approached one of the three directors. Harcourt Morgan, the agricultural specialist, was the most accessible to conservative interests. He considered himself the spokesman for local interests on the TVA board and advocated the principles of decentralization and cooperation with local and state agencies in his writings.[44] The large landowners of the Tennessee valley sought his support. Harcourt Morgan, in turn, frequently supported the conservative economic policies of the Department of Agriculture and the AAA, giving vital support to the decision to pay landowners rather than tenant farmers compensation for land and crops destroyed by TVA reservoir flooding. In addition, this former university president strongly encouraged efforts to improve land grant colleges and universities in the valley. He initially regarded TVA as a short-term experiment that might not last four years, if Congress or the courts chose to terminate it, and he was concerned that nothing tangible would be left in the valley except a few dams after TVA ceased to exist.[45]

While the agriculturalists and land grant colleges had Harcourt Morgan on the board to support their interests, and the advocates for public utilities had David Lilienthal, the civil rights special interests did not have one particular board member to champion their cause. Arthur Morgan, as chairman of the board and the official responsible for almost all the agency's social programs and social planning, was the member most likely to be concerned with the problems of minorities in the Tennessee valley. His reputation for taking risks, his unpopular stands against patronage and political favors, and his willingness to ruffle the feathers of powerful politicians made him the best bet for those who hoped for a policy committed to changing race relations. Indeed, Arthur Morgan was the individual on the board to whom most complaints of discrimination were sent by civil rights groups.

Arthur Morgan, however, officially denied that any racial discrimination existed. When confronted by critics, he flatly denied that TVA discriminated against blacks and implied that the critics were ignorant of and insensitive to the racial mores of the South. In 1935 John P. Davis of the Joint Committee on National Recovery accused TVA of excluding blacks from the TVA town of Norris, Tennessee. Morgan replied, "It is not the policy of the Authority to exclude Negroes from Norris," even though "there are no Negro families occupying houses at Norris at the present time." Although there were blacks living in temporary housing in Norris, it was clear that these blacks would not be permanent residents, because "the fact of the matter is that no applications for houses at Norris have been received from Negro employees." Morgan also stated that all the houses were occupied by employees whose work was centered in that area, there was a waiting list of some 150 employees, none of whom were black, and there was little chance that additional houses would be built. He concluded that it was unlikely that any blacks would be able to live in Norris.[46]

That same year Morgan wrote to Secretary of the Interior Ickes, complaining that "there has been considerable misinformation and misinterpretation of the Negro problem as it is related to the program of the TVA." He suggested that Ickes find "a competent Negro leader" to visit the Authority and observe its work first-hand. Ickes chose Robert Weaver, a young economist and advisor on Negro affairs for the Department of the Interior. As noted above, his report, to the embarrassment of Morgan and the agency, confirmed Davis' charges and added several new ones in the area of employment opportunities. The report was addressed to Arthur Morgan but was also circulated to all of the board members and to the director of personnel, who prepared an analysis of it.[47]

Yet Arthur Morgan continued to deny any knowledge of discriminatory practices in TVA. In 1938 he appeared before the Joint Committee on National Recovery. Quizzed by Senator James J. Davis of Pennsylvania on the "brutal treatment of colored labor" and the "exclusion practices at Norris," Morgan replied that he did not know of any such practices in TVA. He also explained that TVA did not exclude blacks from Norris on racial grounds; rather, blacks were not housed at Norris for economic reasons. He pointed out that under Tennessee laws, if "you have Negro housing, you have to set up Negro schools, and Negro facilities." These facilities had to be separate, by law, and construction of separate black facilities would raise costs needlessly.[48]

Morgan was concerned with more than cost considerations in regard to race relations. Although not a southerner, in many respects his racial views were similar to those of southern conservatives. He stated that deficiencies caused by historical, environmental, and biological factors relegated blacks to a segregated society until they could improve their position. In 1910 he wrote that "the extreme and universal immorality of the negro is a bigger blight upon the country than people realize." In the twenties Morgan became interested in the eugenics movement, which sought the perfection of mankind through the selective breeding of the fit. These beliefs were shared in the 1920s by Margaret Sanger of the birth control movement and an assortment of Harvard-trained social scientists. Morgan, however, continued his support of the eugenics movement into the 1930s, long after it had fallen out of favor with most Americans. He believed that certain races and nationalities were more fit than others and that Asians and blacks were the most unfit of all.[49]

Morgan put the burden of improvement on blacks themselves and in many ways echoed the self-improvement stance of Booker T. Washington. He told the commencement class at the historically black Knoxville College:

> If colored men can depend upon the fellowship and honesty of other colored men in business, if colored physicians and dentists and lawyers can be depended upon for honest and faithful service, if colored people can supply to each other their needs in a spirit of brotherhood—the New Deal will be well on its way for them.[50]

Morgan suggested that blacks should not criticize the racial policies of TVA, because the Authority could only do so much for them. It was not the government's responsibility to provide better opportunities for blacks. Blacks had to create their own opportunities. Blacks were to be the pioneers of the modern Tennessee valley: "building an economy of their own, they may have a better opportunity in life than the white people did here a century ago." Further, they must reject radical or northern concepts of equality and to listen only to their truest friends, "the white people of the South." "Find a man who is working here for a fair deal for the colored people," he told the black college audience, "and you will usually find a native Southerner who knows the colored people and who knows how to work with and for them." [51]

Morgan did not leave many written records expressing his personal views on blacks. He did, in correspondence with both Robert Weaver and John Davis, exhibit a formal courtesy. Yet he did not capitalize the word "Negro," a practice that was being adopted at this time by progressive newspapers and government agencies. In public addresses to black audiences, he preferred to use the term "colored people." [52]

Moreover, he was not above using racial stereotypes and telling a "Negro story" when illustrating a point to a predominantly white audience. To convey the differences between the plight of the North, which had lost its prosperity during the Depression, and the plight of the South, which had never enjoyed any prosperity, he told the following story, which strongly emphasized the use of a supposedly Negro dialect: "A kindly woman visiting a Negro orphanage undertook to help wait on the table. When she said to a little waif, "Will you have more molasses?" he turned to the boy next to him and remarked, "She asked me to have mo' lasses. Can't she see I ain't had any lasses yet?" [53]

Some forty years later, Arthur Morgan attempted to cast himself as a thwarted racial progressive. Despite overwhelming evidence to the contrary, he insisted that under his leadership blacks were given equal pay for equal work and were provided with "identical housing with equal facilities." He regretted that this housing was segregated but had feared at the time that "if I had tried to impose integrated housing, I probably would have been out of TVA." He blamed the absence of a strong, positive racial policy on the conservatism of his fellow board members, recalling a 1933 attempt to establish a three-man commission on race relations, consisting of Morgan himself, the president of Fisk University, and Will Alexander, whom Morgan described as "a white Southerner known throughout the South for his active interest but somewhat moderate views on improving race relations." That Alexander was recommended is no surprise: his name appeared frequently in New Deal circles when the racial views of southern moderates were mentioned. Such a commission was needed "for dealing with thorny questions of race that would inevitably arise in an active public works program in the South," Morgan recalled, yet Harcourt Morgan and David Lilienthal "would have no part of it." [54]

To place Arthur Morgan's racial views and plans for blacks in a proper

1930s perspective, it is important to compare them with those of other social planners working in the South at the time and grappling with thorny racial issues. One such planner was Howard Odum, North Carolina sociologist and fellow member with George F. Milton and Will Alexander of the racially moderate Interracial Cooperation Commission. Although Odum considered Arthur Morgan a rather impractical dreamer, he shared similar racial views and likewise favored economic opportunities over political and social advances for blacks. Both Morgan and Odum felt that blacks had to earn their political rights by first building a secure economic base. Both held Booker T. Washington as the proper model for black achievement. Self-help, industrial education, and proper guidance by southern whites were keys to success for southern blacks. While defending the basic good instincts of southern whites, both expressed regret at the intransigence of poor and middle-class whites who resisted efforts to widen job opportunities for blacks. As planners, both felt that their hands were tied by a conservative majority: Odum was powerless to make significant changes because of his role as an academic planner, and Morgan was unwilling to make changes because of his adherence to "grass-roots democracy." A racially integrated South was for both men only a remote possibility. Neither planned for that possibility, or hoped for that day. To Morgan an integrated society represented a radical concept of equality, while to Odum it represented the beginning of a trend that could lead from social equality to intermarriage to racial suicide.[55]

Yet for all their similarities, there were three important differences in their racial views. Odum and the North Carolina regionalists professed a moral commitment to racial change, a need to do what was just and right. TVA officials, in contrast, displayed almost clinical detachment in talking about race relations, emphasizing practical limits and considerations, and eschewing idealism. Moreover, although both talked about the need to provide greater job opportunities for blacks, they differed on the extent of these opportunities. Odum argued that while industrial education was useful for the majority of blacks, professionally trained blacks were also needed: even in a segregated society, blacks should be found in all occupational categories, from laborer to professional. There was a need for black skilled artisans as well as doctors, lawyers, and academicians to serve the black community. Odum also suggested that southern industry would function better if it would train and employ more black workers. Morgan, as the chairman of TVA and the largest employer in the Tennessee valley, provided only limited opportunities for training and employment in the skilled trades. His quota system was horizontal, applying only to unskilled and temporary positions.

A third difference lay in their approaches to planning for blacks. Odum recognized that blacks were an important and permanent part of southern society. They had to be included in plans for the future South, or they would later present serious problems for society. It would be impossible to ignore the problems of blacks, he argued; their presence and significance were too great in social and economic terms. Morgan, in contrast, having instituted the racial quota system, ignored the presence of blacks, particularly in areas where they made up less than 10 percent of the population. He initiated plans that excluded blacks from model communities and worksites. Planning for the racially homogeneous community of Norris made ideological and economic sense to Morgan: the duplication in facilities required by segregation was too costly; integration was unthinkable; so the exclusion of blacks was acceptable. Blacks were included at many job sites only after protests were made. It is ironic that Morgan, the transplanted northerner, envisioned a more limited future for blacks than the academic from North Carolina.[56]

Harcourt Morgan, a native Canadian, also appears to have adopted the racial mores of the conservative South. He did not correspond with critics of TVA racial policies and consequently did not leave a formal statement of his position on them. But he did record his analysis of the historical precedents for the tenant farm and sharecropper system, along with an unusual interpretation of the effects of slavery on the white and black population of the South:

> The moral question of the slave trade became a matter of very serious debate which under political and economic conditions ended in a civil war. During the period of the slave economy there were several millions of white people who were not a part of that economy and who became jealous of the protection enjoyed by the Negro under the slave economy. Antagonisms between this white population and the slave population became almost traditional. With the end of the war and the liberation of the slaves, these two populations came into conflict under the new economics which evolved gradually into the present tenant and sharecropper system.[57]

Harcourt Morgan regarded the slave legacy as one of the tragedies of the South and one of the serious problems facing TVA social planners. The experience of slavery had established a permanent "anthropological pattern" in the South, which the TVA was obligated as a regionally sensitive agency to maintain. His use of "anthropological pattern" is reminiscent of the justification for racial segregation presented by Howard Odum in 1910.

Significantly, by the 1930s Odum, along with most social scientists, had dropped allusions to anthropological or biological patterns in describing southern racial conditions.[58]

The third member of the board, David Lilienthal, served on it from 1933 to 1946, the last five years as its chairman. Lilienthal came to the TVA with a reputation as a supporter of a variety of liberal causes. He did not, however, support progressive racial policies while on the TVA board. Although his racial views were less rigidly conservative than either Harcourt Morgan's or Arthur Morgan's, he nevertheless carried out a policy maintaining the racial status quo throughout his tenure on the board.[59]

Lilienthal expressed his opinions on blacks in American society in two distinct roles—as TVA chairman, and as a private citizen. In 1941, the year in which he replaced Harcourt Morgan as chairman, President Roosevelt established the Fair Employment Practices Committee. All government agencies, including TVA, were expected to comply with the committee's nondiscriminatory guidelines. Each agency had to file periodic reports, and Lilienthal also answered several letters of inquiry from the FEPC concerning complaints of discrimination lodged against TVA. He stated that TVA had always maintained a nondiscriminatory wage policy, minority employment in proportion to the Negro population of the valley area, and efforts to expand and extend occupational opportunities. He acknowledged, however, that some areas needed more attention and that TVA "has not reached a final solution to this pressing problem by any means."[60]

One area in which TVA acknowledged the need for more compliance involved the cooperation of organized labor. Most trade unions in the Tennessee valley excluded blacks from their locals. In answer to a letter of inquiry from the FEPC concerning discrimination against Negro carpenters, Lilienthal asserted that there was a shortage of qualified Negro carpenters in the Tennessee valley, in part because of blacks' exclusion from apprenticeship opportunities in the unions. He added that TVA did not discriminate against blacks, although out of the 1,900 carpenters it employed, only one was black.[61]

Lilienthal, in his official capacity, wished to present a favorable image of TVA and consequently attempted to present its racial policies in the context of private employment practices in the Tennessee valley. These were highly discriminatory and exclusionary, and TVA, because of its grass-roots philosophy, could not force progressive racial practices on the local white population. Although Lilienthal's assertion of local intransigence could be interpreted as a convenient excuse, his belief in the sanctity of grass-roots governance was real, and it influenced his opposition to initiating progressive racial practices in TVA. He believed that two principles were essential for the effectiveness of TVA: "First, that resource development must be governed by the unity of nature herself. Second, that the people must participate actively in that development." [62]

Lilienthal and the rest of the TVA board were aware of the drawbacks of relying on the will of the people, whom they recognized to be a basically conservative force. In a board meeting discussion, Lilienthal posed a hypothetical dilemma: a local institution strongly supported by the people opposed a vital progressive program within TVA. Did one choose the progressive program for the future good of the people, or did one adhere to the principle of grass-roots democracy? According to Lilienthal, the board decided that the will of the people was more important. Patience was necessary—to educate the population and make it more agreeable to progressive programs. [63]

Although Lilienthal's reluctance to act against discrimination could be attributed in part to his adherence to grass-roots democracy, it could also be attributed to his personal social analysis of America. Segregation and discrimination, while unfortunate in humanistic terms, were for him a part of American social history and would probably remain so for years to come. When his daughter expressed outrage at the segregation at Norris Lake, Lilienthal told her

> the feeling about Negroes by most people, North and South, was a fact and should be approached as a fact. In the South it was more nearly understandable, for it had a sorry history, especially the reconstruction period. There was no use pretending that there would be anything but social distinctions, and with them segregation, perhaps for generations to come. . . . The thing to do was to try, patiently and with considerable difficulty, to remove some of the causes of race feeling, but to stand like a rock on the right of each Negro to an opportunity to work and to learn as much as he was capable of learning on his merits. [64]

Although he acknowledged that blacks were not treated equally and did not have adequate opportunities for work, Lilienthal also asserted that blacks, particularly in the South, were not excessively mistreated. In an argument similar to that advanced by southern moderates like Odum, Lilienthal sought to

> explode the myth that it is in the South that the Negro is most mistreated and downtrodden. The record is not one that satisfies or begins to sat-

43

isfy most of the intelligent, good citizens of the South. But [Gordon]
Clapp tells me that Appleton, Wisconsin has an ordinance of many years'
standing forbidding any Negro to stay in that abolitionist community overnight.[65]

The TVA board as a whole elected not to issue any formal statement of
policy specifically on race. In 1938 the racial issue was placed before the
board in the form of Board Agenda Item No. 622, "Housing and Employment of Negroes for Hiwassee Project." The item concerned allegations of
exclusionary practices against blacks. After some informal discussion, it
was removed from the agenda, with the understanding that the general subject would be reviewed later and discussed among the directors and members of the staff. The item was never formally discussed, nor did the board
take a position on the issue. Instead, it decided to delegate responsibility
for dealing with racial problems to the Personnel Department.[66]

The Personnel Department, under Gordon Clapp, repeatedly complained that it lacked authority to criticize other TVA departments for their
failure to offer equal opportunity. Clapp noted that "it is probable that
other departments have unconsciously or otherwise taken the view that the
Authority's responsibility in connection with racial problems is something
which they can forget." He asked without success for the board to give
some clear statement to all departments, because "there has been little or
no indication of the extent to which the Board or the G.M.'s office considers
the problem important as it relates to the general program." The board
remained silent throughout the war years and failed to issue significant
directives on the formation or implementation of racial policy.[67]

For blacks, the reality of TVA planning fell far short of the initial
promise of nondiscrimination. The reasons for this discrepancy are many,
including a reliance on "grass-roots democracy" in a conservative environment, administrative vagaries, and the impact of conservative special interests. Yet the most important factor was the unwillingness of the TVA board
to formulate a coherently progressive racial policy to offset discrimination.
Although they were outsiders, TVA's board members were in complete
agreement with the racial ideologies of the southern conservatives and moderates. They exerted no pressure to change the prevailing racial conditions
in the valley. Indeed, despite protests, inefficiencies, and racial tensions,
the board did not appear even to appreciate the degree of racial discrimination found in TVA's employment, housing, education, and community
development programs.

CHAPTER III

Hiring and Promotions
for Blacks

DURING the New Deal period, TVA was first and foremost an employer of thousands of skilled and unskilled laborers. Most of the workers were needed for the construction of a series of multipurpose dams along the Tennessee River and its tributaries. TVA sought to integrate its regional planning and development activities with its function as an employer. Indeed, it was as an employer that TVA's vision for blacks in the future planned society was manifested most clearly.

Between 1933 and 1945, TVA began construction on fifteen dams: Norris, Wheeler, Pickwick Landing, Chickamauga, Hiwassee, Watts Bar, Kentucky, Fort Loudoun, Cherokee, Apalachia, Chatauge, Ocoee No. 3, Nottely, Fontana, and Douglas. In addition, Wilson, Hales Bar, and Ocoee No. 1 and No. 2 dams were acquired by TVA and brought into the system. The first two dams, Norris and Wheeler, were designed by the Bureau of Reclamation, but all fifteen dams were built by TVA employees.

Different workers were needed for the three phases of dam construction. The first phase consisted of reservoir clearance work. Men chopped trees, cleared shrubbery, leveled the land, demolished or burned condemned structures, and constructed dirt roads on which vehicles needed for the second phase could travel. The second phase consisted of construction of the outer structure and base of the dam. Workers skilled in carpentry, masonry, and cement finishing as well as operators of heavy construction machinery were needed. The third phase consisted of the installation of the machinery to generate electricity and the mechanism to move the locks that regulated the flow of the Tennessee River during the flood season. Skilled technicians trained in mechanical and electrical engineering were needed for this phase. To the annoyance of the local inhabitants, many of these highly trained technicians were recruited from outside the valley area. The majority of unskilled and semiskilled employees were needed for phases one and two.

The largest number of employees were used for the first phase, and their average period of employment lasted just over six months.

Hiring and recruitment of men for reservoir clearance began in the area near the dam site. TVA hoped to help alleviate the high unemployment caused by the nation-wide Depression and likely to be compounded by the proposed flooding of productive farmlands and commercial areas. It wished, moreover, to provide not only temporary employment but also vocational training and improved living conditions, so that valley inhabitants would be equipped to find better jobs once they left TVA. In order to provide a congenial setting where a new life for the workers could be encouraged and supervised, TVA constructed housing for its employees, ranging in scope from the model community of Norris, complete with experimental schools, craft shops, and individual wooden bungalows, to the barracks-like dormitories of Fort Loudoun and Douglas Dam.[1]

The promise of TVA to provide congenial living conditions did not materialize to a significant degree. The period of employment in TVA was too short to permit most workers to benefit from vocational training and only a limited number could live at Norris Model Community and benefit from its experimental activities. Nevertheless, employment by TVA during its first decade was highly desirable.[2] For employment by TVA meant not only wages far above the average for unskilled labor, but also the possibility of living in a house with running water and electricity, sending one's children to uncrowded and well-supplied schools, and training for a better-paying job or learning modern farming techniques.[3]

Blacks, along with other inhabitants, sought jobs with TVA. The agency's official racial policy, as we have seen, sought to achieve "the same proportion of Negroes to whites in its employment as their proportion in the total population of the area." Concurrently, TVA also sought to conform to the social patterns of a racially segregated society.

The absence of a strong policy statement on nondiscrimination by the board members served to place the responsibility for carrying out racial policy on the middle-level officials and line supervisors who were responsible for hiring, promotion, and on-the-job training in the short-range employment phase of TVA. The actions of many of these men ensured that TVA employment practices remained consistently discriminatory.

In TVA, it was the supervisors who made the initial request for workers. The Personnel Division reviewed the applications for jobs, rated the candidates according to their test results, and drew up a list of those who qualified for the job. The supervisors could then select any person on the list of qualified people, regardless of ranking. If a supervisor did not want anyone on the list, the Personnel Division had to search until it found a person who satisfied the supervisors' requirements. Supervisors were also given discretionary powers of promotion and termination. Requests from the supervisory level for the termination of an employee were, with few exceptions, routinely carried out by Personnel.[4]

Many of the line supervisory personnel were local inhabitants with traditional views regarding the inferior economic and social position of blacks. White supervisory personnel frequently requested that blacks not be included in their requisitions. During the period of the New Deal, the Personnel Division did not attempt to force supervisors to take any minority group members that they did not specifically request. Indeed, unless it was clearly stated otherwise, Personnel generally assumed that supervisors did not wish to have any blacks or other minorities on the list of qualified applicants.[5]

Terminations immediately took the employee off the payroll. Although an appeal apparatus existed through the unions and the Personnel Division, the initial act of termination carried considerable weight, and the majority of appeals were denied.[6] Blacks were adversely affected by the discretionary powers of termination that the supervisors enjoyed. In part because of the traditional racial beliefs of foremen, blacks were singled out for disciplinary rulings and termination. Blacks also were less likely than whites to secure reinstatement.[7]

TVA itself recognized the existence of discriminatory practices in this area and was concerned about the harassment of black employees by supervisory personnel. Prompted by the Joint Congressional Committee to Investigate the TVA, the Authority in 1938 held a series of hearings at Chickamauga Dam to investigate complaints of unequal treatment. Several blacks testified that they had been fired without explanation by white foremen and were not given an opportunity to use the appeal apparatus.[8]

Upon the conclusion of the testimony and investigation, the director of personnel stated:

> There is reason to believe that the attitudes of supervisors, in some instances, has [sic] resulted in a general attitude which has been interpreted by Negro employees as a negative attitude of management with respect to the rights of Negro employees. . . . Largely as a result of the hearing of these complaints, the administrative officers at Chickamauga Dam recognize this situation as one which must be corrected. . . . Effort should continue to be made to make it clear that Negro workers are as much a part of the total working force as any other group.[9]

While he did not call for any reprimands, the director of personnel recommended to the board that an educational program emphasizing race relations be started for line supervisors and foremen. The TVA board, however, elected not to interfere with the prerogatives of the supervisors and did not start a program for improving relations between blacks and supervisors until 1957.[10]

While the actions of supervisors were a problem throughout the system, the treatment of blacks in the construction phase changed depending on the conditions and personnel at each dam site. Norris Dam, in the hills of eastern Tennessee, was the first dam constructed. Begun in 1933 and completed in 1936, Norris, named after Senator George Norris, the early supporter of river system development, was a multipurpose storage dam. It was built in a sparsely populated, hilly area approximately forty miles northwest of Knoxville. Because most of the workers would have to be recruited from outside the immediate Norris area, TVA provided housing, schooling, and recreation for the employees and their families.

Blacks experienced several difficulties at Norris. They were excluded from living at Norris Dam, ostensibly for cost considerations, as we have seen, and unofficially because, according to one TVA official, "the presence of Negroes in the village would lead to racial outbreaks of a serious nature; . . . the 'white South' would not tolerate Negroes at Norris." TVA officials stated that they were only following the advice of Charles S. Johnson, a sociology professor at Fisk University, and Will Alexander of the Interracial Cooperation Commission, who expressed the fear that demands for inclusion at Norris would create a backlash that would defeat more substantial race relations efforts. Johnson subsequently denied that he had ever offered such advice. But John Neely, Jr., secretary of the TVA board, stated in the course of an interview with John Davis and NAACP counsel Charles Houston: "You can raise all the 'rumpus' you like. We just aren't going to mix Negroes and white folks together in any village in TVA."[11]

Blacks were, in addition, effectively excluded from employment at Norris Dam as well. Although theoretically committed to a quota-percentage policy, TVA did not achieve the requisite percentage in its Norris hiring. Blacks made up 4.5 percent of the population in the fourteen counties surrounding the dam. Yet black employment during the peak period of employment (1933 to September 1935) ranged from 1.80 to 2.70 percent, with a mean of 1.96 percent.[12]

After the end of the second phase of construction at Norris, black employment decreased markedly. By 1936 there was only one black employed permanently at Norris Dam. There was also a construction crew consisting of nine black men, who were stationed for several months at Norris in order to extend a concrete access road to the dam. This crew worked in the immediate vicinity of the dam, where, perhaps not by coincidence, "the operation was seen by most of the employees at the dam and most of the visitors passing through." [13]

The relationship between the few black workers and the white workers at Norris appeared to be relatively good. The construction crew was well accepted because "it was evident that these Negroes knew their work and were doing a good job." The personnel representative reported that "to the best of our knowledge, there was no criticism or 'kicks' expressed by the white men on the job." [14] The relative lack of friction between the races can best be attributed to the small number of blacks at Norris: white workers rarely if ever came in contact with them.

A greater percentage of blacks were employed at Wilson Dam, Joe Wheeler Dam, and Pickwick Landing Dam. Over 90 percent of all the blacks employed by TVA worked in this three-dam area. Wheeler Dam was built as an extension of the original Muscle Shoals–Wilson Dam complex. Originally it was to have been constructed by the Army Corps of Engineers. In October 1933 President Roosevelt decided that TVA should take over the immediate construction of Wheeler Dam in order to ease unemployment in the area.[15] The black proportion of the population in the Wheeler-Wilson Dam area was almost 25 percent. TVA black employment in the Muscle Shoals–Wheeler Dam area ranged between 16.2 percent and 20.1 percent, with a mean of 18.9 percent. Many civil rights advocates argued that the percentage of blacks employed by TVA should have been higher, not only to offset lower percentage rates in other areas (e.g., Norris), but also to answer the greater need for work among the black population in the Muscle Shoals area. Excluded from relief rolls by subterfuge and open hostility and forced to bear the brunt of AAA-induced tenant evictions, blacks desperately needed government relief and public works support. TVA's position was that although the proportionate need among blacks might be greater, that need was not its concern, because "the TVA is not a relief project." [16]

In the Wheeler Dam, Wilson Dam, and Pickwick Landing Dam areas, black personnel officers were employed to aid in the recruitment of blacks and to assist in any on-the-job difficulties that arose. In order to make application forms widely available, TVA distributed them to local branches of federal agencies and departments, including post offices. Local white postal officials, however, refused to give blacks the necessary forms. When blacks demanded applications, they were told, in an effort to frighten them away, that "they were signing up with the government for four years." [17]

In the construction phase of Wheeler and Pickwick dams, black personnel officers received only requisitions for unskilled work and could recruit

49

only unskilled workers. Requisitions for men to fill skilled jobs came from the construction superintendent of a particular project and were sent only to white personnel officers. Black applicants with skills like carpentry were automatically excluded. At Wheeler Dam, in the 1935 construction phase, there were 300 white carpenters and no black carpenters, although there were qualified and unemployed black carpenters in the area.[18]

Of the 2,035 blacks employed in the Muscle Shoals area, only 0.8 percent were skilled workers, and 12.8 percent were semiskilled. Three cement finishers and five riggers at Wheeler Dam received the $1.00-an-hour rate. Among those in the semiskilled category were 44 jackhammer drillers and 37 flagmen. TVA also included 144 concrete laborers in its statistics for semiskilled workers, by far the largest number of blacks in that category. Yet concrete labor was only a slightly higher form of common labor and belonged in neither the skilled nor the semiskilled class. If the concrete labor category is excluded from the total percentage, only 8.3 percent of black workers could be considered semiskilled.[19]

Blacks employed as flagmen in the Muscle Shoals area suffered from a discriminatory wage scale. The prevailing wage for flagmen in dam construction was customarily two-thirds of the rate paid crane operators. Crane operators at TVA–Muscle Shoals received $1.50 an hour, so flagmen should have been paid $1.00 an hour. Instead, they were paid 60 cents an hour. The discrepancy in the pay scale was probably due to the fact that the job of flagman in TVA was an almost exclusively "Negro" job. Five white workers hired in 1935 to do the same work as the Negro flagmen were classified as "structural steel workers" and paid $1.10 per hour.[20]

In addition to wage differentials and misclassification, blacks faced other types of discrimination in the construction phase of TVA. Blacks who held skilled jobs were frequently replaced by whites or terminated in groups. The worst of the three dams in this regard was Pickwick, built in an area where blacks made up 18 percent of the population, just ten miles north of the state junctions of Mississippi, Alabama, and Tennessee. Black skilled workers there were frequently terminated in favor of whites. In 1937 Kirk Quarrels, a $1.00-an-hour concrete finisher, was fired so that a white skilled worker who had been temporarily laid off could continue to work for TVA.[21]

In 1935 all the black skilled workers in carpentry, electrical work, and plumbing were laid off at Pickwick Dam. They had been hired to build the "Negro quarters": dormitories, a recreation hall, a school, and twenty-five cottages. It was the policy of TVA to hire black artisans to work only on "Negro quarters." It gave several reasons for this policy. First, designating blacks to work on "Negro quarters" allowed TVA to employ, at least temporarily, relatively large numbers of black skilled workers without incurring the wrath of white skilled workers' unions. TVA could explain to the local unions that no white workers were being replaced, and that the blacks were doing only specified work. Second, TVA was using Pickwick Dam as a test case, under controlled conditions, to see whether Negro skilled labor was as efficient as white skilled labor. The Training Division of TVA concluded that the black workers were in fact less efficient; unit costs were 41 percent higher with Negro labor, more materials were used, and the black crews took longer to complete similar tasks. It attributed some of the inefficiency to the relative lack of job experience among the black crews and noted that the end product was comparable in workmanship to that of the white crews.[22]

TVA did not cite inefficiency when it terminated the black crews. Rather, it stated that these terminations were part of a larger work reduction program. More importantly, the Negro village was finished, and black workers were not used in the construction of the larger white village. Since there were no plans to construct Negro villages at the next dam (Hiwassee), no black skilled workers were retained.[23]

In an effort to ease the drop in the percentage of blacks employed at Pickwick, TVA attempted to hire blacks for jobs once held by whites.[24] Yet these jobs did not involve advancement or increased job opportunity, and they were labeled as "disagreeable" work. For example, blacks replaced whites as "filling-in-men," a semiskilled position that involved continually working knee-deep in water around pipelines.[25]

Unlike Norris Dam, where the presence of a few blacks did not cause much racial friction among workers, Pickwick experienced several job-related racial incidents. Officials stated that separate waiting rooms and entrances to the employment offices had to be established to minimize fights and threats between racial groups. Pickwick therefore became the first dam site to have its personnel offices segregated. There were several complaints by black workers of harassment by whites at the job sites. One young worker at Pickwick, P. T. Marsh, a graduate of Knoxville College, was attacked by white workers when he ignored their racial slurs. Marsh was beaten with a wrench and narrowly escaped being killed. His foreman witnessed the attack and responded by firing him.[26]

Morale among the black workers was particularly low at Pickwick Landing Dam. There was a general feeling of job insecurity and a sense that advancement was impossible. One black worker complained:

I have been a maker of foremen. TVA sends its white laborers to our gang. When they come to us they are green, raw and without a knowledge of the work. We teach them and they soon become our bosses and we keep on teaching them. They make a dollar an hour, and we have trouble in getting a raise to sixty cents. We also run the danger of getting the rap, because when a white man has been taught by a Negro he generally fires that Negro when he becomes boss.[27]

Black personnel officers agreed with the accusations of discrimination and pointed out some of the problems that black employees experienced in having their grievances heard. Yet these officials themselves found it hard to assist in the complaint process because

most complaints on the job, abuse of workers, cases in which the white personnel assistants have overlooked conditions under which Negroes receive lower wages than stipulated by the Authority for workers of this class, have to be submitted by the Negro office interviewer for correction to the same personnel assistants who have been indifferent to such practices.[28]

Black workers complained that blacks of high intelligence and ability were frequently passed over for opportunities for advancement—for example, to the position of foreman. Investigating a public statement by a white personnel administrator that there were no blacks of foreman ability, two black personnel interviewers found "the statement to be in error." At Wheeler Dam they found many black men of this caliber with long years of experience at their jobs, who only needed encouragement and several sessions in leadership training—a provision made for all foreman trainees—to move up. It was observed rather bitterly, however, that giving leadership training to blacks would be in direct conflict with the tradition within TVA "to neglect the younger and more intelligent [black] men and yield to a traditional emotionalism that favors the more docile and smiling Negroes."[29]

Black employees at these three dam sites were provided with housing. At Wilson Dam workers were housed in three villages: two set aside for whites, and one set aside for blacks. The houses had all been built for nitrate plant workers during World War I. The two villages for whites contained a wide range of accommodations, from three-room bungalows to large two-story frame and stucco houses. In addition to living accommodations, recreational facilities, playgrounds, and several elementary schools were provided for the white workers. The Negro village was decidedly inferior. The choice of accommodations was limited—none of the twenty houses were equipped to accommodate large families comfortably. Moreover, the houses had been moved from a location near the white villages to an isolated swamp next to a railroad. When TVA's senior black staff member, J. Max Bond, and a Muscle Shoals black citizens' committee complained about the location, they were told that the houses had originally been in an even swampier area and that the railroad track was rarely used.[30]

Their undesirable location aside, the housing provided for blacks at Wilson was inferior in quality. Each house had electric lights, an indoor bathroom, a kitchen, and two other rooms. Though located in a swamp, they did not have screens, which made it difficult to keep insects out, particularly at night. Families, most of whom were existing on a wage of thirty-seven and a half cents an hour, were encouraged to keep a truck garden in a community area set aside for that purpose. They were also encouraged to bring along a cow—TVA provided a pasture. Yet at Wilson Dam blacks were discouraged from using the pasture lands by a sign that warned: "Niggers keep your cows out of White Folks Pasture."[31]

Housing conditions were little better at Wheeler Dam. The Negro village consisted of a large dormitory and ten separate houses for families. The white village was situated on a scenic bluff overlooking the dam and river, while the Negro village was situated in the swampy woods. A school, library, theater, park, and tennis courts were provided for the white workers, while only one tennis court was provided for the black workers. The whites had a separate recreation hall, while the blacks had a combined dining hall–recreation room.

The housing provided for and built by blacks at Pickwick Dam was comparable to that of white workers. Its location, however, was less desirable, separated from the white village by a ravine that was subject to flooding during the rainy season. The only road leading from the Negro village to the worksite passed by a squatter village inhabited by poor whites not associated with TVA. The squatter village was Pickwick's crime center, with an ample number of brothels, gambling houses, and "speakeasies." The passage between the Pickwick village and the worksite was frequently marked by fights and unpleasantness. Only after frequent complaints by blacks of harassment by white squatters was another road built to the site.[32]

Separate and unequal housing was not unique to TVA; and, indeed, TVA was not the worst employer in this regard. Other employers in the valley who had to provide housing for their construction workers also separated them according to race. Alcoa Aluminum built a plant and company town just outside North Maryville, Tennessee, fifteen miles south of Knoxville. During the pre–World War I construction phase, it housed its black workers in two- and three-room temporary tarpaper shacks on low ground in an area known as "Black Bottom." More permanent homes were built in the 1920s and 1930s in a segregated area named "Hall" after Charles M. Hall, discoverer of the electrolytic process for the reduction of aluminum from its ore. Blacks were primarily employed in the reduction process, the hottest and arguably most unpleasant work in the plant.[33]

The government facilities constructed during World War II at Oak Ridge, Tennessee, also contained housing for blacks. The original plans called for construction of a Negro village comparable to the white village, made up of dormitories, a cafeteria, a church, a school, and stores. These plans were scrapped on the grounds that blacks were not working in occupations that warranted such "substantial housing," that space was needed for white employees, and that blacks did not want to live in surroundings so much above their current living conditions. Although complaints were filed throughout the war, blacks continued to be housed in huts with no running water or glass windows. A report on conditions at Oak Ridge concluded that "the responsibility of the Office of the District Engineer . . . is not to promote social changes, whether desirable or undesirable, but to see that the community is efficiently run and that everybody has a chance to live decently in it." [34]

During the next two years (1936–1938), TVA began work on three other dams: Hiwassee, located in the northwestern tip of North Carolina; Guntersville, located in central Alabama, and Chickamauga, built several miles outside Chattanooga. The Hiwassee employment situation was very similar to that at Norris Dam. The major decision facing TVA at Hiwassee was not how to treat its black employees, but whether there were to be any black employees at all.

TVA was divided on the question of excluding black workers from Hiwassee: the Engineering and Construction Department was against hiring blacks, while the Personnel Division considered their hiring a legal and social necessity. The former department cited several reasons for excluding blacks. The first was cost: given that blacks were less than 2 percent of the population of Cherokee County, the potential black workforce was fewer than 100 to 125 employees. The expense of providing separate dormitories and other facilities for a hundred employees would be a substantial and unnecessary addition to the cost of operation. Construction and Engineering was also concerned over the potential for racial friction in the Hiwassee area. The low black population meant that everyday contact between the races had up to now been kept at a minimum. In addition, the few blacks in Cherokee County were believed by construction division analysts "to be employed as domestic servants and the like . . . but few of them [have ever been] engaged in so-called public works." The local white inhabitants might not appreciate TVA's importing "strange Negroes" into the area.[35]

The welfare of the black workers was also cited as a reason to exclude them from employment at Hiwassee. The analysts calculated that the cost to blacks of rooming in TVA dormitories, having their meals at the cafeterias, and, at the same time, supporting their families back home would be very great. Because the surrounding area would probably be hostile, blacks, unlike whites, could not find cheaper accommodations for their families in the neighborhood. In addition, it was speculated that blacks would not be happy in the isolated areas around Hiwassee. They would have "but little opportunity to mingle with members of their race residing locally. . . . the expense of visiting their families and friends in their idle periods would be considerable."[36]

Even potential medical problems were invoked. The silicosis hazard at Hiwassee was linked to the high tuberculosis mortality rate among blacks (two and a half times the rate among whites). Construction and Engineering speculated that it was probable that blacks would be given excavation and quarry work, where the hazard of lung disease was greatest. When men contracted silicosis, they became more susceptible to tuberculosis. Consequently, blacks should be barred from employment, for humanitarian reasons. Construction and Engineering also suggested that more blacks could be hired at projects closer to large black populations, such as Guntersville Dam. Since "the employment of Negroes would necessitate additional administrative attention," the department concluded, ". . . there can be no real benefits resulting from the employment of colored workmen other than doubtful political expediency."[37]

The Personnel Division countered with several compelling reasons for hiring blacks at Hiwassee. Using arguments provided by the Office of the Supervisor of Negro Training, Personnel stated that although the provision of separate facilities was an added expense, it was "the cost inherent in the race problem itself," and would amount to approximately 2 percent of the budget for workers. As for the contention that blacks would be given added employment at other projects to offset their loss of employment at Hiwassee, it was known that their losses at Norris Dam had never been offset by increased employment elsewhere. The men in the Hiwassee examination zone would not be qualified for employment at any other dam site and consequently would be excluded from TVA employment.[38]

55

Personnel also argued that the danger of racial tensions was exaggerated. Several prominent citizens of Murphy (the nearest town) had been interviewed and expressed the doubt that there would be "serious difficulties in the matter of racial relationships if the employed ratio did not exceed 10 percent and if the Negroes employed were carefully selected." The problem of silicosis-tuberculosis among blacks would be handled by a careful and rigid physical examination that included chest X-rays. Moreover, all employees would be required to adhere to dust-control measures, thus keeping down the hazards for whites and blacks alike. Far from being a matter of "doubtful political expediency," Personnel stated that employment of Negroes at Hiwassee was a necessity, if only to diffuse "criticism directed at the Authority for the exclusion of Negroes from Norris, some of which seemed justified on the basis of the broad principle of nondiscrimination." The division suggested that the entire matter be decided by the board.[39]

Four months later, in March 1937, Personnel issued another series of memoranda repeating the basic argument that, from a public relations point of view, TVA could not afford to exclude blacks. According to Clapp, TVA could be running the risk of encouraging criticism not just from citizens' groups and civil rights advocates, but also from a "national administration that has gone further in the direction of applications of broad non-discriminatory policy . . . than has been true at any time heretofore." [40]

One year later, in May 1938, Personnel was still asking the board to take up the question of blacks at Hiwassee. Clapp noted that if a decision was not reached during the next few months, the peak period of employment would have been reached, and any future decision would be academic. He added that the board's inaction made it difficult for Personnel "to explain matters to Negro groups who write us." [41]

The TVA board, as was its custom, did not rule on this racial matter, and Board Agenda Item 682—"Housing and Employment of Negroes for Hiwassee Project"—was never discussed. Inaction was in itself a decision, for no blacks were hired during the peak period of employment, which ended for Hiwassee in 1939. Rather than proclaim a policy of exclusion, as it had done in the Norris Dam controversy, TVA chose to make no public policy statements and allowed the timetable for completion to take care of any pressure or criticism from outside groups. The situation at Hiwassee was summed up in 1942 by the project manager there:

During the construction of Hiwassee Dam, due to the fact that no Negroes were living in the immediate vicinity and due further to the antagonistic attitude toward the Negro in the copper basin and hill country, no Negroes were used.

> . . . it is probable that we might have been able to place Negroes in these projects in the early stages but this action would have caused a great deal of resentment, and it would have been necessary to use a certain amount of force. The construction schedule is now too far advanced to employ Negroes.[42]

TVA also attempted to exclude blacks from the important reservoir clearance portion of the Guntersville Dam project. In contrast to the Hiwassee area, the Guntersville-area population was 23.7 percent black, and consequently a low percentage of blacks in the area could not be used as an excuse. Here, a particular aspect of regional planning policy was the excuse: TVA stated that in accordance with its emphasis on fostering an empathetic relationship between modern technology and rural heritage, farmers would be employed as part-time workers. In 1936 it announced that "the selection of employees for clearance work would be limited to those men who were engaged in farming and who, by virtue of this fact, would be in position to spend, during alternate weeks, fifty percent of their time on the farm and the other fifty percent as employees of the Authority."[43]

Blacks were not employed, because it was deemed that there were not enough black farmers in the vicinity to form two separate Negro units. Therefore, TVA decided to limit the work personnel to whites only. In August 1937 TVA abandoned its original plan to use part-time farm workers and decided to hire 3,000 men. Yet because 1,500 whites had already been hired as part-time workers, TVA argued that the additional force also had to be white to eliminate administrative confusion and the need to establish integrated work crews. Consequently, no blacks were hired during the early reservoir clearance phase at Guntersville, even though under the 1937 plan there were several hundred blacks who qualified for positions.[44]

TVA misunderstood local customs—it was a common Tennessee valley practice to use mixed work crews when the job demand was large enough. The Authority in effect established a new pattern of segregation hitherto unknown in the Tennessee valley by insisting on segregated work crews. The result was that individual blacks remained out of work unless enough blacks could be found to make up a full crew.[45]

At the Guntersville construction site, blacks were hired on a percentage basis. The quota of 18.1 percent, however, was still considerably below the 23.7 percent population ratio for the county, according to the 1930 U.S. census. Blacks were employed as common laborers, semiskilled construction workers, janitors, and health aides/attendants. TVA had not planned effectively for the blacks employed in the project, and the black dormitories were overcrowded. Many of the men had to sleep in cars and on the side of the road until substitute accommodations could be found in Huntsville, Alabama, the nearest large town.[46]

The highest percentage of blacks on any one dam construction site worked at Chickamauga Dam, several miles outside Chattanooga. Their 25.4 percent representation in the workforce actually exceeded their 18.3 percent proportion in the examination area. They were employed as carpenters, electricians, machinists, reinforcing steel workers, and steamfitters, as well as common laborers in field clearance and quarry work.[47]

It appears that the degree of racial tension and difficulty at the Chickamauga worksite was also greater than that at any other site. Complaints of physical harassment and job discrimination were so numerous that in 1938 TVA was directed by the Joint Committee to Investigate the TVA to conduct a thorough and impartial investigation of race relations at Chickamauga.[48] Personnel Director Clapp held a two-day hearing on complaints from black workers. James Simpson, a black skilled worker, reported that he was kicked by Cliff Farmer, one of the foremen on the job. He was threatened with being fired if he reported the incident, and did not do so until after he had been fired anyway. In his affidavit Simpson stated that he had gotten along well on the job until it became generally known that he was the president of his local union. Another skilled worker, Wallace Butler, a flagman, was threatened with a rock when he refused to follow a white worker's orders. He testified that shortly after that incident he was fired. Butler, also active in his local union, concluded that "if a foreman doesn't like your looks he will fire you."[49] Other men complained that they were fired when they protested against work conditions or the lack of advancement. A concrete finisher stated that he was terminated after he attempted to use the TVA grievance procedure as outlined in the *Employee Relationship Policy*. Another was fired after he attempted to have his status elevated from flagman to rigger. His foreman refused his request, saying, "We will not have any more nigger riggers."[50] Clapp's report concluded that negative attitudes were prevalent among white supervisors, and that black workers were not fully utilizing the TVA grievance procedures, fearful that if they openly complained they would be fired.[51]

The disposition of the cases of terminated workers did little to alleviate such fears. None of the men who were fired was reinstated, even though TVA management concurred that their terminations were unfair. In 1939 Clapp wrote that he was unable to find a job for Simpson at either Chattanooga or the fertilizer works at Wilson Dam. Butler was not reemployed because he would not take the workmen's examination again, contending that he had already passed one test and should not have to pass another to be reinstated.[52]

The largest dam built by TVA was Kentucky Dam, located near Paducah, Kentucky. (The dam was originally named Gilbertsville after the town that was inundated by the reservoir waters.) TVA attempted to avoid problems in the hiring and employment of blacks here by anticipating difficulties. Citing the problems of dormitory overcrowding at Guntersville, TVA officials authorized studies to determine the probable number of black employees, their need for housing, and transportation costs. It was determined that 18.9 percent of the total workforce or 529 workers, would be black, and that 480 of them would be traveling more than twenty-five miles to the site and would therefore need housing. Also citing the criticism of TVA's exclusion policies in the Hiwassee, Guntersville reservoir clearance, and Norris projects, officials attempted to publicize its efforts to recruit blacks to work at Kentucky. Efforts to attract black skilled workmen were made in Nashville, at both the Negro colleges and the local black skilled craft unions.[53] Yet difficulties arose. Plans to employ black waiters in a white restaurant had to be postponed because white workers objected, not to the presence of black waiters, but to their taking jobs away from white waiters. Only after white workers were convinced that no whites would lose their jobs could blacks gain acceptance as waiters and busboys.[54]

Almost all of the dams in the final group—Watts Bar, Fort Loudoun, Cherokee, Apalachia, and Douglas—were all built in areas where the black population was small. All except Watts Bar were built during World War II on a round-the-clock basis. In the construction phase, blacks were used sparingly. There were enough blacks at Watts Bar, however, to need two safety committees: one in charge of "Negro safety" and the other in charge of "white safety." The director of personnel noted that the separation of races was logical and acceptable in the area of housing and work crews; however, it was irrational and inefficient to have separate committees working on the same basic problems. Consequently, the Negro safety committee was abolished.[55] The Apalachia project faced a threatened strike by white workers who objected to the presence of Negro flagmen. The Personnel Department, anticipating difficulty, had attempted to recruit white flagmen, but the recruits turned out to be too inexperienced. For safety, TVA had to hire the more experienced blacks. Because it was wartime and because (unknown to the workers and the general public) Apalachia Dam would be a source of electrical power for Oak Ridge, where important experiments

59

on atomic energy were being conducted, TVA fired the workers who had threatened to strike. The rest of the white workers returned to work without incident.[56]

The last dam to be completed during TVA's first twelve years was Fontana. The treatment of blacks at Fontana differed from the practice of earlier projects in two significant ways: the greater intensity of the racial hatred shown by whites at the presence of black workers, and the presence of a third racial group—Native Americans.

Fontana Dam was located in a relatively unpopulated area of North Carolina near a Cherokee Indian reservation. It was begun in 1942 as a wartime electrical power production station, and construction work went on around the clock. TVA officials projected that in keeping with the Authority's quota policy, there would be 96 to 100 blacks at Fontana Dam, although no blacks lived within a radius of thirty miles. Local residents protested against the importation of blacks from Knoxville and from Asheville, North Carolina, and rumors that blacks would not be permitted to work at Fontana were widely circulated. TVA chose to ignore these rumors and proceeded to bus in black workers. In contrast to the situation at other sites, dormitory facilities for them were completed at approximately the same time as the dormitories for whites.[57]

Only four years earlier threats of a more nebulous nature, along with cost considerations, had prevented blacks from being hired at Hiwassee. In 1942, however, there were two new factors. First, the war had created a worker shortage, and black labor was necessary to fill the around-the-clock work shifts. Second, President Roosevelt had issued Executive Order 8802 in 1941, requiring government agencies involved in defense activities (of which TVA was one) to utilize fully all manpower regardless of race, creed, or color. To exclude blacks from Fontana Dam would be a blatant violation of the order, and TVA officials clearly did not wish to risk the repercussions.[58]

Blacks who reported for work at Fontana Dam were greeted with stones and threats of lynching by a mob of white workers. During the first evening, there was an attempt to burn the dormitory with the blacks in it. TVA public safety officers stopped the mob. The next morning TVA supervisors attempted to read Executive Order 8802 to the mob, without perceptible results. Many blacks requested transportation away from the camp because they had been warned that "the sun should not set on their faces." The rest remained under guard for their own protection for over a week. The tension dissipated only after additional safety officers were imported from other camps. In addition, TVA officials made it clear that any attempt by white workers to disrupt dam operations would be considered a serious federal offense. By the middle of 1943, the direct threat of physical violence had ended, and the black workers' complaints centered on housing, which for many consisted of leaky tents, the inadequacy of their own recreational facilities compared with whites', and the lack of electric fans.[59]

The racial difficulties at Fontana Dam were complicated by the presence of American Indians. TVA had seized some of the Cherokee reservation lands for the dam clearance area. Partially as compensation, TVA promised the Bureau of Indian Affairs to hire American Indian men as unskilled laborers for Fontana Dam.

Their presence at Fontana caused initial confusion among TVA officials. Categorizing the Native Americans was difficult in a status (and race-conscious) society. Educationally, they were perceived as the least well equipped of the three ethnic groups: many were illiterate. Culturally, they were perceived as more adapted to a rural, communal lifestyle and unable to work well in an organized group. Socially, Indians were accorded a status separate from and slightly higher than that of blacks, but they were discouraged from or were not interested in mingling with the whites. Consequently three separate sets of facilities were established at Fontana, one each for whites, Negroes, and Indians. The relationship between whites and Indians remained strained. As for black-Indian relations, Indians experienced a similar discriminatory pattern in TVA, being relegated to unskilled jobs almost exclusively. Yet blacks and Indians did not share a uniting bond of deprivation. Rather, Indians regarded blacks as competitors for the low-paying jobs in TVA and were active participants in the mob that threatened blacks upon their arrival.[60]

The persistence of racial difficulties was evident in the reluctance of blacks to stay at Fontana Dam for any length of time. In the fall of 1943, TVA noted that stepped-up recruitment for Negro workmen skilled in concreting operations was not successful. Although skilled Negroes were available, they did not wish to work at Fontana Dam.[61]

Racial discrimination in employment was not limited to the construction phase of TVA. Blacks who were permanent employees also experienced considerable racial discrimination. Although they held over 14 percent of the temporary construction-related jobs, they held only 3.7 percent of the more permanent jobs with an annual salary scale. In 1939, when the first complete survey of black employees was conducted, there were 115 in occupations other than those of tradesman or laborer: 61 janitors; 13 charwomen; 1 messenger; 1 duplicating machine operator; 3 warehouse laborers; 4 cafeteria attendants; 2 cooks; 9 orderlies; 4 laboratory helpers; and 3 kitchen attendants. In addition to these employees in so-called menial work were 9 semiprofessional employees who worked in the personnel office and were classified as job interviewers, and 4 semiprofessional employees who functioned as instructors in the Negro training unit. The only black professional employee in TVA was the superintendent of Negro training, who made an annual salary of $3,800.[62]

By far the largest number of blacks employed on a permanent basis were in the custodial service. The majority of these employees were at the Knoxville headquarters or at the facility in the Muscle Shoals–Wilson Dam area. In 1933 TVA leased several buildings in downtown Knoxville for its administrative center. When the Authority took over the old post office and the Arnstein building, it also took over a number of building service employees. For the first three years, the janitors in Knoxville were those whom TVA had inherited. Most of them were of advanced age and were becoming physically infirm. More importantly, many of the original janitors were functionally illiterate and had, on average, three years of formal schooling.

In 1936 TVA decided to upgrade its janitorial staff (including charwomen). Citing new cleaning methods involving complicated washing and waxing machinery, TVA officials suggested that black college students be employed as replacements for the older employees. A personnel officer remarked that "a younger, better educated group would probably be able to learn faster, perform the work more effectively, and derive more permanent benefit from employment with the Authority." By employing students, TVA hoped to improve the caliber of its janitorial service, to enable a considerable number of students to earn money for higher education, and to discover among these workers "a few choice Negro employees who might be later utilized in other positions."[63]

To effect this project the services of J. Max Bond, the supervisor of Negro training, several personnel officers, and representatives from Negro colleges were used. TVA recruited most heavily at the all-black Knoxville College. The recruiters were instructed to look for young men (college women were thought to be unsuitable for charwoman work) of "a neat, clean, quiet manner, not slouchy." If possible, recruiters were to "encourage the married applicant for obvious reasons."[64]

The response from the college students, from the perspective of TVA, was not positive. Very few black students responded to the recruitment efforts, and considerable disappointment was expressed that TVA could offer black college students only janitorial positions and not more skilled or suitable opportunities. The frustration engendered by limited job opportunities could be heard in the comments made by an anonymous TVA employee to Roy Wilkins of the NAACP. He noted that after all the years of agitation, "the only tangible result . . . was that [Personnel Director] George Gant called all the camp managers together and advised them to hire 'more Negro cooks in the future.' "[65]

Janitors on the job at TVA experienced job insecurity similar to that experienced by black construction workers. For example, two janitors were dismissed at Guntersville for keeping the Negro dormitories in an unsatisfactory condition. Black janitors worked under different conditions from whites. The white janitors who kept the white dormitories in a more satisfactory condition had two common laborers as full-time help and were warned about visits by health inspectors several days in advance. The two dismissed janitors filed grievances, using the camp's one Negro-owned typewriter, and were rehired. Two days after reinstatement, they were again fired—this time without explanation. The owner of the typewriter was also fired.[66]

In 1939 TVA decided to expand the number of positions open to black annual (i.e., relatively permanent), salaried personnel. The director of personnel, after conversations with Charles Houston of the NAACP, initiated a program to employ blacks as mail clerks and messengers. The announcement that some of the white messengers would be removed and replaced by black messengers caused a critical reaction from several white union locals. A representative of the American Federation of Government Employees (AFGE) Lodge 136 wrote, "We believe that the removal or transfer of the white messengers and their replacement by the Negro is an absolute discrimination against the white race." The union was also concerned that "the mingling of the white messengers with the Negroes, necessitating their working side by side, will create a racial friction which will not only result in loss of efficiency, but will cause much criticism from the people of the South."[67]

The general manager replied that TVA appreciated the union's concerns, particularly on the matter of the "co-mingling of the two races." It was TVA's intention to remove the white messengers and mail clerks as quickly as possible so that the "co-mingling" would be kept at a minimum. All the white clerks would be given promotions and kept in TVA employment. TVA assured the union that it did not intend to alter the Authority's existing pattern of segregation.[68]

The messenger and mail unit became all-black, although it took over two years for the complete racial change to take place. The unit's black employees were all college-educated, and many had bachelor's degrees.

The positions of messenger and mail clerk were more attractive than that of janitor to college-trained blacks because messengers traditionally had more chances for advancement. In a large organization, the position provided a good opportunity for a young person without any particular skills to learn about the different sections and departments. After six to nine months as a messenger, the employee could hope to transfer to a more responsible and better-paying position.[69]

Unfortunately, the pattern of advancement ended when blacks became messengers. There were no promotions beyond the mailroom for blacks. The shop committee of the mailroom complained on several occasions that they were denied advancement. In a letter to the general manager, they wrote:

> In view of the fact that numerous vacancies have been and are being created by the national war effort and realizing that there has been a tremendous increase in the work program of the Authority, we of the Mail and Messenger Unit desiring to become a more integral part of the agency wish to be considered for placement throughout the Authority.[70]

Dissatisfied with TVA's response, which was to ask for a list of staff members to fill openings outside the mailroom as they appeared, several employees in the unit wrote to the NAACP to try to initiate a lawsuit against TVA for discrimination. The NAACP was interested in the allegations but could not offer to pursue a separate lawsuit in 1943 because of a shortage of funds.

The shop committee became one means by which black employees could take their complaints to management. Although there was an official Race Relations Committee within the Department of Personnel, many black employees, even those employed outside the mailrooms, preferred to have the mailroom shop committee, which had developed a militant reputation, argue in their behalf. Complaints of segregation in the TVA buildings in Knoxville and at the recreation centers of Fort Loudoun and Norris were brought before the shop committee, which in turn relayed the complaints to the general manager.[71] The lack of advancement out of the mailroom remained a problem well into the 1970s.[72]

At just over 10 percent, the percentage of blacks in annual trade and labor positions was larger than their representation in annual non-trade and labor positions. Yet this percentage did not accurately reflect the position of blacks in skilled positions. None of the 103 skilled blacks employed by TVA earned a salary of over $1,206, whereas more than 83 percent of the

877 skilled white employees were at a salary of over $1,206. More than 66 percent of the blacks were at $900 or $980 a year, the lowest salary levels for annual trade and labor classifications.[73]

TVA explained that few blacks were employed in highly paid skilled positions because few blacks qualified for them. The Authority pointed to the workmen's examination registers to validate this claim. Of the 9,213 people who took the examinations for skilled craft workers given in 1938 and 1939, only 108 were black, and only a few were considered by TVA to meet the requirements for certification as skilled journeymen. Although there were a few cement finishers, bricklayers, and machinists, the majority of black skilled workers were employed in the so-called Negro trades: as powdermen, jackhammer operators, and wagon drill operators. There were also a number of black helpers who were used in many skilled trades in the Authority.[74]

TVA expressed regret that the employment of skilled Negroes had not been as significant as might have been desired, yet it stated that it had not been given "a special assignment or statutory authority to reconstruct the racial relationships of the population in the area of its operations." It was limited to the obligations specified in the TVA act, it insisted, and these did not include expanding job opportunities for blacks beyond the Authority's normal self-interest.[75]

Yet analysis of data available on black skilled workers employed in the seven major southern cities suggests that TVA did not utilize the existing pool of qualified skilled candidates. Although only one black carpenter was employed in TVA on a full-time basis in 1942, over 2,487 blacks in those seven cities were employed, full time, as carpenters, or 18 percent of the total number of carpenters.[76] No black painters or plasterers were employed by TVA in 1942, although there were 1,445 Negro plasterers (69 percent of the total), and 1,185 Negro painters (15 percent of the total) in the area.[77] In addition, a sizable number of black skilled workers had passed other government examinations and were employed on work relief projects in the area from 1938 to 1941. For example, there were sixty-seven carpenters employed in Memphis and thirty-two in Atlanta on projects aided by the United States Housing Administration.[78]

TVA did hire black skilled workers in three categories not designated as "Negro" trades. Its Department of Chemical Engineering started a program to train chemical operators in the fertilizer plant at Muscle Shoals. There were forty-four trainees in that program, and twenty additional trainees were slated for the Watts Bar Steam Plant, making that location's permanent employment roll over 50 percent black. TVA employed an all-black line crew of electricians, who had been working for the Tennessee Electric Power Company when its facilities were acquired by TVA, and there was an all-black crew of machinists at the Nashville steam plant.[79]

Although chemical operators, linemen, and machinists were not in traditional Negro trades, TVA attempted to create a controlled and segregated work situation involving as little contact as possible between black and white tradesmen. The training of the twenty chemical operators was intended to create a situation in which the majority of individuals working at a plant, in this case the Watts Bar Steam Plant, would be black. The black line crew worked autonomously and rarely came in contact with white crews. An indication that blacks were not considered for jobs when their hiring would entail integration was the rejection of a black graduate student who applied for a job in the TVA chemical labs. Rollins Winslow, a black personnel officer who had been hired originally as a college summer intern, wrote to a black colleague, "You and I know there is no such position for him. Let him down gently." [80]

TVA officials were concerned that the limited number of blacks in skilled positions would decrease rather than increase. The average age of its black skilled employees was over fifty, and most were scheduled to retire before 1940. The Authority did not have an adequate list of replacements for the all-black crews. Efforts to recruit skilled blacks for the positions were unsuccessful.

Recruitment of blacks in TVA had been a problem from its earliest years. The initial problems in the Norris area, where post office employees would not hand out examination forms to blacks, created a high level of skepticism among black inhabitants. TVA enlisted the services of the National Urban League along with black college presidents and heads of local segregated trade unions. Yet even at the height of the Depression (1933–1938), when jobs in the valley were relatively scarce, fewer blacks than TVA expected applied for positions.

One reason was the difficulty of reaching potential black applicants with offers of employment. Complaints came from the black communities that by the time they received word of job openings, the jobs had been filled by whites. This communication gap and the resultant disappointment created a credibility problem for TVA, making black leaders reluctant to work with its officials. TVA also noted that "rumors" had begun to circulate in the black community that TVA discriminated against blacks and employed them only in certain undesirable jobs.[81] Thus, wariness on the part of blacks made it difficult for TVA to fill even the positions that it did offer to blacks. The problem became so marked that local black leaders began to urge more

66

blacks from local unions and colleges to apply for jobs just so "TVA would not have an excuse to say that no blacks apply." [82]

A third factor was the war-inspired prosperity affecting even the Tennessee valley. Private employers began to compete with TVA for workers, and local blacks noted that "Negroes are not employed in certain skills by the Authority but are employed in the same skills by private construction in the Tennessee Valley area." [83]

By 1941 private industries offered more job opportunities and paid higher wages. TVA was unable to attract black laborers to Fontana Dam, not only because of the site's racial problems, but also because the Kaiser Construction Company was recruiting in the same area. Alcoa Aluminum continued to hire blacks not only from the Knoxville area, but from as far away as Alabama, Georgia, and Mississippi, throughout the 1930s. In order to meet the increased demand for aluminum products, Alcoa built a new plant in 1941, which expanded its workforce (black and white) to 12,000. In 1942, blacks could also find employment at Oak Ridge, Tennessee, helping to construct the atomic energy facilities. The Army did only a small proportion of the hiring, most of which was done by private building contractors. The pattern of employment was rather similar to TVA's, and the largest numbers of blacks were unskilled. As a worksite, however, Oak Ridge was closer and more accessible to the black communities in Knoxville and Chattanooga than the remote Fontana Dam construction area.[84]

Unsuccessful in its recruitment efforts, TVA did have the opportunity and the facilities to train its own skilled labor out of the excess pool of untrained but willing black laborers. Yet, with minor exceptions, TVA did not choose this option, because it wished to maintain a good working relationship with the Tennessee Valley Trades and Labor Council, a body of sixteen labor unions affiliated with the American Federation of Labor.

Although TVA was created as an agency of the federal government, Congress gave it many characteristics of a private business firm, including the flexibility to adopt an employee relations policy consistent with current developments on the national scene. Section 3 of the TVA act provided that all contracts requiring the employment of laborers and mechanics should contain a wage provision and that workers receive "not less than the prevailing rate of wages for work of a similar nature prevailing in the vicinity." Section 3 also exempted the TVA board from laws and regulations of the Civil Service Commission regarding the appointment of employees and enabled TVA to enter into collective bargaining agreements. In 1940 the Authority signed a formal agreement with the Tennessee Valley Trades and Labor Council, recognizing the Council as the collective bargaining agent for all trades and labor employees. A joint labor-management committee set standards on wages, hours of employment, work rules, selection and place-ment procedures, apprenticeship training, and other rules and regulations affecting working conditions.[85]

TVA had established a close relationship with organized labor both nationally and valley-wide and was cognizant of organized labor's long-standing support of public control of water resources. Organized labor was a vocal supporter of TVA throughout the 1930s and 1940s. In 1944 William Green of the AFL stated that "labor and . . . TVA have transformed into reality many of the dreams of the American Federation of Labor." The Hod Carriers Union praised TVA for having raised wages and improved conditions throughout the South.[86]

The 1940 agreement with the Tennessee Valley Trades and Labor Council was the result of years of close cooperation with independent unions. There was no specific mention of race in the agreement, nor was there the emphasis on merit and efficiency that had appeared in previous TVA employee relationship statements. Most unions that belonged to the Council excluded blacks from membership. The International Brotherhood of Electrical Workers and the United Association of Plumbers and Steam Fitters, among others, excluded blacks or, like the International Union of Operating Engineers, had southern locals that excluded blacks. Only the International Hod Carriers, Building and Common Laborers Union of America and the United Brotherhood of Carpenters and Joiners had a sig-nificant number of blacks, and these blacks were in segregated locals.[87]

TVA clearly placed a high premium on cooperation with the unions. Although it denied allegations that blacks could not be hired as journeymen unless the unions agreed, it did acknowledge that "unions representing its employees is [sic] indispensable to the accomplishment of the public pur-poses for which the Authority has been established."[88] The extent of TVA's commitment to a "hands off" policy was illustrated in its response to an NAACP complaint that Operating Engineers Local 660 was attempting to increase its membership among workers in a TVA plant for the purpose of eliminating black workers from jobs that came under the union's jurisdic-tion. TVA replied: "The question of representation is a matter for employees to determine and the majority rule is a firmly established principle. . . . It would seem inappropriate for management to attempt to interfere in any way with employee rights of self-organization."[89]

Exclusion by the major skilled trade unions was an acknowledged fact, although discriminatory clauses in the Operating Engineer's constitution were removed at the Authority's request. The road to journeyman was blocked at several points. In order to qualify as a journeyman in TVA, an individual had to have training in a regular apprentice program—four years of actual experience in the craft. Blacks were excluded from non-TVA apprenticeship programs, and even the Authority's own apprenticeship programs were controlled by the very unions that excluded blacks. Consequently, TVA apprenticeship programs in the skilled trades also excluded blacks, with a few exceptions. Blacks were allowed to participate in training programs in such traditional "Negro" skills as drilling, flagging, machinery lubrication, and jackhammer operations.[90]

TVA acknowledged that there was considerable intransigence on the part of the unions. The Council stated that apprentice training programs would "give full consideration to blacks as apprentices for those trades represented by unions which made provision for Negro participation."[91] Yet the unions strongly resisted what they regarded as expanded opportunities for blacks. AFGE Lodge 136, as we have seen, strongly protested against the use of blacks as messengers and mail clerks;[92] the International Brotherhood of Electrical Workers protested against the transfer of Negro linemen from the Tennessee Electric Power Company, despite assurance that "the Negro crew can function independently of other construction or maintenance crews in special assignments."[93]

Excluded from participation in all-white unions, blacks were also penalized in certain instances for organizing their own separate unions. Several blacks at the Chickamauga Dam site were threatened and fired for attempting to organize common laborers. Rollins Winslow, the young personnel officer, was fired because he attempted to organize black janitors at Wilson Dam.[94]

The sense among TVA middle-level supervisors that black unions were to be discouraged was heightened by the aggressive behavior of the black locals of the International Hod Carriers, Building and Common Laborers Union of America and the Brotherhood of Carpenters and Joiners. Both unions functioned as outside pressure groups attempting to encourage TVA to expand its employment opportunities. The Carpenters' Local 2216, Chattanooga, supplied several qualified carpenters for the TVA examination. When these applicants received no word, the local continued to write to TVA until it received a reply: TVA stated that the men sent had qualified and been put in a pool along with over two hundred qualified applicants, to be hired when positions became vacant; yet they were not hired.[95]

The Hod Carriers also pursued tactics. TVA frequently stated that the scarcity of black skilled applicants prevented it from hiring a proportionate number. A vice-president of the Alabama State Federation of Labor and an officer of the Hod Carriers together conducted a survey of black skilled labor in the Tennessee Valley regions. The results of the survey showed an acceptably large pool of skilled black labor and caused considerable discussion within TVA. Several meetings were held among the Hod Carriers, TVA labor representatives, and the director of personnel to discuss the Authority's employment problems. The Hod Carriers stressed the allegations and the evidence that TVA supported discriminatory policies by labor unions and particularly excluded blacks from employment in the defense program.[96]

Black locals also handled grievances from black TVA employees. From 1936 on, TVA employees had the Interracial Race Relations Committee in the Department of Personnel to handle special complaints. Yet as evidenced by the number of complaints written directly to the union locals, many blacks preferred to appeal outside of the Authority. Some asserted that if it became known that they had complained to the Race Relations Committee, they would be harassed on the job. Appealing to the unions afforded a degree of confidentiality and security as well as some assurance that the complaints would be given full consideration. In addition, TVA's black workers appeared to prefer to write to their fellow blacks in trade unions, rather than appealing to a committee comprising black and white management personnel.[97]

Black women experienced particularly limited job opportunities and were the most underrepresented segment of the workforce. TVA, which was essentially an engineering, operating, and construction organization, did not employ many women of either race. As was the custom in the Southeast, women were not employed as skilled tradespersons or as manual laborers in dam clearance or construction, even during the World War II labor shortage. Nor were they represented in management positions, other than as office supervisors, or in professional positions—as engineers, chemists, or agricultural experts. White women were employed as nurses, dieticians, cafeteria workers, charwomen, clerks, and secretaries. Women complained that they were not considered for positions outside traditional "female" job categories, but none filed an official grievance during the first twelve years of TVA operations. Black women were employed primarily as custodians and cafeteria workers. The first black secretary was employed in the office of the head of Negro training to avoid the socially awkward problem of having a white secretary working for a black male professional. Other black women worked in the offices of black job interviewers.[98]

The suspicions of black TVA employees about TVA's commitment to "nondiscrimination on the basis of race, creed, or color" were justified in theory and practice. In the area of short-range planning, TVA showed a clear pattern of discrimination in employment policies, ranging from exclusion from skilled jobs to harassment and violence at the job site. Several factors contributed to these practices in TVA. The attitudes of top TVA officials were important; the board of directors, general managers, directors of personnel, and department heads were all aware of discriminatory practices, but chose to take a muted stance against them. (When TVA did choose to take a firm stand, such as the introduction of blacks at Fontana Dam, the policy was put into effect despite threats of violence.) On-the-job treatment as well as hiring and promotions were greatly affected by line supervisors, many of whom were strongly skeptical of the ability of blacks to do an acceptable job. Exclusionary practices by white skilled trade and craft unions, which prevented blacks from securing skilled employment in TVA, were particularly damaging due to TVA's commitment to cooperation with union policies. TVA's institutionalized reluctance to challenge patterns of racial segregation in the region also resulted in discrimination. TVA was unwilling to introduce blacks into new occupations without a sufficient number to form all-black work crews. Local customs of job exclusion also helped to produce a smaller pool of skilled workers from which qualified blacks could be hired. Yet if TVA had been willing to integrate its forces, it could have provided a greater proportion of black skilled workers. It can be concluded that the shortage of qualified blacks was only relative, but was used more frequently as an excuse by TVA for not hiring any black skilled workers at all.

In comparing the treatment of blacks in TVA employment in 1933 with their treatment in 1945, one can conclude that the pattern of discrimination remained the same, as did the lack of employment opportunities. With the exception of mail clerks, machinists, linemen, vehicle operators, chemical operators, and duplicating machine operators, jobs that blacks were excluded from in 1933 tended to remain out of reach in 1945. There were no black professionals in TVA in 1933, and there were only two black professionals in 1945.[99]

TVA sought to exclude blacks entirely from its Norris workforce in 1934–1935 and from its Hiwassee workforce in 1938. The effect of exclusion was the same in both instances: a small number of blacks were employed as custodians or cooks' helpers but none were employed in the building of the two dams. TVA chose to acknowledge its policy of exclusion at Norris and incurred a negative reaction from civil rights groups. Wishing to avoid a similar response in 1938, the Authority chose to deny any exclusion policies, citing the need for cost analysis and study. Through a strategy of postponement and inaction, it avoided severe criticism while continuing to exclude blacks. Thus, TVA merely became more subtle in its discrimination over the period of the New Deal.

The advent of World War II did not substantially alter TVA employment practices. On the construction site, blacks continued to be underutilized and harassed, as in the case of Fontana Dam, or partially excluded, as in the case of Apalachia Dam, despite pressure on TVA from the War Department to maximize its efforts to produce power for the war industries in the area and the nuclear research facilities at Oak Ridge. The wartime labor shortage made greater utilization of black semiskilled labor a necessity. The first black clerk-typists and chemical trainees were hired because of the labor shortage in these fields. Yet even these modest changes were met with resistance from forces in TVA determined to maintain the racial status quo.

CHAPTER IV

Regional and
Community Development

TVA's relationship with blacks went beyond its role as an emergency employer of unskilled and semiskilled labor. The promise of TVA involved the revitalization of the valley through regional planning and cooperation. Its long-range planning programs included removal and relocation of families living in areas to be flooded by TVA dams, town planning and development, recreational development, and educational cooperation with colleges, high schools, and elementary schools. In all of these areas, TVA was confronted with the problems of blacks.

Sensitive to criticism from conservative politicians that it frequently overstepped its social and regional planning role in the valley, and advised by its own legal division to restrict its redevelopment activities, TVA constructed an elaborate rationale to justify its development program, citing empowerment through Sections 4, 5, 22, and 23 of the TVA act. The Authority argued that it was empowered to provide whatever supportive activity was necessary to implement its program of flood control, power production, and fertilizer manufacture.[1]

Thus, TVA justified its involvement in the removal of reservoir families on the grounds that the construction of TVA dams directly affected and disrupted the lives of those in the path of the reservoir. The flooding of entire towns or parts of towns required assistance in redevelopment and rezoning and led to TVA's involvement in town planning. The increased need for technologically trained personnel led TVA to form cooperative programs with Tennessee valley state colleges and vocational schools. The desire to develop a market for its fertilizer influenced TVA's cooperative efforts with local farmers and agricultural colleges. The influx of TVA personnel involved in the building and maintenance of dams put a strain on local facilities, particularly the school systems. TVA therefore entered into agreements with local school boards to help expand their facilities in order to meet the needs of the children of TVA employees. It also sought to develop parks and resorts to increase the use and profitability of TVA-owned lands and reservoirs.

In 1933 the Department of Regional Planning and Development was given the responsibility for implementing the Authority's long-range planning programs. This department's staff included administrators, social workers, professional planners, geologists, architectural engineers, sociologists, demographers, and geographers. It comprised agricultural, industrial, land planning, engineering planning and geology, social and economic planning, and forestry divisions, all of which were to work with the board of directors to create the long-range planning policy for TVA. The years 1933 to 1935 were the department's most productive period. With Arthur Morgan's encouragement, the department initiated plans for park development near the Norris Dam and Wilson Dam areas, implemented plans for fertilizer distribution and soil-erosion control through terracing, and conducted surveys and detailed studies of the impact of reservoir flooding on the lives of the local inhabitants.[2]

An unstable unit, the Department of Regional Planning underwent a significant reorganization in 1937. This change decreased its influence and organizational strength. Another factor contributing to confusion and decreased effectiveness within the department was the overlapping of the jurisdiction of other government agencies with that of the regional planners. TVA sought to utilize existing local agencies and organizations, such as state planning boards, post offices, and agricultural agents, as part of its "grass-roots" approach. It also used and was used by other government agencies. It used the surveys on appraisal and land valuation done by the Bureau of Agricultural Economics as a basis for compensating owners of flooded lands. The Farm Security Administration (FSA) gave the TVA data and advice on resettlement as well as cooperating in the withdrawal of submarginal lands. The National Park Service supervised the grading, terracing, and seeding of parks in the region and gave advice and data on the initial purchase of lands for recreational development.[3]

The Department of the Interior, which provided funds for the purchase of grass, seeds, and fertilizers, caused the most conflict over jurisdiction, although TVA also had disputes with other departments and the Resettlement Administration (the FSA's predecessor). The TVA board was concerned that Harold Ickes's department might overstep the boundaries of cooperation and seek to control the funding of all TVA projects. Lilienthal particularly expressed hostility toward Ickes and his efforts to influence the internal policies of TVA. In 1941 Lilienthal wrote in his journal, "I learned

. . . that Ickes' plan to absorb all power agencies into the Interior under the guise of defense necessity had reached a stage where it was likely to be put in effect." Lilienthal resisted, expressing frustration at the obstructionist maneuvering of the Interior Department. In 1942 he observed:

> The idea of a regional resources development agency runs counter to the vested interest of the existing departments, the Interior Department, the War Department and the Department of Agriculture. It is almost incredible how powerful these supposed creatures of a democratic government can be in enforcing their vested jurisdictional prerogatives.[4]

Still another disruptive factor was the dismay within the Department of Regional Planning over the limited scope and direction of regional planning within TVA. Several regional planners expressed disappointment that the needs of relocated families were not being met. They submitted a memo detailing many population adjustment problems. They acknowledged that, on an individual basis, TVA provided answers to complaints and solutions for many problems of resettlement, but "there had been no outright and thorough policy adopted in regard to many other problems that are reaching proportions that challenge our attention." Instead, there were such informal "policy statements" as "greatest good to the greatest number," "least harm to the least number," "hope that the population would be left in as good or better condition as they were in before the establishment of TVA."[5]

Unfortunately, the large-scale displacement of farm units and the subsequent relocation of families caused severe economic problems for the families and the overpopulated area in which they were forced to resettle. The tenant and poor landowner bore the brunt of readjustment. Appraisal studies showed that families forced by TVA to move were worse off than they had been before the coming of TVA. The surveys conducted by regional planning staff showed that 69 percent of the farmers in the Wheeler Dam area were relocated to inferior land. The explanation for this unfavorable statistic was twofold: there was very little good land available on which to relocate, and most of the farmers had been tilling soil on the rich river-bottom land, which was flooded. Nevertheless, in light of the Authority's stated goal of bringing a better standard of living to the valley, the unfavorable situation of the relocated families was considerably troubling to portions of the regional planning staff.[6]

By 1937 regional planners were asking, "What is the responsibility of TVA for population readjustment?" They complained that TVA was defining the limits of its compensation too narrowly. Some families in the vicinity of a reservoir depended upon income derived from reservoir lands but did not own these lands. TVA compensated only those individuals who could show a direct, measurable loss; it ignored those who did not have written or formal access to the lands and refused to acknowledge the local custom of informal use of nontitled land as a means for supplementing income. In other cases dams and flooding had cut off individual families "from trade centers, thoroughfares, and other sources of living or made excess [*sic*] more difficult." Land speculators and swindlers descended on the Tennessee valley, involving families in phony or unprofitable investments. The field agents of the Regional Planning Department wanted to know how to answer the "large numbers of families [who] after sale of their land to TVA [made] unwise investments of their money, became disillusioned and [claimed] that if TVA had not forced them to sell their land they would be secure now." [7]

Another unsolved problem was the position of destitutes who could not afford to seek new homes or to move. Many families had been living on these farms for several generations and did not have the knowhow, let alone the money, to manage a move. Many were forced to sell their furniture and family heirlooms to augment the compensation they received from TVA. "Why should the government require them to sacrifice life essentials without compensation?" the planners wanted to know. Finally, they wanted to know what TVA was going to do about "an implied responsibility in the TVA Act or in the public mind that TVA should actively participate in social reconstruction of families affected by its program. . . . Would something be done to deny or affirm the implication?" [8]

An unofficial answer had already been provided in a set of instructions written by A. Snell and distributed in 1936 for an orientation course for TVA agents on the process of removing families from reservoir areas. Agents were instructed that TVA was not empowered to give benefits to reservoir families; its role was one of coordination with other agencies. Snell pointed out that there were other social service agencies helping in the removal problem. Removal agents were not to feel compelled to act on every problem, because agents from other agencies, such as the relocation service of the University Extension Department, the Department of Public Welfare, and the Rural Resettlement Administration were also there to assist families. [9] These restrictions represented a victory for the Authority's legal division. This important division took a cautious position on the legal authority of TVA to become involved in relocation activities beyond the condemnation of property and the payments of a cash settlement to former residents. While Arthur Morgan and regional planners like Levron Howard and Tracy Augur supported an extensive project to relocate families and help them adjust, the legal division, under the direction of the General Solicitor James Fly, argued that the agency should refrain from expending funds to help the families and that the TVA act might limit its financial obligations. During this period (1936–1938) TVA was embroiled in a series of court battles, and the legal division clearly did not want to risk another legal challenge over a few unfortunate families.[10]

Black families experienced particular difficulty in relocation. The relief agencies had a shortage of trained personnel who were sensitive to the special problems of blacks. There was only one black reservoir removal agent, Birdius Browne, for the entire Wilson–Wheeler Dam area, whose population was over 25 percent black. Although he appears to have been an effective and professional worker, Browne's caseload was much too heavy for one person, and he could only offer his services to a minority of the affected black families.[11]

Black families in the Wilson–Wheeler area were already in an economically precarious state. Over 80 percent of the blacks were tenant farmers, and all the black tenant farmers were sharecroppers. Most were not able to make enough from their crops to pay off their expenses and were deeply in debt to their landlords. The quality of life for both black and white farmers was poor. Both blacks and whites owned, on the average, one suit of clothing, suffered from the vitamin deficiency diseases pellagra, rickets, and scurvy, and lived in unheated, unpainted, unsealed dwellings. Sanitation facilities were nonexistent, and many families suffered from lice, worms, and dysentery. In addition, schools were understaffed, were open less than half the year, and offered little opportunity for a different life.[12]

Black families experienced the same conditions of poverty as their white neighbors but also had to contend with a rigid, racially based caste and economic system. Blacks were not an integral part of the rural communities but lived in isolated, difficult-to-farm hamlets. Many were not even on the mail route and lived miles from the nearest paved road. Many did not send their children to schools, primarily because buses were not available or were unable to traverse the dirt roads. In any case, the schools were decidedly inferior to schools for whites and offered only elementary instruction. Blacks were denied access to relief services; black World War I veterans were turned away at Veterans Administration hospitals and often denied their pensions. They were also discriminated against in New Deal agencies, earning an average total of $5.00 each in the Civil Works Administration, while whites earned an average total of $52.00: although paid the same wages in the CWA, whites remained on the payroll many weeks longer than blacks. The annual average income of the valley's black tenant farmers for 1933 was $140.00, while that of white tenant farmers was $265.00. Yet in Tuscaloosa County, Alabama, black tenants paid, on average, $2.08 a year in taxes, while white tenants paid an average of $1.12.[13]

TVA reservoir removal agents were able to assist blacks on an individual basis. For example, Birdius Browne helped a black family move off TVA property. Initially refusing to move, the family contended that their landlord, a white man, held a mortgage on the family's six mules and was threatening to foreclose the mortgage, leaving the family without mules with which to farm. The black TVA worker was able to effect a compromise. Four of the mules were surrendered to satisfy the debt, leaving the family with two. After this adjustment, the family moved off TVA property and, according to a TVA report, was "well pleased, both with this arrangement and with their new location."[14]

The Regional Planning Department was also confronted with more complex problems involving the relocation of entire black communities. TVA had observed that rural blacks and whites lived in rigidly segregated communities, and it was conscious of the need to preserve the racial structure and patterns of the area. Consequently, when forced to relocate a black community, it sought, along with other agencies, to find an isolated area away from whites. While offering initial assistance in planning relocated communities, TVA acknowledged that "it [was] probably not the proper agency to permanently offer planning assistance to small communities." In keeping with its grass-roots approach, the Authority declared that such services should be offered by state planning boards, municipal boards, or other state organizations, with assistance from local agents of the FSA.[15]

Despite its disclaimers, however, TVA was intricately involved in the resettlement of several black communities. One was the Beulah community of northern Alabama, located on the Beeline Highway between Decatur and Athens, Alabama, in the area flooded by the Wheeler reservoir. The community's leading citizen was George Bridgeforth, a former college professor and administrator in the departments of agriculture at Tuskegee and Tennessee State who had been educated at the University of Chicago and Northwestern University. Bridgeforth owned a large portion of land in the unflooded part of the community and decided to subdivide it to provide farms for those flooded out by the dam. He proposed planning a new community with model school facilities, a town church, and a recreation center. He also proposed building town sanitation facilities and having an independent water supply based on a nearby natural spring.[16]

Bridgeforth wrote to Harcourt Morgan in 1933, asking for assistance in planning his community. Bridgeforth was particularly concerned that

TVA might intend to take over the spring that, he said, supplied the town with five million gallons a day. While TVA had compensated individuals for lands lost, he noted, there was no study or concern about the impact the flooding would have on the entire community.[17] Receiving an unsatisfactory reply, he arranged for a white lawyer from Decatur, Alabama, to write to the Regional Planning Department asking for assistance in drawing up plans for the model community. TVA replied as follows: "While this office is not in a position to give official approval or advice on such projects we are always glad to know of them and to do what we can to help private developers coordinate their plans with any plans for road relocations or other matters being studied by this division."[18]

A brief report on Beulah, done by the Negro recreational unit of TVA, showed that the "Negro spring" provided only two million gallons a day, and that the flow would not be sufficient to create a fresh lake. Bridgeforth was portrayed in the report as a wily entrepreneur more interested in selling his tracts of land to relocated families than in building a model community for humanitarian purposes. Bridgeforth should therefore be told that the community could not retain control of the spring or the land around it, because if "they [regional planners] allowed him control of the spring and development around it everyone would want it." The author of the report felt that "it would be disastrous to make concessions which would be contrary to what the Land Acquisition Division had already indicated to them for it [and] would cripple the land purchase program in that section."[19]

The conclusions of the report essentially called for TVA unofficially to discourage the development of the black community. Although more investigation was needed, the report noted, it was clear that without the spring there was not a sufficient water supply for the community. Moreover, the proposed location for the development was unsafe because of a possible earthquake hazard. Above all, the report recommended that TVA offer no advice or assistance that could be interpreted as encouragement or approval of the project.[20]

Bridgeforth, not easily discouraged, maintained a relationship with TVA. In 1934 he and his brother, Isaac Bridgeforth, contracted with TVA to clear brush for its reservoir clearance projects. Yet one contract with Isaac Bridgeforth was withdrawn because he did not have sufficient workers; the Bridgeforths were criticized for not having proper tools or men experienced in log removal work; and a Bridgeforth team of horses was terminated from contract work with the comment that the team was fine, but the driver was constantly late.[21]

In 1935 George Bridgeforth wrote to the Agricultural and Industrial

Division and asked "for some of your fertilizers in some experimental work to be carried on as suggested." It replied that "TVA is making sulphur phosphate, which it is manufacturing in connection with its demonstration farm programs. . . . The distribution is through county agents on the demonstration farms which must be selected and approved by the people in the community." Bridgeforth was told to see his county agent. He was also told that the programs would not suit his needs, because sophisticated farming methods would be necessary to use TVA's product efficiently.[22] Bridgeforth was, of course, former head of the agriculture division at Tuskegee and a man with extensive training and administrative skills; he was capable of using both simple and sophisticated farming methods.

In his correspondence Bridgeforth also raised the question of independent cultivation of TVA land. As stated above, farmers in the region traditionally cultivated crops on unoccupied lands, and these people suffered when TVA took title of such lands. Bridgeforth asked permission for the Beulah community to cultivate TVA land that was lying fallow. TVA refused to give permission, stating that it did not have the power to make exceptions to a valley-wide policy.[23]

Bridgeforth attempted a different tactic to gain TVA cooperation and interest. He began to organize a memorial and appreciation day, scheduled to take place in August 1935, to celebrate the beginning of "a road to recovery." Bridgeforth asked that Harcourt Morgan attend to offer greetings to the Beulah community, and that President Roosevelt send greetings. Arthur Morgan wrote to Roosevelt's secretary, stating that L. N. Allen, head of the Reservoir Clearance Division, would read the following statement at the celebration:

> I am instructed by the President to convey his greetings to you on this occasion. . . . TVA is glad that actual and material benefits have been received by you by reason of your employment and because you have availed yourself of the program of training and education which the Authority has offered you.

The letter informed the president that the "colored people" appeared to be organized in a constructive and socially acceptable manner. In case there might have been any confusion or misgivings in the Roosevelt administration over who would be giving the greetings, the chairman offered the information that "Mr. Allen of course is white and a native Southerner." [24]

Despite his overtures and expressions of goodwill and gratitude, Bridgeforth did not receive much assistance from TVA after 1935. Indeed, TVA showed increased annoyance at Bridgeforth's insistence that his community be given aid and characterized him as a troublemaker who did not behave in an acceptable manner for a person of color in the South.

In 1936 Bridgeforth asked TVA to include Beulah in its demonstration farm projects, particularly in the area of poultry raising. TVA referred the request to the Alabama Extension Service, primarily because there were no TVA assistants employed in "negro work." To a Bridgeforth letter documenting racially biased treatment by the Alabama Extension Service, TVA replied that it had conducted its own investigation into the charges and the "negro county agent and assistants in agricultural training together with the regular county agent were giving the same type of service to the negroes in Beulah Land Community." Investigators had talked with several black farmers who stated that they were "entirely satisfied with the assistance given them by the Alabama Extension Service and were grateful for the interest that was being shown." The investigators concluded that Bridgeforth was a self-serving opportunist, and that the entire question of prejudice could be dismissed.[25]

It is clear that further requests by Bridgeforth were treated with less than full interest by TVA officials, as when the Beulah community asked to use bricks from the "old Bridgeforth house." The land where the house stood had been bought by TVA as part of the reservoir area, but Bridgeforth maintained that the house, which remained unused by TVA, could be dismantled and the wood (including a mahogany staircase) and bricks could be used to build a community center or a school. TVA noted that the house was quickly deteriorating and the roof was about to fall in, but denied the request, despite the recommendations of Birdius Browne, because the Legal Department indicated that a bothersome precedent would be set. In addition, it was noted again that Bridgeforth was a troublemaker with whom the Authority should have as little to do as possible.

After unsuccessful attempts to influence TVA directly, Bridgeforth wrote letters of complaint to outside officials. In a rather bold move, he wrote to Senator John Sparkman stating that after buying expensive equipment to fulfill a contract, he discovered that his more wealthy neighbors had conspired to take his crop away. He asked Sparkman to intercede. Sparkman wrote a heated letter to Arthur Morgan, questioning TVA's callous treatment of Alabama citizens. TVA replied that the Soil Conservation Association had control over the seed growing program and the dispute was not TVA's problem. It added, for Sparkman's information, that Bridgeforth was a "colored man," a fact that Bridgeforth had failed to provide in his letter to Sparkman. There were no further letters from Sparkman on the matter.[26]

Despite Bridgeforth's efforts and, to a certain extent, because of

Bridgeforth's efforts, the Beulah community did not receive much adjustment assistance from TVA. A 1937 memo summed up the Bridgeforth–TVA relationship from the Authority's point of view by characterizing him as "that colored man who has caused the Authority more trouble in the operation of its lands than almost anyone else." [27] TVA regional planners' treatment of other black communities was similar in ultimate impact, although the methods and spirit varied. The Authority appears to have been more cooperative with the community of Orrsville, Alabama, whose seven families were forced to relocate because of flooding from Wheeler Dam. Several factors contributed to TVA's more cooperative attitude. The leader of the Orrsville community was a more retiring, less aggressive black man named Pleas Orr, better known among his neighbors and TVA staff as "Uncle Pleas." A field agent sent to investigate Orrsville noted: "A large sign in the front yard of Orrsville's first citizen, Pleas Orr, announces the name of this community which was conceived and brought into existence by 'Uncle Pleas' as a home for his family and friends and as 'sumpin to stay here after I'm gone.' " The agent went on to describe "Uncle Pleas" as a man who liked to have his friends around him, a civic-minded individual who had helped rebuild the community's Baptist church. Orrsville itself was described as a "nice community . . . the houses are fairly well constructed and nicely separated." The agent presumably intended to compliment the inhabitants when he stated: "One gets the impression that the people are above the average for their group." [28]

Pleas Orr did not demand results but rather requested assistance in nonthreatening tones. His conformity with acceptable racial patterns was a factor in TVA cooperation. Another factor was the nature of his requests. Rather than asking for feed contracts, experimental stations, or other major projects, Orrsville asked to use a portion of the TVA-owned land to which they had been relocated for a community recreation ground. The field agent, Birdius Browne, strongly recommended that Orrsville be allowed to fix up a portion of the land as a playground with a baseball diamond. TVA eventually acceded to that request, and Orrsville, with the aid of the WPA, had a baseball diamond. Yet several conditions were imposed. TVA first sought and received permission from the white citizens who owned land near the proposed park. A tripartite agreement drawn up between the white neighbors, Orrsville, and TVA stated in part that blacks could use the land for a ballpark as long as "their activities were carried out in an acceptable manner to the TVA and to the neighboring citizens." Moreover, if the white neighbors wanted to sell their land and the prospective purchasers objected to having a black recreation center and ballpark near them, the facilities would be removed.[29]

The black families of Kirbytown, near the Guntersville reservoir, presented a special problem in that the surrounding areas were predominantly white. A proposal was made to "have some Federal agency assist the Negro families to purchase the remaining holdings of the white families of the Kirbytown Peninsula to make the community all Negro." The FSA was contacted, and the readjustment problems of the black families were turned over to that agency.[30]

Overall, the black communities affected by TVA reservoir removal were not given substantial help in reordering their lives. Several regional planners with considerable power to approve or reject requests held racial views that did not allow for equal treatment of blacks. The personality of George Bridgeforth offended regional planners, who labeled him a troublemaker and rejected his requests in part because he had the temerity to ask for fair and equal treatment. Even communities whose leaders conformed to local standards of acceptable behavior were treated unequally, as when the use of the Orrsville recreational park was made dependent on the personal wishes of white neighbors and future land buyers.

Yet racial prejudice was not the only factor. The entire department was understaffed, but the effects of the shortage were felt most sharply in the black communities. When Birdius Browne left TVA in 1937, those communities lost a vital and sympathetic liaison, and TVA did not provide a replacement. George Bridgeforth's problems illustrate another factor: the confusion created by overlapping agencies. Conflicts over jurisdiction created inefficiency within the Regional Planning Department, and, more importantly, the many agencies involved in the same general work caused confusion among the evacuees. In many instances the displaced individual did not know where to write to get help. In addition, TVA was not above creating additional confusion by shifting unpleasant or complicated issues to other agencies and claiming "a lack of jurisdiction."[31]

Although all these factors served to exacerbate the black communities' already severe problems, the limited scale of the reservoir removal project itself was the major factor. TVA regional planners did not significantly aid any relocated families, regardless of color. TVA did not keep records on the fate of its reservoir removal families; there were no follow-up studies to measure adjustment and living conditions after removal. Unless presented with an insistent resident, as in the case of George Bridgeforth, the correspondence between communities and TVA lasted for only a period of months. A shortage of data made it virtually impossible to arrive at an active plan for readjustment. Each issue was treated as it arose, and no clear policy developed. TVA was reluctant to involve itself in long-term projects and preferred to offer assistance in the form of advice for initial adjustment only. It carefully limited its actual responsibilities to compensation for owned land and was not concerned with the hardship caused by loss of access to traditionally used yet unowned land, or with the psychological or emotional damage caused by uprooting. Not given substantial support, many families just moved away.[32]

Reservoir flooding affected towns as well as rural communities, and these too sought TVA advice on planning. Guntersville, Alabama, was the flood plain of the Guntersville reservoir, and a major portion of the downtown area was flooded. The Guntersville Planning Board, consisting of the town's leading white citizens, attempted to effect a modern, efficient zoning plan for the restructured town. It requested information from TVA on Gunterville's industrial needs and future growth. TVA referred the board to the Commerce Department, which had completed a study. Yet it was evident that the Planning Board really wanted advice from TVA on another planning matter—the question of racial zoning.

Without input from TVA, the Guntersville Planning Board drew up a zoning ordinance. Section I established districts: Class A for detached one-family dwellings for members of the Caucasian race, Class B for detached one- and multi-family dwellings for persons other than members of the Caucasian race.[33] The ordinance was introduced as a progressive measure intended to bring order and logic to the rapid growth anticipated for Guntersville as a result of cheap TVA-produced electricity and TVA-inspired recreational activities. Another aspect of the new ordinance was its creation of an ordered residential pattern built on race. The old Guntersville had a general area where blacks congregated and lived, yet residential segregation was built on custom and tradition. The Guntersville planners sought legally to restrict blacks to certain areas in order to prevent the possibility of residential integration. In planning for the two areas, certain allowances were made for the presumed differences in lifestyle and interests of the two races. Both A and B districts allowed churches, schools, libraries, and recreational clubs. Boarding houses were allowed in Class A districts with written permission from the neighbors. Boarding houses were allowed in Class B districts without written permission from the neighbors. Class A allowed a minimum of 12,000 square feet for a family dwelling; in Class B, there only had to be 6,000 square feet per family unit. Apartments and hotels were allowed in Class B, while Class A, to avoid overcrowding, did not allow multifamily dwellings.[34]

The racial zoning aspect of the Guntersville ordinance caused much controversy. The Guntersville Planning Board used the advice of Charles Edward of Alabama Polytechnic Institute, A. L. Thomas of the Alabama

84

State Planning Board, and D. A. Johnson of the TVA Planning Division. Johnson forwarded the ordinance for review by the TVA board of directors, since the Authority owned and controlled certain recreational areas of the new town. He had earlier advised the Planning Board that "there be created in the Guntersville zoning ordinance separate zones for white and negro residents." Johnson maintained that he was following TVA's policy of sensitivity to local customs and that the racial zoning ordinance "was probably in line with other municipal zoning ordinances in Alabama." [35]

TVA regional planners, after seeking legal advice from the TVA counsel, recommended that the city planners delete the section on racial zoning on the grounds that it might be found illegal by the courts: "We would like to call attention to the fact that racial zoning has been held unconstitutional by the U.S. Supreme Court." [36] But the city planners were undeterred by the legal defeats of similar ordinances. Charles Edwards, on behalf of the Guntersville Planning Board, suggested in a letter to TVA that a constitutional issue might be avoided if the ordinance was revised to read: "Residences A-1 District . . . recommended for but not restricted to use by persons of the white race. Residences B-2 District recommended for but not restricted to use by persons of the negro race." Moreover, it noted that most racial ordinance defeats occurred between 1924 and 1930, "when the Supreme Court of the United States was quite different in membership from the present . . . the present court might hand down an entirely different opinion." Regardless of the legal difficulties, the Planning Board was determined to maintain racial restrictions for the future safety and well-being of the South. It was certain that even if illegal, the ordinance would never be challenged in court, and neither the city government nor the Guntersville community would make an issue of it. The only danger, as far as the Guntersville board was concerned, would come from a suit initiated by an outside agency or influence.[37]

TVA chose not to reply to this letter—the Legal Department and the Regional Planning Department suggested that the Authority write "no comment" and file it—and issued several memos to "put on our record against the validity of racial zoning." [38] It had earlier determined that none of the lands owned by TVA would be subject to local zoning and building ordinances and, consequently, that it would not become a participant in any potentially illegal discrimination.[39] The Guntersville city planners, receiving no reply from the TVA, announced that their city council had accepted the ordinance and that the final authority rested not with TVA, but with the state planning commission, whose member Charles Edwards had given advice on the original ordinance.[40] In this case TVA, because of its self-defined role as advisor, had no ultimate influence on the final decision to implement the racial zoning ordinance. The controversy illustrates the problems inherent in cooperating with local planners and businessmen even more reluctant than TVA itself to change customary racial attitudes.

The development of recreational parks was another responsibility of the Regional Planning Department that touched the lives of blacks. The reservoirs created by TVA dams flooded much farmland. TVA's long-range plan called for the replacement of income from farming with income generated by tourists attracted to TVA parks and lakes. Displaced farmers could be hired to run concession stands and rent out boating and fishing equipment. An increase in tourism would also spur the growth of support facilities like restaurants, stores, and hotels, creating hundreds of new jobs. TVA regional planners investigated and recommended feasible sites for recreational facilities and, with the aid of population and economic surveys and maps, determined the probable number of park users and whether rustic cabins or conventional cottages and lodges would be more suitable there. The park facilities were to be run as a nonsubsidized part of the TVA corporation, and although they were not expected to make as much money as the fertilizer or electricity plants, they were not expected to lose money. Once the parks were open, their usage was constantly monitored.

Two aspects of recreational planning involving segregation and economics particularly affected blacks. In conformity with local practices, TVA planners as a matter of course drew up plans for separate recreational facilities. Yet while plans for a white recreational facility were drawn up for almost every reservoir, plans for black recreational facilities were delayed until economic feasibility studies were made. The construction of a separate black facility was considered an additional cost outlay, and surveys had given regional planners the impression that blacks were less inclined than whites to use recreational facilities. TVA therefore frequently turned down proposals for Negro parks on the grounds that not enough blacks would use the facilities.

The proposed Norris Negro Park was one park that was ostensibly turned down for economic reasons. Yet other factors were also involved. Norris Dam had already become an area of racial controversy because of the exclusion of blacks from the Norris Model Community in 1934. By the time the Norris recreation park was proposed in 1937, civil rights groups were watching the Norris area for further signs of exclusion. Consequently, when the Norris recreational proposal (without facilities for blacks) was announced, civil rights groups quickly voiced their criticism. TVA officials replied that feasibility studies done on the Norris lake area had concluded that only 4 percent of the population was black, a percentage too low to sustain an adequate usage rate. In addition, the general manager stated that "the Authority will not be able to develop a recreational park for Negroes due to lack of state participation."[41] By "lack of state participation," the general manager was referring to the refusal of the Tennessee Department of Conservation to construct a demonstration park in the Norris area. TVA stated that it could not operate its own demonstration park for blacks, because a demonstration park—Big Ridge Park—already existed nearby. Although it was for whites only, the Big Ridge Park was judged by the Legal Department to be too similar in conditions and operation to the proposed Negro demonstration park at Norris to justify the expense.[42]

The final policy decision as released by the general manager in 1938 and again in 1940 stated that there were no plans to provide Negro facilities at Norris. Yet this public statement did not reflect the divided opinion of the departments within TVA. The Department of Regional Planning Studies (formerly the Regional Planning Department) recommended that blacks be provided with a park at Norris Lake, accurately predicting that unless the matter was immediately considered by the board, the future cooperation of the National Park Service, the CCC, and other state and local agencies would be difficult to obtain. It further noted that although only 4 percent of the population of the area surrounding Norris was black, the sizable number of blacks living in Knoxville and Knox County were within driving distance. In addition, the economic level of blacks in Knoxville was relatively high, in part because of opportunities within TVA and the presence of eight black colleges employing over a thousand teachers. Interest in recreational activities was high among these economically secure blacks and would ensure adequate usage of the park.[43]

Altruism and equality were not the most compelling reasons for TVA development of recreational facilities for blacks. Regional planners also perceived a need "to relieve the present tendency on the part of Negroes to use Norris Park facilities," and recommended locating the Negro park area on Norris Lake far away from the Norris Dam area. At that time, blacks, while excluded from overnight facilities and camping grounds, were theoretically allowed, although not encouraged, to use the remaining park facilities. Thus, regional planners hoped that when a segregated alternative was presented, more blacks would be more easily persuaded to keep within the segregated pattern.[44] They suggested that the Negro park include a day-outing area with a boathouse and constant-level pool, overnight accommodations for Negro tourists, "who now find decent stopping places almost non-existing," and camp grounds and simple cottages for low-income families.[45]

In the end, the regional planners were overruled. The general manager cited surveys that maintained that the Norris area was "off the beaten path" and would not be attractive to a large number of blacks, who were fleeing the rural areas and seeking the comforts of urban life. Blacks were no longer interested in camping out. Given these migration patterns, it was unlikely that the demand for Negro facilities would increase. Moreover, Gordon Clapp stated, "It is the desire of Negro groups that separate facilities be provided." Integrated facilities would be unacceptable not only to whites, but to blacks as well. This contention was heatedly denied by black TVA employees, the NAACP, and local black organizations, as well as members of the Personnel Department.[46]

Another reason given for the refusal to construct recreational facilities at Norris was the plan to build Booker T. Washington Park in Chattanooga. Surveys showed that 405,000 black persons lived within a 200-mile radius of Chattanooga, and the site chosen was also close to the intersection of four federal highways. TVA agreed to furnish the land, and the Tennessee State Department of Conservation and the National Park Service cooperated readily to develop the park.[47] The park, once constructed, had facilities for swimming and boating, picnic areas, a pavilion, playing fields, a camp ground, and vacation cabins. The last two features were provided because no private tourist areas admitted blacks. The initial complaint regarding Booker T. Washington Park involved its proximity to an industrial site, which diminished its esthetic value and hampered the park's development. The park proved to be an even greater disappointment in the 1940s, when it was not properly maintained: for example, the swimming pool remained closed for lack of pumping equipment. In addition, there were no lavatories in the park.[48]

Other, smaller parks were provided for blacks. Wilson Negro Park served blacks in western Tennessee and northern Alabama. TVA regional planners noted that it was underutilized during the week but that the facilities were strained on weekends and holidays. A survey measuring the use of TVA parks on 4–5 July 1940, however, noted that only 45 persons visited the park on those days. Respondents noted the absence of such facilities as ballparks, swimming pools, and a dance pavilion. The park also suffered from not providing overnight accommodations. Unlike Booker T. Washington Park, Wilson Park had no cabins to attract the tourist trade, so its users were all local. In fact, in an analysis of the recreation potential of the northern Alabama area, planners recommended only day-outing facilities because the "accent should be on facilities that will satisfy the gregarious nature of the Negro rather than on those designed to promote close association with nature; in other words, 'lively' as against 'contemplative.' "[49]

Planning based on these stereotypes ignored evidence to the contrary supplied by the patronage of Booker T. Washington Park and the requests of the black citizens near Norris Dam. The practice of planning around a stereotype revealed the limitations of long-range planning. The ideal of so-called scientific or rational planning, based on survey results and "hard data," did not hold up in the area of recreation, where conclusions were reached on the basis of subjective impressions or personal prejudices.

There were also instances in which statistics and surveys were manipulated or at least overemphasized. The economic feasibility survey for the establishment of Negro parks was one such example. Although TVA kept meticulous records of attendance at parks operated for blacks, no comparable records were kept at parks operated for whites. While blacks were placed in the position of having to prove interest and the probability of profit for TVA, whites were given the right to expect facilities at almost every dam site regardless of costs.[50]

Economic feasibility served to cloud another important issue within recreational planning: the desire to discourage blacks from congregating in new, nontraditional areas. We have already noted, for example, how TVA sought to discourage blacks from using the Norris area: employment of blacks in the area was kept at a minimum; no blacks were allowed in the Norris Model Community; no provisions were made for blacks at Norris Park, not even sanitary facilities or water fountains; TVA refused to approve a separate park in the area for blacks; and when blacks did venture into Norris Park or nearby Big Ridge, "their use of picnicking areas . . . [was] questioned and their presence discouraged."[51]

Recreational facilities, while a factor in the growth of economic prosperity, were only fringe benefits in the future planned society. A more essential ingredient in the development of the valley was the improvement of educational opportunities. TVA recognized the importance of education in creating a new environment and devoted considerable effort to aiding public schools and land grant colleges and promoting adult education.

The Authority operated schools for workers' children in most of the isolated dam sites. In addition, there were three laboratory schools, one each at Norris and Wilson Dams for whites and one at Wheeler Dam for blacks. The Norris school system was the first and most ambitious laboratory project. The secondary school attempted an innovative approach to education and hoped to attract students who ordinarily would not have continued in school. Concerned with the widespread apathy toward school, TVA educators placed considerable emphasis on the practical nature of school and its usefulness in later life. Science students took field trips to learn about weather forecasting and local geography; math classes visited banks, where bookkeeping systems, financial contracts, and investments were explained.[52] To counter the atmosphere of failure and inferiority in which valley children had been raised, TVA educators attempted to create a comfortable, noncompetitive school environment. Children were encouraged to talk freely in classroom discussions. In place of written grades and report cards, parents received letters from the school indicating their children's progress. A child never repeated or skipped a grade. The curriculum was sufficiently flexible to allow various levels of proficiency in each classroom.[53]

The innovative programs of Norris lasted only ten years. After the completion of Norris Dam, TVA gradually withdrew its support for the school. Without government support, the local school board had to curtail the special programs and shorten the school year from ten months to eight. The school also returned to the grading system and the practice of failing or skipping students.[54]

Similar to Norris in its overall experimental educational philosophy, the Wilson school was even more pronounced in its advocacy of the rights of the child. It placed the interests, problems, and desires of the child ahead of the need for conformity and adherence to a standard curriculum. The school experimented with different ways to encourage interest in learning, such as using "Alley Oop" comic books to develop reading skills. Despite protests from parents, TVA discontinued the Wilson school in 1942 and sent the workers' children to the inferior Sheffield, Alabama, county schools.[55]

The elementary school provided by TVA for blacks during the construction of Wheeler Dam had only one room, where a teacher taught grades one through six. Previously the black workers had obtained the services of three volunteer teachers and had held classes in their homes. After they requested a school for their children, TVA hired a black teacher for 1935 and converted a small house into a school with a small library, a nature museum, and an arts and crafts shop. The curriculum addressed the perceived special needs of black children. Along with the standard elementary subjects, the teacher stressed hygiene and placed a special emphasis on music appreciation and the playing of the piano. She observed that "music plays an important role in the daily life of the people. . . . For this reason there is a high correlation between leadership and the ability to play the piano. . . . I therefore decided to provide free instruction to those students who were interested." [56]

In addition to new definitions of leadership abilities, the teacher at Wheeler relied on standardized IQ tests to evaluate her pupils. Although most students at Wheeler were judged capable or above average on the basis of school assignments, most also scored below average (between 76 and 90) on the Binet-Simon intelligence tests. The teacher noted that one boy whom she had considered to be very bright, an excellent worker, and the school leader, tested as having an IQ of only 76. Regretting her mistaken initial appraisal, the teacher welcomed the "more exact measure . . . of the Binet-Simon intelligence test." [57]

While a program for black children that relied on the questionable pedagogic beliefs of one teacher for one year did not compare with either of the two extensive programs for white children at Wilson and Norris Dams, additional proof of TVA's policy of separate but unequal education can be seen in the different school buildings provided for blacks and whites. At Kentucky Dam, the school for white children was a brick building constructed from plans prepared by a private architect with assistance from TVA staff. Black children on the other hand used a reconditioned wooden farmhouse of "reasonable substantial construction." When asked about the lack of TVA-sponsored schools for blacks, TVA officials stated that they preferred to contract with local school boards for the education of the children of black TVA employees.[58]

Indeed, it was the policy of TVA to contract with local school boards to educate most children of TVA employees. To offset the costs of increased attendance in local schools, TVA provided tuition vouchers on a per-pupil basis. In order to raise the standards of the local schools, TVA provided additional money to school districts for supplies on the condition that they lengthen their school terms to at least 156 days.[59]

Providing education for the children of black employees presented certain difficulties to the planners within TVA. While local white schools were judged substandard, most black schools were rated even lower. The school boards in the seven Tennessee valley states traditionally spent less on black schools, and the facilities and level of instruction reflected the disparity.

To educate the black children of workers at Watts Bar Dam and Reservoir, an agreement was made between Rhea County, Tennessee, and TVA. The county promised to provide adequate materials and instruction and to keep schools open at least 156 days a year. The school board also provided transportation in TVA-approved metal school buses with licensed drivers carrying $10,000 worth of insurance. In return, TVA agreed to pay $60.00 for each pupil assigned. The school board was free to use any money above the actual expenses per child on purchasing additional books, equipment, and trucking materials. TVA also entered into an agreement with the city of Benton, Kentucky, on behalf of the black and white children of employees working at Kentucky Dam. It agreed to pay $80.00 for each white pupil and $135.00 for each black pupil. The higher cost for black children was due to the unavailability of black schools at Benton; consequently, Paducah and other communities were paid extra money to take them. On the other hand, in keeping with the local practice of spending less on education for blacks, TVA paid the school board of Sheffield, Alabama, $55.00 for each white child and only $30.00 for each black child.[60]

The expense of educating black children was used as an excuse for not hiring blacks at certain work sites, particularly Hiwassee and Douglas Dams. The former was located in an area where there were few blacks, and TVA argued that the number of black children on the site would not be enough to warrant a TVA-operated school. And yet there were no schools for blacks in the vicinity of the dam site.[61]

Despite this use of the school issue, TVA contributed substantially to the improvement of both black and white schools through direct tuition and indirect guidance and consultation. Each school district was assigned a TVA education consultant, who worked closely with the school board to attack educational deficiencies in the district. The consultant offered advice on such matters as qualifying examinations for schoolteachers and the selection of proper schoolbooks. Unfortunately, all contracts between TVA and school districts were terminated by 1945. The terminations caused some hardships for school boards, and some questioned the equity of the discontinuance, complaining that they had not been given adequate notice and consequently did not have enough money appropriated to educate unsubsidized TVA children. TVA consistently replied that it had no legal responsibility to continue the subsidies.[62]

Adult education was also part of the Authority's long-range planning and another area where TVA was willing to accept the status quo for blacks. Trade unions, in cooperation with TVA, organized job-training and apprenticeship courses, yet these were for whites only. Working for the most part independently of skilled unions, TVA established its own program to improve the skills of its black workers so that they could become more productive citizens in a modern Tennessee valley society.

The classes that blacks were allowed to take emphasized janitorial training for men and homemaking and housekeeping training for women. Black men were given elementary training in plumbing and electrical wiring—not enough to become apprentices in either field, but enough to become more efficient and knowledgeable handymen. There were classes for medical orderlies and medical aides, classes in blueprint reading and practical mathematics for tenders, in first aid for chemical plant workers, and in problems and practices in reservoir clearance. In the last-named class instructions were given in how to use a pick and shovel most effectively. Whites were at least given the option of learning technological skills that offered the possibility of permanent employment by TVA. Blacks were for the most part trained to occupy the same menial or semiskilled positions that they already had in the valley.[63]

In offering a course in bookkeeping methods geared to sharecropping, the Training Division explained that it was taking a pragmatic view of future job opportunities for blacks. TVA argued that it was being realistic rather than idealistic in setting limited goals for black adult education. J. Max Bond, supervisor of Negro Training, noted that "Negroes in North Alabama were always in demand as odd-job men." Indeed, there were no opportunities for blacks as hydraulic technicians in the valley, and TVA did not risk setting a precedent by hiring any blacks in the new technologies.[64]

TVA also ran a community education program aimed at the employees' leisure time. Social workers visited employees' homes and instructed the women on basic hygiene and ways "to improve the standard of the home." There was a major effort to remove illiteracy among both black and white employees. TVA acknowledged that many workers, both black and white, read on a first- or second-grade level. These men were trained in simple English, with an emphasis on the spelling of common words, and arithmetic skills.

There was also an informal attempt to give black workers a sense of community by developing pride in practical training and self-sufficiency. TVA clubs were organized in northern Alabama to discuss serious problems in the black community, such as high infant mortality, inadequate housing, and crime. Yet while social issues were discussed in the clubs, criticism of the larger society was not encouraged. Rather, criticism was directed at the black community's failure to take advantage of existing opportunities within a segregated society. For example, there were discussions on how to develop dependable work habits to offset a negative image within the white community.[65]

In a similar, though larger, program in Chattanooga, TVA cooperated with the Chattanooga Community Council, a group of black schoolteachers, ministers, and skilled laborers, in sponsoring a "People's College," which held a series of public lectures and discussions. Its purpose was "to acquaint blacks with their problems, to encourage the organization of permanent study groups, and to develop a group of volunteer leaders." Over eleven hundred people attended the lecture and discussion sessions. The largest numbers came to hear Rayford Logan, a black historian, speak on "Fascism, Communism, and Democracy as Each Relates to American Minorities," and Ira D. Reid, a former member of Roosevelt's "Black Cabinet," lecture on "Social Security and the Negro." When Reid spoke in 1938, he was very enthusiastic about federal programs, including TVA. He asserted that "TVA will raise standards of living among the lowest and unskilled classes. . . . Those in areas affected will be lifted from their present state of economic slavery and be nearer the utopia of economic security." Although no transcript is available of the discussion after the lecture, it was described as very lively.[66]

TVA sought to expand the impact of its adult education program by cooperating with black colleges in an internship program. In 1934 it reserved a hundred summer intern positions for blacks and sent requests to Fisk University, Knoxville College, Tennessee Agricultural & Industrial, Clark University (Ga.), Talladega College, Lane College, Jackson College, Morehouse College, and Tuskegee Institute. TVA stated that the students would be employed as janitors and laborers and should have demonstrated leadership ability and high scholastic achievement and be in good physical condition. Only Fisk, Tuskegee, and Knoxville College participated in the program to any significant extent, and the goal of a hundred interns was not met.[67]

TVA also occasionally requested assistance from the black colleges in recruiting for permanent jobs. In its search to find black electricians and plumbers to build Pickwick Village, TVA asked Tuskegee to compile a list of qualified craftsmen.[68] There were other forms of cooperation. TVA and Fisk University exchanged speakers. Floyd Reeves, the first director of personnel, was a frequent lecturer at Fisk, and Charles Johnson, a Fisk sociologist, was a frequent visitor to TVA, for which he conducted several studies. One was "The Negro Personality Changes Under Conditions of Race and Culture in the Tennessee Valley Area"; another was "Negroes in Skilled and Professional Trades in the Tennessee Region."[69]

There was also limited cooperation in academic areas. Blacks were prevented from taking many courses in the TVA extension program because the courses were taught at white universities. TVA managed a compromise, encouraging university professors to allow blacks to enroll in correspondence courses. Although the universities would still not give credits to black students, TVA secured college credit for them from Fisk University.[70]

Fisk professors occasionally sought advice on courses and examinations. Floyd Reeves, who had been a professor at the University of Chicago, was sent several masters' degree examinations. Students were asked to write essays on "The Married Woman as School Teacher"; "The Depression and Education"; "Teachers as Members of Labor Unions"; "The *Einheitsschule* Movement"; and "The Oversupply of Teachers." Reeves replied, "The objective and subjective scores would differ, but would pass six without question if they were at U. of Chicago—fail one and conditionally pass three." By sending Reeves these papers, Fisk established an early relationship with the director of personnel and obtained written legitimization of its own standards and the quality of its students, although the college was unable to translate approval of standards and quality into TVA employment.[71]

In addition to such informal correspondence with black educators, TVA sought to establish more formal and complex cooperation with two black schools, Alabama Agricultural and Mechanical College and Tuskegee Institute. Alabama A&M had developed a cooperative homesteading project. The college president sought funding from the FERA to establish a 200- to 250-family cooperative on land adjacent to the campus, and the proposal stated that professors and students from the college would assist the families in choosing the correct fertilizer and methods. The self-help community would then farm the land as a unit and divide the profits according to the number of hours put in by each person. With the aid of the FERA, Alabama A&M was able to establish a small black cooperative. TVA became interested in the project when several black families in nearby Riverton, Alabama, had to be removed from the flood plain of a TVA dam; their relocation to Alabama A&M would have been "a happy solution to the removal problem in this community." TVA offered to provide advisors from its Regional Planning Department. However, the effort at cooperation did not succeed, primarily because the black families of Riverton did not wish to move to a cooperative farming community.[72]

Tuskegee Institute was the only black college with which TVA made an effort to establish a research connection: the Authority did not consider other institutions to be worthy. One TVA official stated: "So far as we are able to determine at this time, the Tuskegee Institute is the only Negro institution with which we may cooperate." Schools like Alabama A&M College were considered to be advanced high schools that sent their best students to either Fisk or Tuskegee to finish their undergraduate degrees.[73]

TVA sought in particular to arrange a cooperative relationship with the Tuskegee laboratories of Dr. George Washington Carver, the world-famous black chemist. From 1933 through 1939, it attempted to contact Carver about a series of experiments Carver was conducting on outdoor paint. The extremely cautious Carver questioned TVA's interest in his research projects. Regional planners themselves were divided over the wisdom of cooperating with Carver: some noted his uncooperativeness and questioned the legitimacy of his scientific credentials. Perhaps expressing the views of his boss, the executive secretary to Arthur Morgan wrote: "From sources of information we understand the chemist is somewhat of an eccentric genius whatever that might be and that he has hit on several things that have possibilities of being developed into industries with commercial value."[74]

To offset Carver's negative image within TVA, letters praising his scientific contributions were written by non-TVA academics. Ernest Seeman of Duke University wrote:

> Personally I think there is a great misunderstanding about this man Carver in that he is "said to be an eccentric genius" and "has hit upon several things." . . . He has worked industriously long hours for long years and if his skin had been white he would now have a high place in the annals of science. . . . He is the same kind of eccentric genius as were Galileo, Langley and Edison.

Seeman also sent a copy of Carver's entry in *Who's Who* and suggested that the president of Tuskegee be contacted for help in pressuring Carver to cooperate.[75]

TVA followed Seeman's advice and, using a variety of intermediaries, finally succeeded in establishing a small cooperative research project for the development of low-cost paints. TVA hoped that through its rural electrification program, more homes in the poorer regions of the Cotton Belt would use electric power, equipment, and appliances. There would also be a growing need for low-cost paint for interior use to improve lighting. Through cooperation with Carver's laboratory, which had developed an organic paint, TVA hoped to develop a market for inexpensive paint that would result in a new industry of paint manufacture.[76]

TVA and Tuskegee conducted the research project from 1939 through 1941. The Authority contributed approximately four thousand dollars to the project, but later retrieved all equipment purchased for it and reserved control over any inventions or new processes developed during the period of cooperation.[77] After 1941 TVA did not have cooperative programs with any black college until 1949, when it concluded an agreement with Tuskegee to provide a study of the effects of rapidly changing economic conditions upon six Negro communities in northern Alabama.[78]

In comparison with the money spent and energy expended on white colleges, black schools—including Tuskegee—were virtually ignored. In connection with TVA's announced program of agricultural development and watershed protection through improved fertilization, Tuskegee asked for a carload of TVA fertilizer for experimental purposes. TVA replied that it could not comply with Tuskegee's request for several reasons. First, all requests for experimental work had to be cleared with the state-controlled Alabama Experimental Station, and no guarantee could be given that Tuskegee would be accepted. Secondly, Tuskegee had requested nitrate fertilizer, and at the time of the request, TVA was manufacturing only phosphate fertilizers.[79] Finally, TVA chose to interpret Tuskegee's proposal as being more suitable for a demonstration farm project than an experimental project. In a demonstration farm project, several chosen farmers were given fertilizers and instruction in growing techniques. An experimental project involved the cooperation of several academic departments and brought thousands of dollars, along with the latest research techniques and equipment, to the college.[80]

Indeed, TVA had established extensive cooperative programs with white land grant colleges and universities in the area, in both research and extension services. Except for the small-scale Tuskegee paint project, black colleges were excluded from research projects and they were also discriminated against in extension services. Despite protests from Tuskegee, J. Max Bond, and the NAACP, TVA continued to exclude blacks or relegate them to minor positions in the extension services. It was later observed by two political scientists that

> after allowance has been made for such factors as the utilization of the service of white county agents in behalf of Negroes' interracial meetings, and the segregation in research reports of the data for the races and the more recent attempts in the work of experiment stations to give attention to the racial problems peculiar to the Negro, there is still evidence that in research and extension there has been discrimination against the Negro.[81]

The quality of life for blacks in the Tennessee valley improved somewhat over the period of TVA's first decade. Yet this improvement can be ascribed to a general economic improvement within the valley and the lessening of overt racial discrimination on a national scale, and cannot be directly attributed to the long-range planning programs of TVA.[82] In fact, in such areas as reservoir removal, recreational parks, agricultural extension services, and land grant college cooperation, the policies of the Department of Planning actually diminished the quality of life. Reservoir removal disrupted the economic and social lives of black families without providing adequate readjustment services. TVA, while providing several all-black parks, excluded many blacks from enjoying parks near their homes. Agricultural extension services and land grant college cooperation improved the quality of the white farm industry and higher education for whites, while denying equal benefits to blacks.

The failure of TVA regional planning for blacks can be attributed to several factors. The first was the inability of the Department of Planning to function as a generator of long-range plans. As stated earlier, the department was hampered by a confused social and political mandate emanating from the TVA act. In addition, adherence to a "grass-roots" philosophy hindered the construction and implementation of long-range, coherent plans. Particularly in the area of reservoir removal, education, and recreational parks, TVA's strict policy of local and state collaboration resulted in a rigorous self-restraint in community and regional planning. Rather than developing a far-reaching or coherent series of long-range plans for the valley, TVA was forced to initiate plans that attempted to solve existing problems. Moreover, its planners adopted a pragmatic attitude that emphasized political awareness of the wishes for powerful interests. Only a few planners took a more idealistic approach that emphasized significant change in social and economic areas. The latter group noted that the Authority's planning for recreation areas was characterized by a "haphazard approach which reflected negatively on the entire planning program." [83] This inability to develop long-range plans prevented TVA from formulating a unified approach to the specific problems of marginal ethnic and economic groups in the valley.

The specific manner in which TVA planned for blacks was another factor. Its planners envisioned blacks as an inferior, monolithic group without distinctions in personality, class consciousness, political inclination, economic status, or educational attainment. TVA assumed that facilities intended for their use could be shifted around without causing much hardship, as in the case of the substitution of Booker T. Washington Park for the all-white Norris Park. TVA assumed that the exclusion of black colleges from significant land grant projects did not greatly harm these institutions, nor was it particularly concerned over the plight of the black communities uprooted by the reservoir removal program.

Ironically, while TVA catered to political interests on the state and local levels, it virtually ignored the possibility of serious lobbying efforts on the part of civil rights advocates until it was confronted with their protests. Although initially taken by surprise, TVA treated such protests seriously and as a result modified several discriminatory practices, such as overt job exclusion and harassment on the worksite. Yet to TVA, protests from civil rights advocates represented an immediate crisis and were not seen as reflecting a far-reaching problem that dictated a reexamination and modification of its policy of bending to the status quo.

Jackhammer operator, Wheeler Dam, 1935. One of the few semiskilled positions in construction, jackhammer operation was considered a "Negro trade." *(TVA Technical Library)*

Construction work on Wheeler Dam, 1935: black work crews and white supervisors and crane operators. *(TVA Technical Library)*

Water fountain for whites,
Pickwick Dam, 1939.
(TVA Technical Library)

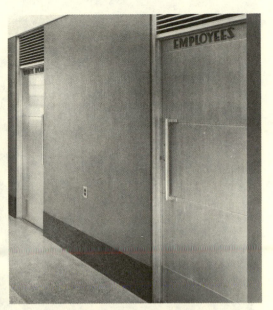

Restrooms for white women and
"employees," Wheeler Dam, 1938.
(TVA Technical Library)

Restroom for colored women behind
mural describing improvements TVA
will make in flood control, TVA dam
site, 1930s. *(TVA Technical Library)*

Digging phosphate in a non-TVA worksite in northern Alabama, taken by
TVA photographer, 1934. *(TVA Technical Library)*

Alabama farmer, 1935. *(TVA Technical Library)*

Sharecropper family, 1933. *(TVA Technical Library)*

Black camp area, Fontana Dam, 1943. Tents were erected adjacent to the black dormitories to accommodate an increase in the black workforce in 1942. *(TVA Technical Library)*

Mule-drawn wagon. In the 1930s there were still areas in the Tennessee valley where mules were used instead of trucks for transporting goods. *(TVA Technical Library)*

Harcourt Morgan, member
of the TVA Board of
Directors.
(TVA Technical Library)

Gordon Clapp, director of
personnel, general manager,
and chairman of the TVA
Board of Directors.
(TVA Technical Library)

Arthur Morgan, first
chairman of the TVA Board
of Directors, 1933–1938.
(TVA Technical Library)

David Lilienthal, member of
the TVA Board of Directors,
1933–1945.
(TVA Technical Library)

CHAPTER V

Critics of TVA's
Racial Policies

THE final test for planning in a democratic society is whether the targeted population accepts and supports the plans. New Deal planners characterized totalitarian and communist regimes as imposing plans from above, while democracies strove to reach a workable consensus: the contrast captured the essential difference between their political systems. Yet TVA officials committed to "democratic planning" found themselves confronted and criticized by advocates of civil rights, both within the Authority and outside it, who felt that TVA's plans were at best insensitive and at worst racist and exclusionary. These attacks took several forms, including critical newspaper reports, investigations by civil rights organizations and the Fair Employment Practices Committee, threats of legal action, protests from valley civic committees, and even complaints by black TVA employees.

Blacks who were advocates of civil rights and were employed by TVA experienced a particularly difficult dilemma. They were torn between anger and dismay over TVA's racial practices on the one hand, and a desire to retain a relatively well-paying and prestigious position on the other. Early in 1934 TVA decided to hire a black professional whose official title would be "supervisor of Negro training," but whose real position would be that of assistant personnel officer. His function was "to plan and promote useful training programs based on the specific needs of Negro employees."[1] In the course of a nationwide search, TVA asked the Interracial Cooperation Commission for suggestions and recommendations. Will Alexander recommended J. Max Bond, a thirty-two-year-old teacher and civil rights worker living in Kentucky and working for the Julius Rosenwald Foundation. He was the brother of Horace Mann Bond, an educator at Atlanta University, and was to become the uncle of the civil rights activist and State Senator Julian Bond. J. Max Bond had recently been laid off by the foundation. Hired without an interview, Bond was sent immediately to Wheeler Dam, where he established a Negro training section in the Employment Office of the Personnel Department.[2]

Although his official job description involved heading the Negro training section, Bond's function in TVA was infinitely broader and more complex. He became the liaison between TVA and the black communities in the Tennessee valley. He met and worked with those communities and promoted training activities for TVA workers and their families within them. Black communities in turn began to designate Bond as their spokesman within TVA and sent him letters of complaint or requests for aid. TVA took advantage of Bond's unofficial function and sent him throughout the valley to speak before Negro gatherings.[3]

During his tenure as the Negro training supervisor, J. Max Bond experienced the conflict between personal conscience and organizational loyalty. Bond expressed the desire to effect changes within TVA by pointing out inconsistencies and open discrimination in its racial policies. Working within the TVA system, he hoped to meet frequently with section heads and supervisors, "to frankly discuss the program, clear up unexplained details, and establish a better understanding and confidence."[4] Bond was asked to keep track of and interpret TVA employment figures and make reports to top-level administrators. He listed the latest tangible results of TVA policy with regard to the hiring of blacks. Although he noted the statistical imbalance of hiring within TVA and the lack of advancement within the ranks, Bond was careful to camouflage his opinions. In an early report he wrote:

> During the history of the project there have been no highly skilled artisans employed, that is, carpenters, brick-layers, mechanics, mechanic helpers, foremen and others in positions requiring a great deal of skill. . . . The one writer [Bond] does not desire this statement to be construed as criticism of the policy of the TVA.[5]

Publicly and in print, Bond was a supporter of TVA racial policies. Within TVA, he functioned as a moderate critic who took stands against the exclusion of blacks from the Norris Model Community, Norris Park, and the Hiwassee Dam site. He protested against the TVA practice of cutting costs by not building segregated facilities—a practice directed at exclusion, rather than integration. As a moderate within TVA, however, he did not criticize the existence of segregated facilities, and he adhered to the TVA rationalization that the time for racial integration had not come for the Tennessee valley.[6]

There were two sides to Bond. Throughout his tenure as a TVA employee, Bond encouraged and aided NAACP investigations of the Authority.

In 1935 Bond wrote a confidential letter to his friend and brother-in-law, Rufus Clement, asking that the NAACP initiate an investigation into the racial discrimination practiced at the Wilson-Wheeler Dam area. Bond wished to keep his role as instigator private, of course, and requested that correspondence from the NAACP be sent in a plain envelope to his home address. He was particularly upset that TVA was building an "inferior type of house" for black workmen at Wilson Dam, and that the black housing there was not to be developed into a model village on the level of the Norris Model Community, as had apparently been promised. The Wilson Dam housing, he told Walter White of the NAACP, was

> so poorly planned that the white foreman himself refused to continue with the work . . . indeed, most of the houses are old structures built during the War as temporary homes for workers. . . . These houses are being moved to the new village site. . . . To "cap the climax" white labor is being used exclusively on the construction work in the Negro village at Wilson Dam. . . . The Negroes are digging the ditches. . . . I've done all I can do to remedy these gross perversions of the plans proposed in Knoxville: conferences, protests are availing us nothing. . . . The white southerners in charge go on unheeding. . . . They feel that they can "get away" with anything. . . . The Negro public is always asleep.[7]

The tone of the letter was one of dismay bordering on bitterness. The TVA social and economic program was not including blacks, and Bond felt all alone: "We ought to get more out of it than we are getting. . . . My protests, without the support or interest of any Negro organization, are futile. . . . The press is silent; Negroes don't seem to care what happens down here. . . . They just aren't interested and the whites 'get away with murder.' " He expressed the dilemma of the black, socially conscious worker in TVA, along with a bit of egotism, when he stated:

> I'd wire Walter White from here to come down and investigate, but you can see what that would mean. . . . There'd be no more "Bond" in the TVA. . . . Now for myself I wouldn't give a d—— but what would become of the Negro Program? Some weakling would be put in my place and the Negro in the TVA would be "sold out."[8]

Clement forwarded the letter to Walter White, who sent John P. Davis and Charles Houston to investigate Bond's charges. Bond met secretly with Houston and Davis, supplying them with the statistical information needed to evaluate the TVA program. While cooperating with the NAACP in private, he maintained his public position as advocate for TVA. In a letter written on TVA stationery and sent to his immediate supervisor for approval, Bond restated his belief that "those who are directly in charge of the program in which some feel that the greatest neglect has occurred . . . are sincere in their desire to see that justice is done." Gordon Clapp had asked Bond to write to Walter White to dissuade the NAACP from pursuing the lawsuit that Houston and Davis were threatening. TVA officials were concerned that a lawsuit would be seized upon by partisan and ideological detractors and used to destroy the Authority. In his letter to White, Bond went on to suggest that the most beneficial approach was one that "involved collective bargaining and the presentation of definite facts through the medium of peaceful consultations." A more militant or forceful approach, particularly any legal action against the Authority, "would do nothing more than crystallize public opinion against the Negro."[9] This statement was almost the exact opposite of one he had made privately to the NAACP, which called for militant Negro reaction because "this situation should be exposed." Clearly Bond's official letter to the NAACP was written to deceive TVA officials concerning his true feelings and not to dissuade the NAACP from suing.[10]

Bond survived in TVA, playing a dual role, for four years. In the course of these years he was criticized by blacks within TVA who felt that he did not present the case against discrimination in a strong enough light. He frequently received letters from black TVA employees who shared the sentiments expressed in the following letter:

> As you are the only Negro within the Authority who is in a position to have direct contact with the head officials of the Authority, we have been under the impression that you were somewhat a mediator, and relationship [sic] man, and your designated function was to look out after the welfare of the Negro in general who were being employed by the Authority. Of course this would concern his social, educational and economic status, . . . For the last twelve months it seems that you ceased to function in your capacity. So far, you are not even a figure head with the Authority.[11]

Bond occasionally defended his role and the role of his staff in effecting change. Charles Cowan, who became the head of the Knoxville NAACP, wrote a seven-point criticism calling for sweeping changes in TVA racial policies, including raising the status of the Negro supervisor to that of a Negro coordinator, who would be employed as an assistant to the general manager and given responsibility for developing plans throughout the various divisions and departments. Although he agreed with Cowan's suggestion for reorganization, Bond replied rather defensively that Cowan was unfairly implying that the Training Division was inefficient and disorganized:

> I am not contending for a whitewash of the Training Division. I am requesting that the Negro staff be given credit for the very noteworthy work that they have accomplished under conditions that under ordinary circumstances would have resulted in the complete frustration of these employees. . . . I don't believe you can say that this program in its approach to some of the problems has not made a unique contribution to the general field of Adult Education.[12]

Bond received criticism in a veiled form in a *Crisis* article, "Alley in the Valley," written by Rollins Winslow, a former member of Bond's staff. Winslow contended that the TVA training section had encouraged the establishment of a small library in the black community solely to discourage the use of the TVA library by blacks. He later wrote to Bond that he was criticizing the behavior of white officials and was not attempting to belittle Bond or his staff; rather, he wished to "paint the picture of how difficult it is." Bond replied that he had not read the article and probably would not have taken offense at the statements.[13]

Bond resigned at the beginning of 1939. In 1937 his position had been changed to general supervisor of Negro training and personnel relations, and his staff was enlarged to include a junior supervisor of Negro training.[14] Despite the enlarged staff, however, Bond continued to feel that he was unable to reduce the incidence of discrimination in TVA in any significant way. Thus, when the NAACP announced that it would conduct another investigation of TVA and requested information and material from Bond, he readily complied. By 1938 his belief in his own indispensability had changed, and he was willing to cooperate more openly, and thus risk his job. He acknowledged that he was "the leak in the TVA" and had given information to the NAACP, and declared that he could no longer honestly work for an organization that he had exposed. Bond's departure was rather acrimonious, and he was prevented from taking personal papers and private correspondence.[15]

TVA now began a search for Bond's successor. The director of personnel wrote to a number of people and agencies, including the Interracial Cooperation Commission and the National Urban League, to assemble a file of suitable candidates. Although the NAACP was not contacted, it maintained a close interest in the progress of the search. Charles Houston expressed the hope that a person who was primarily concerned with racial equality would be appointed. There were several candidates, and finally, after months of searching, TVA settled on J. Herman Daves, a Knoxville College sociology professor who had worked with TVA on cooperative training programs.[16]

Daves assumed the position of supervisor of Negro education and training. He contrasted sharply, in personality and political inclinations, with Bond. Whereas Bond cooperated with the NAACP and counted the head of the local chapter as one of his friends, Daves sought advice from the National Urban League, a more conservative organization that stressed individual consultation and bargaining rather than direct confrontation. The NAACP was somewhat disappointed in the choice of Daves; it considered him too unaggressive, and believed that he was handpicked by TVA officials for precisely that personality trait.[17]

Daves, like his predecessor, experienced considerable frustration at the lack of discernible progress in ending discrimination, but he adopted a patient attitude and was an advocate of gradual change. In retrospect he noted three factors that hampered his efforts in TVA. First, the Authority was located in a region with traditional patterns of segregation, which TVA could not or would not change. Second, there was a reluctance on the part of blacks to apply for jobs that were not traditionally held by blacks in the South, and a decided timidity about challenging stereotypes and seeking out competition. In the rare instances when TVA offered blacks new positions, it was hard to find blacks willing to apply. He deplored as defeatism the view held by many blacks that TVA was insincere in its recruitment efforts, even though there was ample evidence to support their cynicism. Finally, Daves acknowledged the small number of blacks in so-called white-collar positions in comparison with the number in trades and labor jobs, but stated that the disproportion was not due to discrimination, but to the extreme shortage, if not complete absence, of well-qualified black applicants.[18]

Given these hindrances to equal employment, Daves attempted to seek gradual redress of grievances. In addition to his official duties, he was used as the TVA representative to conferences on civil rights and was designated as an official TVA spokesman before the black communities of the Tennessee valley.[19] Daves remained with TVA from 1939 until his retirement in 1963.

Both Bond and Daves experienced divided loyalties and priorities in working for TVA. As employees of a large and powerful government corporation, both experienced pride in their positions and defended their staffs from attacks, whether the attacks came from TVA officials or civil rights organizations. The process of becoming part of the system as well as one of its victims presented a real dilemma, regardless of personal philosophy. Both the activist Bond and the accommodationist Daves experienced serious conflict between loyalty and social conscience. Bond resolved his conflict by resigning; Daves preferred to emphasize patience and remained in TVA.[20]

TVA employed ten to twelve Negro "semiprofessionals" on the staffs of the Employment and Training Sections of the Personnel Department. Comprising interviewers, recreational assistants, labor officers, and junior supervisors, the staff were more vocal in their dissatisfaction with race relations in TVA than were their supervisors, perhaps because they were closer to the work areas and came in contact with workers and their problems and complaints. They expressed frustration at the lack of power inherent in their jobs. Job interviewers complained that they were not informed of many openings and, consequently, could not offer a wide variety of positions. Labor relations officers and junior supervisors observed that black employees who had complaints could not go to employment representatives of their own race but instead had to complain to a white supervisor, who in many instances was the perpetrator of the racial discrimination. During the first decade, the staff filed critical memoranda and compiled extensive documentation based on interviews and investigations.[21]

Two separate committees within TVA were concerned with the treatment of blacks: the Committee on Negro Training and the Race Relations Committee of the Personnel Department. The Committee on Negro Training was formed in May 1938. Its chairman was J. Max Bond, and other members were Walter Goldston, labor relations officer; Ralph Martin, recreational instructor; and Lloyd Huntington and W. J. McGlothlin, two white staff members of the Employment and Training Sections. The findings of the committee emphasized the restricted opportunities available to blacks within TVA and in the surrounding valley. It suggested that the Training Division concentrate on the basic educational needs of the illiterate or semiliterate black worker. Yet, in a departure from previous TVA training objectives, it also recommended that more sophisticated and technological training be offered to those who aspired to higher-paying jobs. It was observed that a morale problem had developed among black workers and educational instructors, since there was no guarantee, or even any reason to hope, that blacks would be given jobs upon successful completion of courses.

Although willing to maintain physical segregation in courses, the committee was opposed to designing special courses just for Negro employees: such singling out would only solidify educational distinctions. The distinction made was to be in degree rather than kind. Courses for blacks were to correspond to courses for whites, from the basic to the more sophisticated level. Black educational officers were to be retained because they were more apt to be sensitive to the needs of black employees. Yet to increase racial understanding, white supervisors were to be used occasionally as instructors in Negro training. After submitting its report, the Committee on Negro Training disbanded.[22]

The Race Relations Committee of the Personnel Department had a more important role as a "specific instrument designed for the express purpose of identifying problems in connection with the employment of Negroes." The earliest evidence of the functioning of the Race Relations Committee is dated 4 October 1937. Yet the Personnel Department had earlier served, informally, to identify the problems of blacks throughout the TVA system. The department noted that it was already being designated as the race relations department by blacks who sent their complaints to the director of personnel and by TVA supervisors and branch chiefs who referred their racial problems to it. It was logical, therefore, that the Race Relations Committee be located within the Department of Personnel.[23]

The formation of the Race Relations Committee was prompted by a greater awareness by TVA of racial problems, which, in turn, occurred as a result of criticism, investigations, and threats to sue by civil rights organizations between 1934 and 1937.[24] Lloyd Huntington, a white personnel officer, was appointed chairman. The rationale for appointing a white as chairman instead of J. Max Bond or another black employee was clear: Huntington's role was to interpret the needs of Negroes to other whites in the Authority. TVA believed that Huntington would be able to approach recalcitrant supervisors and division heads more forcefully than a black could. His presence as chairman of the Race Relations Committee somewhat diminished Bond's role in TVA. Huntington was the advocate for fair treatment who talked with white officers and administrators within TVA, while Bond could only receive complaints from black employees and translate TVA policies and positions back to black workers and interested civil rights groups outside the Authority.[25]

The Race Relations Committee's role was purely advisory, and it could only recommend changes within TVA to the director of personnel. It criticized exclusionary practices in the Norris and Hiwassee areas, opposed the restrictions on job opportunities imposed by TVA and the craft unions, deplored the failure to anticipate the problems that blacks experienced in TVA, and even suggested that TVA should no longer arrogantly ignore the findings of civil rights investigators and critics. It discounted the contention that the low percentage of blacks in white-collar positions was due to lack of qualifications; rather, lack of recruitment and discriminatory barriers were the key factors.[26]

TVA committees, established specifically to foster better race relations, appear to have had little effect. Their failure was due to the lack of a positive racial policy statement and the clear prejudice of a significant number of TVA administrators, including members of its board of directors. In addition, the Race Relations Committee was handicapped by its bureaucratic position within the Personnel Department. That department recruited, hired, and fired all employees and consequently was involved in discrimination cases. In effect, the Race Relations Committee was asked to investigate and criticize its own department and its practices, an action that would strain the members' sense of loyalty as well as their instinct for survival. Moreover, no committee member was above the rank of staff supervisor. In criticizing the practices of the Department of Personnel, the Race Relations Committee was forced to criticize by implication the policies of the director of personnel, who was the superior of everyone on the committee. Although directed to investigate TVA practices freely, the committee set limits on itself, as when Lloyd Huntington turned down an opportunity to review the NAACP transcript of interviews with TVA workers before it went to the Joint Congressional Committee.[27]

The Race Relations Committee was abolished on 10 November 1942, ostensibly because it had completed "the main planning functions for which it was established." A more compelling reason was the need for restructuring the racial grievance apparatus in TVA to comply with the directives of Executive Order 8802, issued in September 1941. TVA reestablished the Committee on Negro Training to facilitate compliance with the order, and directed it to analyze the scope of training for blacks and identify the impediments to its expansion. It recommended setting up special training programs for blacks, keeping in mind "their importance in meeting the Authority's needs and in feasibility of execution."[28]

The many critical articles and reports about TVA during the New Deal years attest to the level of concern and disillusionment among TVA's external critics, the civil rights advocates who had in 1933 expressed hope for progressive racial practices in the Authority.

The first article criticizing TVA in these terms appeared in *Opportunity*, the monthly magazine of the Urban League, and was written by Cranston

Clayton, a southern white clergyman. Clayton was also a member of the Interracial Cooperation Commission of Tennessee. The editor of *Opportunity*, Elmer Andersen Carter, wrote in the introduction to the article: "A white Southerner herein accuses the Federal Government of almost criminal neglect in the plans of the Tennessee Valley Administration [*sic*]." [29]

Clayton noted TVA's failure to include blacks in its long-range planning and especially criticized their exclusion from the Norris Model Community. He pointed out with considerable irony that although southern state governments practiced blatant racial discrimination, they at least allowed "their outcast population to lie in dirt and shacks down by the creek or the railroad tracks." It was left to the federal government to exclude Negroes entirely.[30] Presenting a moderate, progressive view, Clayton defined change in the status of the Negro in terms of more job opportunities and better pay. He advocated neither social change nor social integration; he did not even criticize the policy of racial segregation in TVA. He merely insisted that racial inequalities had an adverse effect on life in the South in general.

The Clayton article represented the Urban League's only public statement on TVA. Although it had branches in some southern cities, including Louisville and Atlanta, the Urban League was primarily devoted to opening job opportunities for blacks in northern cities. It focused on problems in urban New Deal agencies like the Federal Housing Administration and the PWA, and consequently did not devote much time or energy to publicizing the problems of the mainly rural, decentralized Tennessee valley. Despite Clayton's article, the Urban League and TVA remained on cordial terms. TVA wrote to the Louisville chapter for help in recruitment, not only for positions like Negro supervisor, but for skilled and semiskilled trade positions as well.

The Interracial Cooperation Commission also kept on reasonably cordial terms with TVA throughout the Authority's first decade. The commission as a whole had expressed concern over the discriminatory practices of various New Deal agencies in the South, specifically the AAA and the NRA. It observed that blacks were not getting a proportionate share of jobs and accused the NRA of paying employees according to a "Negro differential" in the belief (promoted by southern politicians) that equal wages for blacks would threaten the entire southern economy. Will Alexander, the commission's president, suggested in his private correspondence that if equal wages in government-sponsored relief projects *would* undermine the basis of the southern economy, then perhaps the southern economy should be closely examined and restructured through long-range planning.[31]

Throughout the New Deal, the Interracial Cooperation Commission sought to find sponsorship for what it termed an "enlightened" segregated South, a South where blacks and whites might enjoy equal economic and educational opportunities in a racially segregated society. The commission saw in TVA, an agency that subscribed to a similar concept of regional planning, a tool to effect social change along these lines. Although influential members, including Will Alexander and Howard Odum, privately criticized TVA for not being concerned enough with the problems of blacks, the commission did not publicly criticize the Authority. Rather, it sought other means of influence. Like the Urban League, it referred black candidates to TVA for staff positions, and it was, as we have seen, instrumental in recommending J. Max Bond for the job of supervisor of Negro training. Both Charles S. Johnson and Howard Odum maintained correspondence with TVA officials and conducted surveys and made reports for it as part of the Authority's program of cooperation with southern colleges and universities.[32]

As part of the commission's effort to establish a more institutionalized relationship with TVA, Gordon Clapp was asked in 1940 to become a member.[33] Clapp refused the invitation, stating that he had to devote all his time and energy to expanding the TVA program to meet the needs of national defense. He added that his response was in no way

> an indication of lack of interest or appreciation of the exceedingly important work of the Commission . . . on the contrary our organization has encountered the interracial problem at significant stages in the development of a regional program. . . . We have sought in a number of ways to consider [better race relations] as an inseparable part of the process of development in the Tennessee Valley and the Southeast. . . . I hope that at some later date there may be an opportunity to assess the thinking of the Commission for its applicability to our problems and to pass along to you such of our experience as may have a bearing on your work.[34]

Unlike the Urban League and the Interracial Cooperation Commission, the NAACP maintained a consistently critical view of TVA. It conducted two investigations of the Authority (in 1934 and 1935), and articles based on the resulting information were published in *Crisis* in October 1934 and October 1935.

John P. Davis, a young, Harvard-trained lawyer, and Charles Houston, special counsel to the NAACP, spent two months during the summer of 1934 in the Tennessee valley. They interviewed black and white workers, and TVA officials gave them policy statements and statistics on Negro em-

ployment. The article they published in the October 1934 *Crisis* was highly
critical of TVA's quota system and the all-white town of Norris. The investigators ridiculed the TVA policy of proportionate hiring, stating that "the
TVA treats the Negro only as a labor commodity," and they called for a
relentless attack on TVA discrimination with "pitiless publicity, politically,
at law, and whatever other means are at [one's] disposal." [35]

The NAACP continued to monitor TVA practices and prepared in
1935 to make another investigation. The 1934 trip had been considered
exploratory and incomplete. At that time, moreover, TVA had only begun
operations, and its racial practices had not yet been firmly established. The
NAACP observed in the spring of 1935 that new and more complex racial
practices were emerging at new dam sites, and that another investigation
had to be made. J. Max Bond's request for a TVA investigation served to
solidify the plans. Davis was commissioned to make another trip to the
Tennessee valley to interview Bond, visit Wheeler, Wilson, and Pickwick
dams, check housing projects at Norris, interview personnel and labor relations officers, and check relief and relocation conditions. He kept his letters
and official interviews with Bond on a formal basis and did not reveal that
he or the NAACP had earlier corresponded with Bond.[36]

Davis as an investigator used an antagonistic approach that evoked a
pronounced reaction from TVA officials. In an exchange with Arthur Morgan concerning the exclusion of blacks from Norris, Davis threatened that
"a legal suit to test the authority of TVA to exclude Negroes from Norris
will speedily be brought unless there is a satisfactory solution of the problem in the immediate future." [37] In his subsequent visit to the valley, his
questions were framed so critically that TVA officials made

> no attempt to define a policy for the Authority nor did we make any
> attempt to state the objectives the Personnel Division has in mind with
> regard to the Negro race . . . it was obvious at the beginning of the dis-
> cussion that statements of this character would have no effect upon Mr.
> Davis . . . he is interested in results and facts and not in good intentions.[38]

From the beginning of his second visit, Davis took the position that
cooperation between the NAACP and TVA was no longer possible. From
that point on, the NAACP adopted a strategy that emphasized possible legal
suits. Recognizing this, TVA officials were instructed to speak in general
terms and not even to express their personal agreement with any of Davis'
allegations.[39]

The NAACP announced that it wished to acquire "nuisance value, in order that the minority race might force the Authority to give more consideration to Negro problems." It hoped to embarrass the Authority through congressional pressure, litigation, and adverse publicity.[40]

Though officials were instructed not to agree with Davis, in an interdepartmental analysis TVA officials acknowledged the substance if not the spirit of his criticisms. In answer to an eleven-point critique by Davis, a TVA official acknowledged that he was correct on eight points, possibly correct on one point, and incorrect on only two points: "(1) the content of our Negro training program was weak in that it placed too much emphasis upon recreation and hobbies; and (2) segregation was an indication of unfairness in racial relations." These two points that TVA would not accept even privately are crucial to an understanding of the ideological impasse between civil rights advocates and TVA. TVA did not consider segregation as discrimination, but mainly a regional characteristic desired by the majority of blacks as well as whites. On the function of Negro training, TVA chose to accept only part of J. Max Bond's position—the idea that training had to start at the elementary level to reach the illiterate black worker. It did not advocate the preparation of skilled black workers in order to pressure trade unions to accept them.[41]

The interdepartmental analysis, marked "confidential," agreed with Davis that

(1) TVA had no consistent policy with regard to the Negro race . . . its policy is totally inconsistent and dependent upon specific sympathies and prejudices of individual members of the staff. . . . (2) No plans to include Negroes at Norris. . . . (3) No Negro in a major staff position. . . . (4) No input in planning the Negro program by present Negro staff. . . . (5) Job discrimination in semi-skilled and unskilled positions. . . . (6) Job discrimination in professional positions and skilled trades. (7) Possibly racial discrimination in the undesirable location of the Negro Village at Wilson Dam. . . . (8) Humiliating treatment of the Negro staff at Muscle Shoals.

In the ninth part of the analysis, it was acknowledged that TVA was insincere in its proclamation of a policy of nondiscrimination.[42] It is interesting to note that this memorandum, which was clearly written solely for the information of TVA, was obtained by the NAACP from its TVA sources.

TVA was not willing to allow allegations of discrimination to be published without a rebuttal. Arthur Morgan requested that Harold Ickes send a "competent" Negro leader to visit the Authority and observe its workings firsthand, in order to "understand the way in which we are approaching the problem." Morgan hoped that the negative effects of the Davis visit and his anticipated report would be offset by a positive and laudatory report by Ickes's advisor on Negro affairs and Davis' former associate in the Joint Committee on National Recovery, Robert Weaver.[43]

Weaver was given statistical data and free access to TVA officials. He submitted his report to Arthur Morgan in November 1935. It was critical, yet it avoided the antagonistic tone of the Davis report. The Weaver report agreed with Davis on the major points of wage discrimination, lack of policy, exclusion, and hostile treatment. It also offered positive suggestions for improvement. Weaver felt that TVA, as a federal agency, should not employ segregated work crews. It was poor labor policy and set an unfortunate precedent. Having analyzed the problem of Negro skilled labor, he suggested a quota based on a given percentage of the payroll. It had to be impressed upon union officials and TVA labor relations officers that Negro skilled labor was to be proportionately employed. He also suggested that TVA issue a boldly worded statement against discrimination.[44]

Weaver noted that his suggestions were neither radical nor unprecedented in government agencies: they had been carried out by the Housing Division of the PWA, and the program was operating successfully in Atlanta and Montgomery. The Resettlement Administration also practiced a modified program of racial nondiscrimination.[45]

The negative Weaver report came as a surprise to TVA officials. Yet it was considered a mild rebuke compared with Davis' second investigative article and full report. After his second visit, Davis had proceeded to compile his data and write a forty-one page critique of the Authority. The NAACP distributed the report to politicians, statesmen, activists, and newspaper columnists, including Heywood Hale Broun and Drew Pearson, Senators Robert LaFollette, William Borah, and George Norris, and Congressmen Maury Maverick, Vito Marcantonio, and Edward P. Costigan, as well as to the three members of the TVA board and the director of personnel.[46] A press release directed to the white press was distributed on 16 September 1935. It began, "TVA projects called of little benefit to Negroes. Investigator declares workers suffer not only in jobs, wages, and housing, but that the whole plan offers Negro citizens no future." The release was sent to the Associated Press and the United Press International as well as the International News Service, *New York Times*, *New York Herald Tribune*, *New York Post*, *Washington Post*, and *Daily Worker*.[47]

The second Davis article and the Davis report repeated the charges made in 1934. However, these later articles revealed a more clearly defined ideological basis for Davis' criticism. Unlike the criticism of the TVA by Cranston Clayton or the private opinions of academic regional planners, Davis' analysis traced the poverty and economic chaos of the valley not to racial discrimination, but to the capitalist system. Racial discrimination was a built-in element of capitalism, which fed off the weak and disadvantaged. Black and white workers, who had been brainwashed into believing each other inferior, had to work to bring about a different economic system following the principles of socialism. In this restructured system, planned and controlled by the government, blacks, who had been most exposed to the antisocial practices and "exploitation of the region, would be guaranteed economic and political equality."[48]

Davis believed that TVA, while not an example of socialist planning, came as close as the United States would ever permit. Consequently, he was particularly disappointed that the Authority was not going to include blacks in its long-range plans. In 1935 he believed in the promise of TVA, which offered increased hydroelectric power production, flood control, and economic and social rehabilitation for the entire valley. He quoted Arthur Morgan's speeches emphasizing its social planning aspects, and interpreted these broad statements as a strong commitment to reorder the Tennessee valley. Interestingly, on the basis of his observations in the valley, Davis concluded that the TVA program itself was progressing toward a planned society—complete with industrial development, educational opportunity, and model communities. His only criticism was that blacks were not allowed to share in the benefits of the program.[49]

Davis also assumed that TVA's perceived success would encourage the Roosevelt administration to implement social and regional planning in other river valleys, such as the Missouri, the Ohio, the Columbia, the Mississippi, and the Connecticut. In that case, he feared, the practice of racial discrimination and exclusion could easily be carried intact to other regions. He concluded that TVA, unless changed, threatened the very economic survival of blacks in the region, because it was training whites for the new technological society in the valley while equipping blacks with archaic skills for subservient roles.[50]

Inherent in Davis' discussion of TVA was the assumption that its social programs were having a significant and beneficial effect on the white population. Davis did not examine in detail the opportunities for whites under the Authority's social program or question the practical gains made by whites in training skills, living conditions, and economic security. His examination of TVA took place in 1934 and 1935, which was still very early in its history; yet there were already signs that its promise of social rehabilitation was not becoming a complete reality for whites either, particularly in the areas of reservoir relocation and tenant farming. The emphasis on the benefits for whites and disadvantages for blacks in TVA employment and social planning might be seen as a useful tactic—the plight of blacks would appear worse if TVA planning for whites appeared to be successfully implemented—yet Davis' argument was in fact based on an assumption of TVA's success. One of the few black critics to express skepticism about the TVA social planning program was Ralph Bunche, who maintained that the entire New Deal social planning program served only to refurbish the "old individualistic-capitalistic system." [51]

Davis acknowledged the need for blacks and whites to work together for a better society and called for an integrated labor movement within the valley, for he felt that the lack of organization among black workers contributed to their economic plight. Political education was needed to politicize and radicalize the workers.[52] And he suggested that the NAACP both sue TVA for infringement of the fourteenth and fifteenth amendment rights of valley residents and pressure Congress to investigate it for racial discrimination. The NAACP attempted to act upon Davis' suggestions but had to abandon its plans for an investigation and suit in 1935 when it could not raise the necessary $2,500 for preliminary work.[53]

TVA reacted to the second article and report with anger and concern. Officials bitterly resented Davis' allegations of duplicity, manipulation of statistics, and a hidden goal of destroying the economic position of blacks. For example, Gordon Clapp called Davis a liar in marginal notes on his copy of the report, even though he had agreed with nine of the eleven points Davis made in his first article.[54] Despite this emotionalism, however, TVA reacted most strongly to the threat of a lawsuit.[55] The director of personnel, Floyd Reeves, expressed his fears to individuals outside the Authority, particularly to his friend Will Alexander. Alexander wrote:

> I have thought of many of the things about which we talked, particularly the threatened suit. I think I know why they are threatening to push that now. The same people who are making the threat were back of the Costigan-Wagner antilynching bill. [They] tried to get Roosevelt to break it . . . [and were] disappointed so are now agitating around Norris.[56]

TVA officials formulated a strategy in order to make certain that the Authority would be in a strong legal position in the event of a suit. They suggested that the TVA board issue a short statement "emphasizing that TVA had formulated its policy for the Negro carefully and with his best interest in mind . . . and that these policies were formulated after frequent conferences with interracial groups, and are considered fair and wholly within the spirit of the constitution." [57]

TVA was spared a legal fight in 1935, but in 1938 the NAACP was able to participate in the Joint Congressional Committee to Investigate the TVA. The committee had been established primarily to investigate charges made by Arthur Morgan that his colleagues Lilienthal and Harcourt Morgan had shown dishonesty and lack of integrity in the Berry land-speculation case (see Chapter II). A well-organized group in Congress, consisting mainly of conservative Republicans, called for an investigation into TVA affairs. Despite pleas from Roosevelt and Democratic leaders, Congress passed a resolution creating a special joint committee of the Senate and the House to look into all Morgan's charges as well as countercharges of obstruction and sabotage brought against him by his colleagues on the board. It was further authorized to examine all programs and divisions of TVA, particularly the power program. The sum of $75,000 was appropriated to finance the hearings. Francis Biddle of Philadelphia, a wealthy lawyer with a reputation as a liberal, was selected as counsel.[58]

The appointment of Biddle was very convenient for the NAACP, since he was a member of its National Legal Committee and a close acquaintance of Charles Houston. The NAACP secured an opportunity to testify before the committee by writing to influential and sympathetic congressmen, including H. Styles Bridges of New Hampshire, Maury Maverick of Texas, Bertrand Snell of New York, and Vic Donahey of Ohio, the committee chairman.[59]

Materials for an investigation had been continuously gathered by the NAACP from 1935 through 1938. Anticipating an opportunity to contribute to the congressional investigation, the NAACP in the spring of 1938 had ordered "all branches to assemble at once all evidence in your hands or available to you concerning the TVA and its treatment of Negroes." [60]

The NAACP sent Charles Houston and Thurgood Marshall, the associate counsel, on an extensive research trip to TVA. The 1938 investigation concentrated on allegations of harsh treatment and blatant discrimination at the dam sites. A list of experts and informed persons in the Tennessee valley was compiled, and these people were contacted. C. E. Leslie, a black labor leader and critic of TVA, was asked to supply information as well as be a witness. Charles Cowan, J. Herman Daves (at the time a Knoxville College professor), J. Max Bond, and other black leaders in the valley were also contacted. Houston also issued inquiries and received favorable replies from sympathetic white union leaders about discrimination in skilled labor.

Both Burton Zien, a labor organizer and a representative of the Southern Youth Congress, and Jacob Bucker, a national labor leader, offered to be witnesses for the NAACP, even though Bucker feared a possible drop in membership in his own union.

Bucker's union was the liberal United Public Workers of America, and he feared a drop in membership not because he would be testifying for the NAACP, but because he would be participating in a congressional investigation that many liberals and progressives considered to be a Republican witchhunt. Zien, the local organizer for the Congress of Industrial Organizations, eventually refused to testify because he felt that the committee would play into the hands of Roosevelt's opponents, and the CIO had to support Roosevelt. The NAACP itself experienced a tactical dilemma. It was aware that some members of the committee were looking for an opportunity to destroy TVA. Walter White cautioned that "we should gather and present our material in such a fashion as not to give comfort or aid to the utility and other interests who don't want to see a social and economic experiment like TVA succeed." [61]

The NAACP announced that it was not part of the campaign to destroy TVA; it admired the Authority—particularly for its stand against private utilities in the effort to lower electricity rates—and was only concerned that blacks be given an equal opportunity to secure jobs and benefit from TVA improvements.[62] Its officials desired changes in TVA, not its destruction. Congressman James Mead, a member of the congressional committee, wrote to Roy Wilkins that "after considering personal matters in the TVA set-up I am of the impression that this agency should be brought under the rules and regulations of the Civil Service Commission." Wilkins expressed an interest in the suggestion and saw it as a possible solution for racial problems involving common and skilled labor: the Civil Service Commission, as a Washington-based agency, would be less subject to southern pressure and could administer personnel matters more fairly than the southern-based TVA.[63]

The NAACP prepared the case against the TVA, accumulating as much evidence as possible. Houston collected affidavits from disgruntled workers and numerous other documents. Each sore spot or area of discrimination, when investigated, revealed other layers of harm and neglect. Houston remarked that just gathering affidavits kept his staff busy from 6 A.M. until midnight.[64]

Before Houston testified, he offered to submit a summary of his investigations to J. Max Bond and Lloyd Huntington for comments and corrections. Bond, who had already decided to leave TVA, made certain corrections of fact in the statements. Huntington, as we have noted, refused to see the summary. Houston observed that Huntington "was afraid to discuss the statement or even to look at it because he did not want to lay himself open to sanctioning any statements therein which he did not object to." Huntington and L. N. Allen, who refused to admit any discrimination in the regional planning program until presented with signed affidavits, were following TVA instructions first developed in response to John Davis' probing questions in 1935.[65]

Houston, although working eighteen-hour days, felt that he had not presented a completed and finished case before the congressional committee. Nevertheless, he presented forty-five exhibits consisting of letters to TVA officials, TVA memoranda, particularly from the legal staff, published NAACP articles from *Crisis*, affidavits, and statements from black TVA workers and black leaders in the valley communities. Congressman Charles Wolverton of New Jersey, a strong supporter of private utilities, and Senator Jim Davis of Pennsylvania, asked the most penetrating questions and expressed the most profound outrage against TVA after hearing Houston's testimony. Houston repeated the accusations of John Davis and Robert Weaver, maintaining that TVA had consistently and willfully discriminated. Patterns hinted at in 1934 and 1935 had become a reality in 1938. He also attempted to show that the testimonies of Arthur Morgan and Gordon Clapp, who had appeared before the committee earlier in August, were not candid in the area of race relations, and he stressed the particularly brutal treatment of black workers at Chickamauga Dam.[66]

Gordon Clapp was given a chance to reply to the Houston charges. He flatly denied that there was any discrimination in rates of pay, housing, work assignments, or general job conditions. When closely questioned by Francis Biddle, Clapp admitted that one could interpret TVA policy as discriminatory; however, TVA only sought to recognize local traditions and racial customs.[67]

The committee, after hearing Houston's and Clapp's testimonies, suggested that TVA, with Houston's aid, investigate the charges of brutality at Chickamauga Dam. Houston expressed confidence that Clapp would make a thorough preliminary investigation and stated that the director of personnel appeared to "be decent on the matter of protecting workers." Besides, Houston told NAACP colleagues, Clapp "will be scared not to order a real investigation."[68]

The investigation, held in September, called twenty black workers, who testified that they were brutally treated and intimidated from joining a union. The public and press were excluded, and Clapp explained that in this internal procedure, "we are going ahead as though grievances were submitted to the personnel department." Yet, despite Clapp's promise and Houston's optimism, the results of the investigation were, as stated above, negligible from the perspective of the NAACP and the aggrieved black workers. None of the black workers who had been released because of race-related incidents were reinstated. The climate of fear at Chickamauga remained until the termination of the project. Only one of the TVA supervisors and foremen accused of brutal treatment was reprimanded for his actions. Clapp's single recommendation—that supervisory sensitivity training be established—was not acted upon until 1957.[69]

The NAACP was able to generate considerable publicity through its counsel's appearance before the congressional investigation committee. It also sought to create an opportunity for the representatives of the black press to mingle with the white press in the valley. Invitations to attend the Knoxville-based congressional investigation were telegraphed to the *Pittsburgh Courier*, the *Baltimore Afro-American*, the *Chicago Defender*, the Associated Negro Press, and the *African World* as well as the black papers in Knoxville and Chattanooga. But, Houston sadly noted, "after all our work, no Negro press representatives were in court."[70] The response from the white press was more positive. In addition to coverage by the northern dailies during the hearings, both the *Chattanooga News* and the *Chattanooga Times* ran news stories and issued editorials calling for an end to discrimination. The NAACP sent a letter of thanks to George Fort Milton, editor of the *Chattanooga News*, complimenting the paper "on the manner in which the hearings were brought before the public."[71]

In April 1939 the Joint Congressional Committee voted to uphold the work of the agency and dismissed the charges of Arthur Morgan. In its written statement, the majority moderately rebuked TVA for permitting discrimination in the employment and treatment of blacks:

> On paper the Authority policy toward Negroes is one of no discrimination and a proportionate share of jobs. . . . In practice the Authority has not felt able to enforce this policy as fully as could be desired. . . . The Authority cannot solve the race problem in a year or in 10 years, but it can and should do more for the Negroes than it is doing.

The majority report went on to suggest that a nationwide recruitment program be instituted to hire well-qualified blacks for some of the better-paying jobs to offset the pattern of hiring blacks only for low-paying ones. It also suggested that blacks be admitted to Norris, that black skilled workers be hired, that supervisors showing racial bigotry be disciplined, and that a director of Negro work be appointed.[72] Despite the political power of the congressional committee and the publicity generated by the investigations, none of the suggestions were put into effect during TVA's first twelve years.

One positive result of the investigation from the standpoint of the NAACP was the heightened sense of purpose generated in the black communities of the valley. Although the funding and the investigative impulse were largely generated by the New York NAACP office, valley black leaders were given credit for valuable cooperation and information. The impetus for the establishment of a Knoxville branch of the NAACP was attributed to the feeling of unity and pride generated by the organization's success in making a large and powerful institution at least listen to the grievances and complaints of black workers. Knoxville activists secured the requisite number of members for an NAACP charter in 1938 by canvassing TVA employees and members of Knoxville's original 1918 branch. This new branch also drew members from the growing number of young college-trained blacks settling in the Knoxville area, and its efforts were supported and publicized by the black *Flashlight Herald*. During the 1940s the branch continued to expand, to the extent that by 1945 there were over a thousand members in the adult division and an equal number in the youth division.[73]

Members of the valley branches of the NAACP were the most vocal in their protests against TVA, although some of their protests were tempered by regional and economic constraints. For example, the Tri-Cities Branch of the NAACP, representing the Muscle Shoals-Tuscumbia, Alabama, area, was mainly composed of women, for many of the husbands were employed by TVA and feared that they would lose their jobs or face serious repercussions if they joined.[74]

During its first decade, TVA interacted with other black organizations and leaders in the Tennessee valley and the southeast region. The presidents and professors of valley colleges, as we have seen, communicated with TVA on the possibility of academic cooperation. C. C. Spaulding wrote to the Authority, inquiring about discriminatory practices and offering his assistance in recruiting skilled blacks. Spaulding was the president of North Carolina Mutual Life Insurance Company, one of the nation's largest black-owned businesses, and a member of the Interracial Cooperation Commission. He was one of the black leaders TVA consulted to find a successor to J. Max Bond. The Louisville Urban League also showed concern over TVA employment practices.[75]

The local black leadership, although fragmented into often competing branches of national civil rights organizations, coalesced around the question of TVA discrimination. In Knoxville, even before the impetus of the congressional investigations, local black leaders had formed the Knoxville Civic Committee, which addressed itself primarily to the exclusion of Negroes from Norris Park. The actual reason for the formation of the committee remained an area of controversy. Critics contended that it was established at TVA's behest: the Authority had allegedly requested the local Negro community to establish a committee that would write it a letter setting forth a demand for separate park facilities.[76]

The controversy over its origin reflected serious ideological fissures in the committee itself over the question of segregation. At least one member of the committee, Charles Cowan, an attorney, wanted to demand unrestricted access to Norris Park. He expressed the opinion that if TVA was allowed to establish a policy of park exclusion or segregation, that policy would be adopted in other national parks in the South.[77] He and the other integrationists were opposed to any request for an equal and separate black park. Other members, including N. A. Henderson and J. Herman Daves, contended that the integrationists were unrealistic and were advocating a position certain to lead to no park at all. These members advocated cooperation with TVA to achieve a Negro park near Norris. They submitted to the Authority statistics showing that the Negro population of Knoxville desired and could support a separate park. Requests by black YMCA and Boy Scout leaders for camping grounds were also forwarded to TVA by the committee. The Civic Committee resolved its ideological split through a compromise. It agreed to request a separate park one mile from the dam, but also demanded full use and enjoyment of Norris Dam Park with the exception of swimming facilities and cabins.[78]

The Civic Committee met with representatives from the TVA Regional Planning Division and the Personnel Department, as well as representatives from the state of Tennessee and the National Park Service, on 23 November 1937. They discussed Norris Park and blacks' right to use TVA recreational facilities. TVA agreed to take the matter under advisement, and said that it would reconvene the conference if and when a decision was made.[79]

The Authority continued to correspond with the Civic Committee, although it was clear from interdepartmental memoranda and discussions that TVA had decided early in 1938 not to build a separate Norris Park for blacks and to exclude blacks from the Norris Model Community. No Negro park was ever built for the Knoxville area, nor were blacks welcomed into Norris Park until 1955.[80]

The Civic Committee was informed in June 1938 that TVA had decided, without consulting it, to build a black park in Chattanooga. Some members felt betrayed and decided that "TVA officials have not acted in good faith in taking their present position." TVA acknowledged that the Negro park in Chattanooga would be "somewhat further from Knoxville than a location on Norris Lake. . . . The advantages of location with respect to Negro population, attractiveness of lake expanse and topography and the expectation of a better economic return would offset the inconvenience." [81]

The Knoxville Civic Committee, along with other valley civil rights advocates, experienced difficulty in getting TVA to take it seriously. Not having the staff or the experience of national organizations, such local groups initially relied on personal contact, feelings of trust, and the paternalistic bonds of regional solidarity, none of which amounted to much when dealing with the TVA bureaucracy. Moreover, the fear of losing employment or being prevented from gaining employment at TVA was a serious deterrent to organized protest against the Authority. It was no accident that the two leading figures on the moderate Knoxville Civic Committee were N. A. Henderson, a doctor, and Charles Cowan, a lawyer. Black TVA employees did, however, play important if quietly supportive roles.

By 1945 Chattanooga blacks had also become better organized, primarily through their battles with TVA. TVA had sought to cultivate a positive image among blacks in Chattanooga, in part to counteract the negative publicity resulting from accusations of discrimination in the Knoxville and Wilson areas. TVA also recognized the potential usefulness of the 30 percent black population of Chattanooga as supporters of New Deal programs, and particularly of TVA itself. In 1935 TVA openly courted black political support for a referendum calling for the city to buy electricity from TVA. Blacks controlled five of the nineteen wards in the city, and as in any efficient machine, the political bosses could be counted on to deliver the vote. To ensure a large turnout of blacks, TVA got the poll tax waived for this special election. The importance of the issue of public power versus private utilities, combined with the waiving of the poll tax, produced the heaviest registration in the city's history. Bad weather kept the actual voting down, but public power won easily, 19,056 to 8,096. Encouraged by the large registration, blacks organized the Hamilton County Negro Democratic Club, which conducted voter registration campaigns in the still predominantly Republican black wards, many of which had been Republican since Reconstruction.[82]

Disappointment over the lack of employment and training opportunities at Chickamauga Dam, experiences garnered from unsuccessful campaigns for better facilities at Booker T. Washington Park, organizational techniques learned from participation in the Democratic Club, and issues raised in the TVA-sponsored People's College led to a new aggressiveness within the Chattanooga black community. In 1939 a group of Chattanooga teachers, along with a few TVA employees, successfully revived the local chapter of the NAACP. Attempts to start a chapter between 1923 and 1939 had foundered on community apathy and fear, but this time over two thousand Chattanoogans, the majority of whom were black, joined the organization. The new chapter called for an end to job discrimination and an increase in voting opportunities. Another organization, the Young Negro Civic League, called for blacks to demand their full share of jobs from TVA, noting that there were no blacks in "an appreciative position" in the Authority. [83]

Of all the private civil rights organizations examining TVA, the NAACP was the most successful in modifying its racial practices. The NAACP utilized its traditional resources—influential friends, media coverage, and threats of suits—to effect some changes in practice if not in attitude. The use of influential friends, particularly congressional, resulted in the inclusion of the NAACP complaints in the agenda of the Joint Congressional Committee. The NAACP also had sympathizers within TVA itself. Along with J. Max Bond, the organization utilized an unidentified informant in the office of David Lilienthal who regularly provided information on policy decisions and attitudes that even civil rights advocates within TVA did not know about.[84] Thus, the NAACP did not suffer from the information void experienced by the Knoxville Civic Committee. It could base its strategy on privileged information and ignore TVA's disclaimers. For example, the NAACP knew about the Clapp analysis of John Davis' report and the areas of discrimination that Clapp acknowledged, despite his public statements that TVA did not discriminate against blacks. The NAACP also included TVA memoranda as exhibits in its argument before the congressional committee.[85]

The most effective tactic employed by the NAACP was the legal threat. TVA officials noted the threat of a lawsuit in John Davis' early articles and developed a policy of circumspection and deniability as protection. Policies of exclusion, while allowed to continue (as in the case of Hiwassee Dam), were less overt and defiant than the earlier, clearly articulated position on exclusion at Norris Dam. The post-1935 training programs and concentration on proper percentage quotas were substantially influenced by the need to eliminate grounds for an NAACP suit.

The NAACP succeeded in making TVA aware of the needs of blacks and other minorities in the social and economic structure of the Tennessee valley. Although TVA for the most part chose to ignore the organization's complaints, it could not openly ignore the existence of blacks or the need for their inclusion within TVA planning. In an agency that planned for the homogeneous majority, a critical and dissenting voice representing a racial minority was necessary to ensure inclusion even in an inferior position. The NAACP perceived the challenge in dealing with TVA to be twofold: inclusion within the future planned society, and equal treatment and fair job opportunities in the present. The all-white Norris Model Community and Park represented to the NAACP the future for the blacks in the valley if civil rights organizations did not agitate.

Perhaps the success of the NAACP and other civil rights critics could best be measured not in terms of explicit changes in policy or a decrease in the number of instances of discrimination, but in terms of the negative policies prevented and the exclusion practices not proposed by TVA. TVA recruited blacks for employment at Kentucky Dam to offset criticism. Moreover, although there was considerable pressure not to hire blacks at Fontana Dam, and precedents for exclusion were conveniently present, TVA stated that the Executive Order mandated full utilization of the population, including blacks. It surely did not want to risk a lawsuit, in view of the public outcry concerning Hiwassee and Norris.[86]

Yet there were problems with the NAACP efforts against discrimination in TVA. Although the NAACP used the threat of a lawsuit with some success, it remained only a threat, and the anticipated lawsuits did not materialize until 1974. The NAACP chose to rely on embarrassment to provide significant results: by exposing TVA practices, it hoped to shame the agency into a more just policy. TVA, however, had developed a rationale that elevated it above embarrassment or strong national criticism. It argued that as a regional agency it could not alter existing racial patterns or customs without disrupting its operational base.

TVA acknowledged that it had to comply with federal regulations and statutes, and when local custom was in violation of federal statutes, federal statutes took precedence. However, during the period from 1933 to 1945, federal statutes based on the fourteenth and fifteenth amendments were not uniformly enforced. TVA discrimination did not generate much outcry or dismay in a nation that perceived the South as a region of lynchings, peonage, poor or nonexistent education, tenancy, political exclusion, and the Scottsboro trials.[87] The tactic of embarrassment and shame that worked relatively well for Martin Luther King and other later civil rights leaders needed a climate of national scrutiny and disapproval. The misdeeds of TVA did not involve criminal abuse and were not sensational enough to evoke national embarrassment.

133

Ironically, the civil rights advocates took the promise of TVA as a reality much longer than did the politicians or media. In 1938 Charles Houston based his complaints of discrimination on the premise that TVA was engaged in a vital rehabilitation of the valley and leaving blacks out. The civil rights critics examined only TVA's failure to provide for blacks, and left the impression that the Authority was providing adequate training programs and job opportunities for whites. Upon examination, it becomes clear that TVA did not provide as many benefits to local white inhabitants as civil rights critics believed. In the area of reservoir relocation, the vast number of relocated families were white, and over 70 percent were displeased with their new location. Regional planners complained about a lack of policy in regard to overall social planning and severely limited benefits to the entire population. Farm tenancy, a major economic problem in the southern Tennessee valley, was not attacked by the TVA but was in fact consciously supported by its practice of paying landlords rather than tenants for flooded land. Although it indisputably provided thousands of jobs for the valley, the vast majority of these jobs, for both black and white, lasted only six months.

The training programs, while providing a wider selection of choices for whites, were not well equipped with the necessary training tools, nor were they of sufficient duration to turn semiliterate white farmers into skilled carpenters or electricians. Indeed, many skilled workers in technological positions had to be recruited from outside the Tennessee valley. Before 1945 most employees in the engineering division were outsiders. Valley residents were even more underrepresented in the higher levels of administration. The first three directors of the board, the first two directors of personnel, and the first general manager were from northern states or Canada. Donald Davidson's observation that TVA was Washington's colonial experiment was no exaggeration.[88]

Finally, the town of Norris that had excluded blacks did not develop into the model community that civil rights advocates described. When Norris Dam was completed in 1936, the construction crew moved on to the next job. Many residents moved out, and there continued to be such a rapid turnover that people other than TVA employees were accepted into Norris. The sections reserved for future businesses were never filled. The town became independently administered in 1938–1939 after residents complained of TVA neglect, and TVA finally sold the land to a real estate developer in 1948. At that point only three of the original inhabitants remained.[89]

The reduced program of social planning and rehabilitation for the valley served to mitigate some of the harmful effects of the TVA-inspired racial discrimination there. Although the Authority's racially discriminatory policies caused hardship and suffering for blacks, their effect was less harmful in the context of the failure of the social planning agenda. Programs designed to train whites in technologically advanced skills were not sustained or effective enough to significantly widen the gulf between whites and blacks in the valley. The model community of Norris did not have the success anticipated, and no other model communities were built to perpetuate the exclusionary policies. Given the policy of racial discrimination and planning for a racial status quo inherent in the philosophy of TVA officials, the failure of these officials to effect a significant rehabilitation program actually prevented a disaster for minorities in the Tennessee valley.

CHAPTER VI

The Fair Employment Practices Committee

ALTHOUGH the NAACP and other civil rights organizations, local civic committees, and the Joint Congressional Committee to Investigate the TVA were largely ineffectual in their efforts to change the Authority's racial policies, the government's Fair Employment Practices Committee (FEPC), coupled with the exigencies of war-related manpower shortages, had a modicum of success in eroding TVA's status quo position on employment opportunities. It did so through the use of public antidiscrimination directives, private negotiations, and correspondence.

The FEPC was established in the Office of Production Management (OPM) to "receive and investigate complaints of discrimination" in private industries under contract with the federal government and government departments and agencies, including TVA, as outlined by Executive Order 8802. Executive Order 8802 declared that "there shall be no discrimination in the employment of workers in defense industries or government because of race, creed, color, or national origin, . . . and that it was the duty of employers and of labor organizations to provide for full and equitable participation of all workers in defense industries." [1]

Roosevelt issued the order in response to pressure from A. Philip Randolph and other black union and civil rights leaders. Citing an increase in racial discrimination and racial exclusion in defense plants during 1940 and 1941, Randolph threatened to lead a hundred thousand protesters in a march on Washington in the summer of 1941 unless Roosevelt took a stand against discrimination. In a lengthy proposal, Randolph called for an end to discrimination in defense industries, in vocational training courses for workers in those industries, and in the federal government itself. He also called for an end to segregation in the armed forces. His proposal included an enforcement clause—if discrimination continued, "the government could take over the plant for continuous operation by virtue of the declaration of a state of national emergency." [2]

Roosevelt refused to address several of the points in Randolph's proposal, including the desegregation of the armed forces. Indeed, it was not until 1948 that President Truman issued an order to integrate the armed forces. Nor was the option of government seizure of defense plants that violated antidiscrimination directives addressed by Roosevelt. The committee, as designed by the order, did not have any punitive powers of its own. It could only recommend and advise the president on specific violations and on overall policy.[3]

Randolph registered his disappointment that all six points were not accepted, but acknowledged that Executive Order 8802 was a step in the right direction. Accordingly, he called off the proposed march, although he continued to criticize the efforts of the government. He noted in 1942 that "Ex. Order 8802 and the FEPC have as yet only scratched the surface by way of eliminating discrimination on account of race or color in a war industry. Both management and labor unions in too many places and in too many ways are still drawing 'the color line.' "[4] Randolph continued to organize marches and mass protest meetings throughout the war.

During its brief, five-year history, the FEPC engendered considerable controversy in its efforts to fulfill its mandate. In 1943 its opponents found a champion in Representative Howard Smith, Democrat from Virginia, who formed the ad hoc Select Committee of the House of Representatives to Investigate Acts of Executive Agencies. Companies and unions that felt victimized by the FEPC had a sympathetic ear in Congress, and conservative senators and congressmen led a successful fight to phase it out in 1946.[5]

From another perspective, civil rights organizations complained that FEPC was not doing enough to end discrimination. Several black members of the committee, including Charles Houston, legal counsel for the NAACP, resigned in protest over its slow progress. The first chairman, Mark Ethridge, editor of the *Louisville Courier-Journal*, came under sharp criticism from civil rights advocates after he publicly assured southern businessmen that the FEPC did not intend to alter or undermine the racial system of the South. He also characterized the expectations of the march on Washington leaders as unrealistic and foolish. In a letter to Stephen Early, executive secretary to the president, he wrote:

> As you know the Negroes wanted the executive order as a sort of second Emancipation Proclamation. They wanted the setup entirely outside OPM with LaGuardia [mayor of New York] as chairman, and I suppose

somebody like Winston Churchill would have satisfied them as executive secretary. . . . I think the agitators had got themselves into such a position with a threatened march that they wanted to make the abandonment of the march appear to come as the result of a great victory.

Ethridge suggested that Roosevelt in future speeches downplay the FEPC's potential to bring about significant change: "It would be helpful if he [Roosevelt] would point out that discrimination is as old as the world and its eradication cannot be brought about except by persistance [sic] and patience over a long time."[6]

Ethridge resigned as chairman in May 1942 and was replaced by Malcolm Maclean, president of the Hampton Institute. In 1943 Monsignor Francis Haas, a dean at Catholic University in Washington, was appointed. Later that year, Malcolm Ross, former information officer of the National Labor Relations Board, was appointed chair, a position he held until the FEPC was dissolved in June 1946.

The committee did not get Winston Churchill as executive secretary. Ethridge appointed Lawrence Cramer, whose responsibilities were those of chief negotiator and administrator of policy. Most of the FEPC's paid staff consisted of investigators and interviewers located in the twelve regional FEPC offices scattered throughout the United States and territories. An effort was made to find staff members from a cross section of racial and ethnic groups, including Mexican Americans in the Southwest, Jews in the North-central region, and blacks there and in the Northeast.

Although the committee lacked enforcement powers, it did have avenues of persuasion at its disposal. After an individual or sympathetic organization filed a complaint, a member of the regional staff investigated and filed a recommendation. If the staff member decided that the case had merit, he or she negotiated with the employer in an effort to arrange a satisfactory adjustment. An adjustment was satisfactory only if it included a written promise to eliminate discrimination against the complainant, to cease other acts of discrimination, and to implement a fair employment practice program to prevent future acts of discrimination.[7]

If the field investigator was unable to obtain a satisfactory adjustment, the case was referred to the FEPC board in Washington. Only 5 percent of cases ever reached this stage. If negotiations and efforts failed with a private company under contract with the government, a public hearing was held. The FEPC lacked the power to subpoena witnesses or records but counted on negative publicity to bring recalcitrant employers to a negotiated settlement. Some, although not all, employers yielded on a case rather than risk an open hearing that might result in their being labeled racists or bigots.[8]

The FEPC did not have the option of an open hearing when investigating complaints against government agencies, which made up over 20 percent of all cases. Such hearings were closed to the public. The FEPC found that winning compliance from government departments and agencies was slow and frequently frustrating work, complicated by issues of jurisdiction, civil service requirements, and bureaucratic turf wars.[9]

The relationship between TVA and the committee illustrates the conflict, frustration, successes, and failures that emerged from its efforts to gain antidiscrimination compliance from government agencies. Upon receipt of a September 1941 directive informing all government agencies of their responsibilities under Executive Order 8802, TVA designated the director of personnel as the respondent to the FEPC. The personnel director was a logical choice from a public administrative perspective, but he was, in effect, being asked to evaluate his own policies in the hiring and promotion of those individuals covered by the executive order. TVA shifted responsibilities for antidiscrimination compliance from Personnel to the Office of the General Manager and back again during the next decades with mixed results.[10]

In October 1941 the FEPC informed TVA that four complaints had been filed against the Authority for racial discrimination. It was accused of refusing to hire blacks as public safety officers, machinist helpers, laboratory assistants, and journeymen in many skilled craft positions. After investigating the allegations, TVA replied in December 1941 that the complaints were either exaggerated or completely unwarranted. The failure to hire a black applicant for a public safety officer's position was not racially motivated, TVA asserted; the complainant had passed all the written tests for the position and had been placed in a pool of 530 candidates, of whom 235 were hired. The complainant, however, would not be hired, since the public would not accept blacks in a position of authority that involved contact with the public, maintaining order, and guarding life and property. The laboratory assistant position was not filled by blacks because it was a stepping-stone for advancement to the position of lab technician. A black lab technician would have represented "a departure from the employment patterns in the area and therefore present[ed] problems of time and efficiency of the unit." Black machinist helpers and journeymen were not hired because many of the skilled craft unions had exclusionary clauses, and TVA did not want to alienate these white workers.[11]

140

TVA did promise to explore new avenues of cooperation and seek new opportunities:

> Negroes should be employed in as many different occupations as may be feasible—feasibility being determined by the qualifications of available candidates and by work opportunities when employment patterns in the area of the Authority's operations make it possible to add occupational opportunities to those previously available to Negroes.[12]

Executive Secretary Cramer was not satisfied with the reply from the director of personnel and ordered a review of TVA's employment policies. Of particular concern was TVA's decision to adhere to the existing patterns of Negro employment within the valley. The FEPC felt that an agency of the federal government should not be governed by local patterns and practices, "particularly if these patterns are at variance with the principle of nondiscrimination." It found TVA's reason for not hiring black public safety officers—"the public would not stand for it"—to be unacceptable and considered TVA's *a priori* decision to follow local custom discriminatory in itself.[13]

The exchange of letters in 1941 and 1942 signaled the beginning of a correspondence that lasted until the dissolution of the FEPC. TVA remained consistent in defense of its racial policies. Personnel Director Gant sought to place the exclusion of blacks within a societal framework, noting that "judgements cannot be made in a vacuum or outside a context of concrete experience." TVA also cited the merit and efficiency clause in the *Employee Relationship Policy* of 1934. Merit was judged on the abilities of individual candidates; efficiency, in contrast, was based not on the individual's ability to work well, but rather on the degree to which he or she added to the efficiency of the work unit. Therefore, policies limiting blacks to positions consistent with the status quo "are not felt to be discriminatory in a placement program based upon individual merit and efficiency of operations." [14]

TVA contended that one of its priorities as a regional agency was to establish community trust and support. Because segregation was well entrenched within the TVA region, any attempt by the Authority to transform the economic and social position of blacks would have caused unrest and anger among the white majority. Gradualism, therefore, was felt to be the more practical approach toward equal opportunity. TVA refused to acquiesce to the FEPC's directives and did not hire any of the original complainants.[15] It did bend to the pressures of the war shortages and the entreaties of the FEPC and hired four black building guards for Wilson Dam in 1943. They were described as essentially watchmen who did not interact regularly with the public, as a public safety officer would. A building guard was also not authorized to carry a gun. TVA did not hire its first black public safety officer until 1960.

The FEPC continued to correspond with TVA throughout the war, not only on issues of hiring and promotion, but also on racial quotas and the use of racial identification and pictures on application forms. The committee examined TVA's well-publicized quotas based on population ratios in the valley with considerable interest. It commented favorably on TVA's efforts to set goals for unskilled black employment, but expressed the reservation that an emphasis on maintaining a constant overall percentage camouflaged the lack of progress in permanent and skilled positions. One staffer noted that "like many other government employers, the TVA seems to be able to cite large numbers of Negroes employed as indicative of no discrimination on its part." [16]

The committee was concerned that quotas, when rigidly adhered to, were in themselves a form of discrimination. The FEPC feared that in order to fill a quota, a company might base its decision to employ an individual on considerations other than qualifications and availability. Thus, the committee ruled that it was not necessary to employ blacks or the members of any group in all areas or at all levels of skill in proportion to their membership in the general population. It emphasized the concept of open opportunities rather than proportionate representation.[17]

The question of quotas had been a matter for discussion in the White House in the months prior to the issuance of the executive order. In May Roosevelt wrote that the OPM should "take negroes [*sic*] up to a certain % in factory order work. Judge them on quality. 1st class negroes are turned down for 3rd class white boys." The reply to Roosevelt's note was quick and direct. William Knudsen of the OPM promised to "get manufacturers to increase the number of Negroes on defense work . . . [However,] if we set a percentage it will immediately be open to dispute; quiet work with the contractors and the union will bring a better result." [18] Knudsen not only articulated the OPM's policy on quotas but previewed the position that the FEPC took as well.

The FEPC also examined TVA's application forms for evidence of improper identification of an applicant's race, religion, or national origin. The committee had indicated to private industries and government agencies that an applicant need only supply citizenship and that employers could not inquire into race, religion, or national origin. It also sought to discourage employers from requiring photographs from applicants. Complaints were filed by many ethnic and religious groups, particularly Jewish Americans, who stated that they were denied employment after they revealed their religious preference. The FEPC questioned TVA's requirement that an applicant send a picture and declare his or her racial origin. TVA responded that the racial designation was used only for record keeping and not for exclusion or discrimination. The FEPC elected not to press the Authority on this issue, stating that its "explanation seemed to be thoroughly sound." The situation had not been resolved at the time of the FEPC's demise, and TVA continued to use applications that required racial identification until 1955.[19]

To encourage TVA to change more rapidly, the FEPC sent it a report entitled "The Employment of Negroes in the Federal Government" to show that some government agencies were cooperating with FEPC directives. The committee noted that lofty assurances of nondiscrimination did not count; it was the number of blacks employed and the spread of occupations available to them. Given the added and important factor of World War II, several government departments made dramatic progress in the hiring of blacks: in 1941 the War Department, for example, employed 9,469 blacks, or just over 20 percent of its staff. Significantly, 6,667, or 70 percent, of the number of blacks held clerical, administrative, or fiscal positions (CAF). The Treasury Department in 1942 employed 6,754 blacks, or 23 percent of the total, and 73 percent of them were in classifications other than custodial. For the Treasury Department, 80 percent of all employees were in classifications other than custodial. The FEPC noted that 52 percent of the total workforce of the Federal Works Agency was black, but "all but a few of these are in custodial classifications." The federal agency with the lowest percentage of blacks was the Agriculture Department, with blacks constituting only 4.7 percent of its workforce. Yet even that department, which had a close working relationship with TVA in agriculture extension work and fertilizer development, had 45 percent of its black employees in CAF classifications.[20]

The FEPC singled out the Civil Service Commission for special praise. The committee considered the CSC a key agency for scrutiny because the commission influenced personnel policy in a host of government agencies. The CSC had originally been embarrassed and stung by the committee's allegations that it discriminated against blacks. Before the September 1942 review, the commission employed 265 blacks; by 30 November there were 500 black employees, or 13.4 percent of the total personnel. Seventy-four percent of the blacks were in CAF or professional classifications.[21]

Despite its detailed and critical directives as well as the more subtle attempts at pressure through comparison, the FEPC was not able to reduce significantly the various forms of discrimination practiced by TVA. Yet there were some changes. The most important was a reversal after 1942 of TVA's policy of exclusion at dam construction sites when there was a low percentage of blacks in the immediate area. As previously noted, the Authority ignored public outcry and threats of violence and hired blacks to work in the construction of Fontana Dam in 1942, asserting that Executive Order 8802 required the full utilization of all the valley population.[22] TVA also, as we have seen (Chapter V), reestablished the Committee on Negro Training to facilitate compliance with the order.[23]

In order to reply more accurately to FEPC inquiries and charges, TVA began to keep careful records and statistics on the number of blacks in various occupations, their rates of promotion, hiring and firing percentages, complaints of harassment, types of training programs, and lists of "firsts or breakthroughs" in occupations previously closed to blacks. For example, in 1942, the first black chemical plant operator trainees were hired; the first black apprentice, personnel clerk, and building guard were hired in 1943. All black personnel officers were required to make monthly reports on the progress of Negro placement and to keep careful records.[24]

The TVA boosted the number of its black employees from 7.8 percent in 1942 to 11.1 percent in 1943 by filling temporary labor positions. Yet the percentage of blacks in clerical, administrative, and professional categories remained almost constant. In 1942, 7 professional, 8 subprofessional, and 46 clerical positions (or 1.5 percent of the total) were filled by blacks. In 1943, the figures were: 1 professional out of 1,200, 13 subprofessionals out of 823, and 44 clericals out of 2,300—or 2.1 percent, an improvement of only 0.6 percent.[25]

Critics of TVA racial policies considered these changes to be cosmetic at best. One TVA employee—a black personnel officer, not J. Herman Daves, who for obvious reasons wished to remain anonymous—wrote to the NAACP about a directive entitled, "Personnel Department Responsibilities for Negro Employment": "Frankly we feel that it is another effort to hoodwink the FEPC or any other investigating body. It may appear OK on paper, but we are apprehensive that any substantial results will be obtained in the field or even in the Knoxville office." It was at this time that the anonymous employee reported George Gant's call (quoted above) "to hire 'more Negro cooks in the future.' "[26]

The failure of the FEPC to change TVA racial policies in any significant way can be attributed to several factors. Executive Order 8802 and the FEPC signaled the beginning of a conflict between the policies and directives of the federal government, with its national perspective, and those of TVA, which sought to remain independent of all federal control over employment policy, whether racially oriented or not. TVA had, since its charter was written, maintained an employment policy independent from the Civil Service Commission. The FEPC represented to TVA an intrusion not only of outside racial mores and practices, but also of unwanted federal control. Resistance to the FEPC's suggestions was based as much on a fierce sense of independence as on a desire to retain the racial status quo. The conflict, present from 1941, became more intense as the Fair Employment and Equal Employment Opportunity committees that succeeded the FEPC in the 1940s, 1950s, and 1960s became more closely associated with the Civil Service Commission.[27]

Mixed signals from the FEPC to TVA also complicated their relationship. Although the FEPC pronounced TVA's employment policies unacceptable in its official correspondence, individual members of the committee, in private meetings with TVA officials, expressed a more tolerant attitude. Mark Ethridge, while chair of the FEPC, wrote to David Lilienthal to assure him that "it seems to me that you are doing the usual intelligent job of TVA. . . . As a matter of fact, I don't see how you could do much more to give the Negroes an opportunity." Ethridge, perhaps mindful of his dual allegiance or the possibly awkward frankness of his letter, included a notation: "Please destroy after reading." Not only was the letter filed instead, but copies were made for Gordon Clapp and TVA's Washington lobbyist, Marguerite Owen.[28]

Most importantly, the FEPC was not in existence long enough to have more than a negligible impact on TVA policies. Only in 1943 did the committee begin to stabilize its personnel policy, bureaucratic structure, and national mandate. On 20 June 1944 Congress passed an appropriation act for the fiscal year 1945 that contained an amendment requiring congressional approval for any "executive order" agency that had been in existence for more than a year. Congressional control of the FEPC budget translated into a severe reduction for 1945 and an expiration date for the committee of 30 June 1946. By the summer of 1945, many field offices—including some that had been open for less than a year—had closed. FEPC's greatest weapons were persuasion and perseverance, both of which needed time. Efforts by civil rights organizations to forestall the end of the FEPC failed. The committee never had time to pressure TVA, or many of the major industrial employers, for better compliance. Nor was it around to analyze the nation's shift from a wartime economy to a peacetime economy and criticize the resulting impact on blacks and other minorities.[29]

CHAPTER VII

Beyond the New Deal

THE term "watershed" has been vastly overused by historians, but 1945 was one of the few years in U.S. history that could qualify for such a characterization. The death of Roosevelt on 12 April 1945, and the end of the war with the surrender of Germany on 8 May and of Japan on 14 August, marked the end of the old era and the beginning of a new one.

The impact of both events was clearly felt in the valley. There were changes in direction and scope within TVA. It was a time to relinquish old ideas and develop new approaches to old problems. One old idea that was effectively abandoned was the regional planning program within TVA. By 1945 the Regional Planning Office had become the Regional Studies Department (compare Figure 5 with Figures 3 and 4 above). Introduced during the period of the New Deal as the chief means for the social rehabilitation of the South if not the rest of the country, regional planning failed to outlast the Roosevelt administration.

There are no easy answers to the question of why TVA regional planning failed to produce lasting results for all valley inhabitants and most especially for those from racial and economically marginal groups. There were noticeable weaknesses in the Authority's theory and in its implementation of regional planning in general. There were also limitations in its planning for racial change in a democratic framework and in an environment where planners shared an ideology of racism and, at best, espoused an "enlightened segregation."

The future society to be achieved through the expertise of government regional planners was ill-defined and confusing. Regionalism was the belief that a region and its people were shaped by a common topography, culture, history, and climate. Yet TVA used regionalism to define an administrative unit shaped by a common topography—a river valley. TVA was established to administer and plan programs of water control, power development, fertilizer production, agricultural and industrial development,

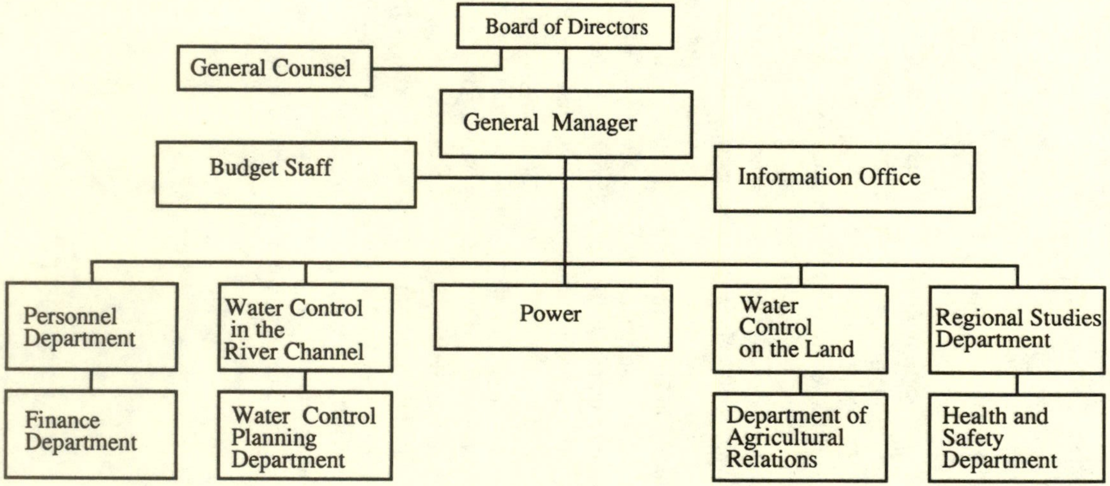

FIGURE 5.   Partial Organizational Chart of TVA, 1945

Source: TVA Technical Library, Knoxville, Tennessee

reforestation and soil erosion control, land planning, and social and economic research. Although some of Arthur Morgan's homestead and home craft projects projected a romantic link between valley farmers and a mystical culture, the basic image of TVA was that of a serious and practical venture in planning, proposing only the programs that it could efficiently and responsibly complete.

TVA's planning approach was oriented more to engineering than to sociology or philosophy. It stressed the structural and administrative challenges of a future society over humanistic goals. TVA planners spoke in terms of efficiency and practical and logical development rather than in terms of morality, compassion, or justice.

The scope of regional planning was limited by the mandated powers of Sections 4, 5, 22, and 23 of the TVA act and the warnings of its own legal division. In the face of legal action by power companies, TVA became reluctant to propose even small-scale projects. In addition, the long-range planning impetus ended when Arthur Morgan was ousted from the chairmanship in 1938. World War II accelerated the shift away from social planning to power and fertilizer production. By 1945 TVA had become a major supplier of power for war industries and the national laboratory at Oak Ridge, and of nitrates for explosives. Social planning projects were phased out, the most significant event in this process being the sale of the Norris Model Community to a real estate developer. When David Lilienthal left TVA in 1945 to become the head of the Atomic Energy Commission, the last original link to the promise of 1933 was broken.

Planning in TVA was also limited by societal expectations and fears. The fascist states of Italy and Germany and the communist Soviet Union had created an unfavorable image of planning, and New Deal planners had to operate under its constraints. The American public had to be convinced of the validity of government planning and assured that no five-year plans would be forced upon them. The idea of planning had to be sold in small, democratic, nonthreatening chunks.

TVA planning was particularly susceptible to pressures from local political and economic organizations. Operating in the framework of "grassroots democracy," TVA was obligated to seek local cooperation for city planning, agricultural projects, and recreational park development; therefore, local citizens sat on cooperative planning committees. Programs could be changed and plans vetoed by influential groups. Special interests, such as large landowners, were able to secure plans sensitive to and supportive of their needs. Economically marginal groups such as tenant farmers and displaced valley inhabitants, on the other hand, did not figure prominently in the ideas of TVA planners, who planned for either the most powerful, the least complicated, or the most homogeneous groups.

The role that blacks were to have in the restructured society was illustrative of the limitations of democratic regional planning as an instrument of social change. TVA's plans for blacks fitted the region's accepted racial customs of segregation and discrimination. Any significant attempt to end racial discrimination by TVA would have created, in its opinion, new and more dangerous problems involving the loss of political and community support. Recognizing that segregation in itself was inefficient, TVA, for the sake of simplicity, attempted in areas with a small percentage of blacks to exclude them from model communities and employment. The Authority had no moral commitment to end social problems and consequently could argue that it was justified in following a rational and cost-efficient plan that discriminated against or excluded blacks.

The belief in the inferiority of blacks shared by many regional planners also reduced the possibilities for a change in race relations. Arthur Morgan and David Lilienthal noted that social distinctions and segregation were a justifiable part of American history and would remain for years to come. However, both considered themselves to be racially progressive and allowed for the need to provide economic mobility and racial dignity and pride. Both believed in planning for an enlightened segregation.

Yet this goal was in itself a limitation. Planners sought to remove gross inequalities while maintaining a segregated society. TVA announced that blacks, although segregated, were to be given equal pay for equal work and were to be employed in proportion to their population in the valley. In reality, there was no enlightened segregation. Blacks were misclassified and paid lower wages than whites doing the same job, and they were employed proportionately only in temporary, unskilled work. Even here, statistics were manipulated to show the highest percentage possible for black employment.

Blacks rejected the concept of enlightened segregation. Through national and civil rights organizations, they formed a vocal and organized pressure group that threatened legal action and participated in congressional investigations. Although they did cause a modification of exclusion policies and spurred the opening of more job opportunities, blacks could not pressure or persuade TVA to change its overall discriminatory practices and plans. From the TVA perspective, granting equal rights to blacks would not increase the Authority's efficiency and would only incur the wrath of powerful local and regional politicians, many of whom were allies in TVA's battles against private utilities.

In 1933 the Roosevelt administration showed considerable interest in regional planning, as evidenced by the establishment of TVA, which was to be only the first of many such valley authorities. By 1945 it was clear that regional planning had ceased to hold the interest of the administration or the American public. No other valley authorities on the scale of TVA were authorized by Congress for the postwar period.

By 1945 there had been a shift in the national perspective away from regionalism to government centralization and control. World War II, with its government-imposed rationing and regulation of war-related industries, helped convince the American public of the efficiency of centralized planning. Blacks in particular began to believe that the most significant hope for change in race relations rested not in regional control, but in a strong central government that could impose a national standard of fairness on all regions of the country.

Truman set the tone for greater centralization and a sharper focus on Washington leadership. He brought this centralized approach not only to economic planning through the Council of Economic Advisors, which was established by the Employment Act of 1946, but also to civil rights. Roosevelt allowed individual departments and agencies to practice their own brand of race relations without substantial interference until the advent of the FEPC. Truman, on the other hand, called for national action, including legislation to provide federal protection against lynching, to protect the right to vote, and to establish a permanent FEPC. He authorized the establishment of the Committee on Civil Rights, and following receipt of its recommendations, issued in 1948 both an executive order directing the armed forces to abandon the practice of segregation and discrimination and a directive that desegregated federal facilities in Washington, D.C.[1]

The area that civil rights advocates deemed most in need of a national standard of fairness was employment. NAACP leaders and A. Philip Randolph lobbied Congress and led a national campaign to create a permanent FEPC. Despite support from Truman, the congressional bills were defeated by a well-organized group of southern and midwestern senators and congressmen, including members of the Alabama, Mississippi, and Tennessee Democratic contingent.[2]

Between 1946 and 1948 there was no federal body charged with fair employment review, and private industries and federal agencies easily slipped back into old discriminatory patterns. The expiration of the wartime FEPC in 1946 and the return of white veterans combined to push postwar unemployment of blacks to dramatic levels. The late employment of blacks in the war effort had left them with less seniority than most white workers, and when the workforce was reduced, blacks were the first to be let go. Federal employers felt free to use a host of rationales for not hiring or keeping black employees, even in traditionally "Negro jobs." Some administrators went so far as to admit that black people were only hired during a time of war. The FBI in 1946 announced the need for 2,000 new clerical workers and made it clear that it wanted only white workers. When the Justice Department posted new openings, it listed them as for "whites only." In its final report, the FEPC noted that black unemployment in the last months of 1945 and the first six months of 1946 was "alarming" and that the wartime gains had dissipated through an unchecked revival of discriminatory practices.[3]

In 1948 Truman, under pressure from blacks who threatened civil disobedience and nonparticipation in the coming presidential election, issued Executive Order 9980, which created a Fair Employment Board within the Civil Service Commission, with employment officers for every department and independent agency. The board's duties were to receive reports from agencies and advise them on problems and policies relating to fair employment. The scope of Executive Order 9980 covered only discrimination in individual personnel actions, and did not address the problem of class discrimination, such as the exclusion of blacks from certain occupations or the maintenance of segregated facilities.[4]

The end of the war had a direct and significant impact on TVA, but the changes in national civil rights policies did not have such an impact. The construction frenzy that characterized the first twelve years of TVA was not sustained in the next fifteen years. The workforce changed from thousands of temporary laborers to a smaller but more stable group of permanently employed technicians and skilled craftsmen, as well as career bureaucrats who administered the flood control, hydroelectric, and later nuclear power plant systems. The wartime labor shortage that had compelled TVA to hire blacks for nontraditional occupations dissipated as returning white veterans and new migrants flocked into the Tennessee valley.

The decline in the percentage of blacks in the workforce from the 1941 high point of 11.8 percent was gradual but unremitting. The percentage decreased from 8.9 percent in 1946 to 6.2 percent in 1963, with the vast majority of blacks in 1963, as in 1946, employed at the three lowest pay scales (see Table 1).[5]

Indeed, for all the dramatic changes that 1945 wrought, some things remained familiar. In the postwar years, TVA's racial policies changed only when pressures from the federal government or civil rights organizations became irresistible. From 1945 to 1955 the few changes that occurred were noted in the annual report of the TVA fair employment officer as "break-

TABLE 1. Blacks Employed by TVA, by Service and
Classification Title, 1950

Service and Classification Title	No.	Service and Classification Title	No.
Professional Service		*Trades and Labor Service*	
Research chemist II	1	Ash car operator	1
Specialist in Negro education		Ash drag and pump operator	1
and relations III	1	Assistant gas- and oil-fired	
TOTAL	2	boiler operator	8
		Bagger and weighter	12
Sub-Professional Service		Bagging and shipping laborer	21
Biological aide I	1	Boiler room helper	33
Chemical aide II	1	Boilermaker helper	3
Draftsman II	1	Bricklayer tender	8
Laboratory aide	2	Car dumper operator	1
Materials tester I	1	Car unloader operator	3
Materials tester II	1	Cement finisher	6
TOTAL	7	Classifying and drying laborer	3
		Coal and ash handler	2
Custodial Service		Construction laborer	282
Building and grounds custodian	1	Conveyor operator	40
Cook I	5	Deckhand	1
Cook II	6	Fertilizer loader	7
Cook III	1	Fertilizer trucker	4
Elevator operator	7	Flagman	13
Gardener I	1	Fusion furnace laborer	5
Gardener II	1	Fusion furnace tapper	4
Janitor I	168	Garage attendant	18
Janitor II	1	Gas and diesel mechanic helper	3
Janitor III	7	Gas house laborer	10
Laundry worker II	1	Groundman trainee	1
Messenger	22	Jackhammer operator	125
Orderly	7	Labor foreman	2
Shipping supervisor	1	Laborer	350
Waiter	7	Lineman	4
TOTAL	236	Lineman apprentice—4th period	1
		Loading checker	7
Clerical, Administrative, and Fiscal Service		Loading machine operator	1
		Machinist helper	1
Bindery worker I	3	Manufacturing laborer	2
Clerk-typist I	2	Metaphosphate tapper	4
Clerk-typist II	1	Monorail operator	2
Duplicating machine operator I	1	Mortar mixer	2
Duplicating machine operator II	1	Nitrate mixer operator	5
File clerk I	3	Oiler	14
File clerk II	3	Phosphate laborer	16
Mail clerk I	3	Phosphate shipping shift foreman	1
Mail clerk II	4	Phosphorus furnace head tapper	4
Mail clerk III	2	Phosphorus furnace tapper	19
Personnel officer II	2	Pilot plant laborer	8
Stores clerk I	2	Pilot plant operator I	6
TOTAL	27	Powderman	10

TABLE I—*Continued*

Service and Classification Title	No.	Service and Classification Title	No.
Trades and Labor Service (continued)			
Power shovel operator	1	Truck driver III	1
Raw materials laborer	18	Truck helper	5
Relief operator I	3	Truck operator—power system	
Relief operator II	2	maintenance	1
Senior coal drag operator	2	Truck tractor operator	2
Senior turbine operator—hydro	1	Wagon drill operator	39
Storage shed powderman	1	Warehouseman	6
Storage shed shovel operator	1	Washer laborer	6
Track walker	1	TOTAL	1,172
Tractor operator—under 50 H.P.	1	GRAND TOTAL	1,444
Truck driver I	4		
Truck driver II	3	*Source:* Tennessee Valley Authority	

throughs" in hiring. In this ten-year interval, TVA hired its first black draftsman, economist, engineer, statistician, and analytical chemist. The reports do not indicate the retention rate among these breakthrough employees. Six black engineers who had graduated from Howard University's School of Engineering were hired in 1952. By 1953 all six had left TVA, complaining of harassment within the Authority. Most also noted that they had received better offers in northern urban environments, where "they would not have to subject their families to segregated schools and water fountains." [6]

The issue of segregation was not resolved until the 1960s, when students from Fisk University and Knoxville College spearheaded efforts to integrate public accommodations, and local colleges and training institutes used by TVA for its training programs began to accept black students. As a government agency, TVA had been pressured to desegregate by directives from the Truman administration, inquiries from liberal political forces, and Supreme Court decisions. The Authority began the process reluctantly in 1951 with the removal of signs from drinking fountains and washrooms at Fontana and Norris dams. The official TVA policy on segregation was inspired by the same philosophy as its policy on Negro employment opportunities. The policy was to follow local custom and provide separate facilities for white and black personnel. General Manager John Oliver stated in a letter to Senator Paul Douglas of Illinois that segregated facilities appeared to be "one way of ensuring that the projects would be visited by all of the people." TVA's priority, he indicated, lay not in directly changing social values but in providing equal wages and employment opportunities: "TVA inaugurated and maintained a policy of nonsegregation in the more basic matter of employment and wages, on the ground that economic equality is essential to the eventual elimination of conditions under which segregation prevails. We deliberately tried to avoid sharp issues over surface manifestations."[7]

In 1951 Oliver promised the senator that all signs would be down "by the beginning of the next tourist season." In 1954 TVA was still in the process of taking signs down from the newer facilities, but it acknowledged that the recent Supreme Court decision in *Brown* v. *Board of Education* had given additional urgency to the process. It was not until 1962, when the cafeteria in the Powell Building in Chattanooga was desegregated, that TVA could claim to be an integrated agency.[8]

The 1960s and 1970s were years of change in the expectations of and opportunities for blacks living within the valley. Schools were integrated from the elementary level through the University of Tennessee and the University of Chattanooga, and new neighborhoods were open to blacks who could afford the cost of a middle-class home. In TVA, blacks made more breakthroughs, perhaps culminating in the appointment of a black woman, Marilyn E. Taylor, as the director of personnel in 1983.

For all the obvious changes, there were less obvious reminders of the past. Until the appointment of Taylor, the highest-ranking black in TVA was the director of the Equal Employment Opportunity Office. In 1938 the highest-ranking black was the head of Negro training. The EEO director, while having much more power and prestige, nevertheless also held a racially specific job. In 1975, after a series of unfavorable reports by black newspapers and the National Urban League and a critical internal report by the director of EEO describing continued racial discrimination in TVA, the general manager, Lynn Seeber, acknowledged that the Authority's record for employing minorities and women was not good. He compared TVA's statistical position with that of the Atomic Energy Commission, an agency that had recently been criticized in congressional hearings for not reaching its affirmative action goals. If the AEC with its 14.9 percent minority and 33.9 percent female workforce had been criticized, then, Seeber reasoned, TVA with its 7.2 percent minorities and 9.0 percent women was clearly in danger. When Seeber examined the Authority's percentage of minorities and women in classifications over GS-12 (approximately M-5 in TVA's internal structure, at the bottom of the management supervisory scale), the differences between TVA and the AEC became even greater. In the AEC, staff members over GS-12 were 5 percent minorities and 5 percent women. In TVA, there were 0.9 percent minorities and 0.5 percent women over

M-5. Seeber concluded that TVA—in 1975—still had "much work to do in the area of equal employment opportunities."[9]

This study has focused on the years 1933 to 1945 in an effort to understand the parameters of government involvement as a social planner for and an employer of blacks in an agency self-defined as socially progressive. That discrimination existed in TVA during the New Deal period is not particularly surprising, although the forms it took were innovative. But the fact that after all of the legislation had been passed, the Supreme Court decisions had been rendered, and presidents had come and gone, discrimination in TVA continued to exist in similar and publicly acknowledged forms into at least the 1970s does give this historian pause.

Several factors contributed to the lack of progress for blacks within TVA. Two closely related factors—lack of turnover in the workforce and company loyalty to the promise of 1933—served not only to create a climate of stability, high morale, and a sense of purpose, but also to block self-criticism and prevent new voices from emerging in important policy-making positions. An example of loyalty to and longevity within TVA, Gordon Clapp served as director of personnel in the 1930s, was promoted to the position of general manager during the war years, and was elected chairman of the board from 1946 to 1953. In all, Clapp served a total of twenty-one years in TVA. As we have seen, in the 1930s Clapp initiated many of the Authority's early employment policies on blacks. While he brought an insider's knowledge to the position of chairman, Clapp the chairman was not inclined to revise or repudiate policies initiated by Clapp the director of personnel or Clapp the general manager.[10]

In *The TVA: An Approach to the Development of a Region*, Clapp acknowledged his loyalty to TVA, called for a renewed sense of faith in the TVA promise, and exhorted his former colleagues to resist attacks on TVA by hostile outsiders, particularly those who labeled it an example of "creeping socialism."[11] Clapp was following the tradition of TVA chairmen from Arthur Morgan through David Lilienthal who equated criticism of the Authority with disloyalty to the ideals of democracy. The marshaling of forces against outsiders' attacks enabled TVA to withstand and survive potentially crippling lawsuits and congressional investigations.

A similar energy was used against other forms of criticism, including allegations of racial discrimination. Inquiries from the NAACP, the National Urban League, and newspapers, and investigations by the FEPC during the war years, the Civil Service Commission during the 1950s, and the President's Committee on Equal Employment Opportunity during the 1960s were also treated as hostile attacks that had to be blunted or defused.

Damage control rather than detailed analysis of the basis for the criticism was the traditional response, beginning with Clapp's reaction to John P. Davis' critical articles in 1934 and 1935.

In 1966 the Civil Service Commission conducted an extensive investigation of TVA's racial policies. An inspection team consulted with over three hundred TVA officials and employees and over thirty community leaders and reviewed policy statements, administrative releases, and other information. The report concluded that although TVA had increased its employment of minority group members despite the difficulty of finding and attracting well-qualified minority candidates, it did not have a broad-based internal plan to end racial discrimination. The report noted that "self-evaluation methods have not identified major problems and need substantial improvement." [12]

The Civil Service Commission report required a reply from TVA, just as directives from the executive secretary of the FEPC had. TVA was thus forced to reexamine its program, at least to the extent that it had to in order to reply to the charges. It acknowledged certain charges as accurate and vowed to do better, promised to develop a better and more critical system of evaluation, and also vowed to introduce more managerial involvement in the EEO programs. In 1968 the Commission recognized improvements in TVA and said that the biggest improvement was in securing management commitment.[13]

Despite some sincere efforts by TVA over the years, the most persistent obstacle to equal employment has been what the Civil Service Commission called the burden of a discriminatory past. During the New Deal TVA established a policy of hiring blacks in unskilled or semiskilled and traditionally "Negro" jobs. Many blacks hired in those positions in the 1930s and 1940s remained in these jobs into the 1950s and 1960s. They had been barred from training programs that might have allowed them to compete for the broadened opportunities of the 1960s and 1970s. TVA recognized the need to identify underutilized personnel and in 1967–1968 conducted a survey of all black annual employees to identify those who wished to be retrained or promoted. Although several blacks were able to train for better positions, however, the majority had in effect been left behind.[14]

Another aspect of that legacy was the continued exclusionary practice of skilled craft unions, which effectively barred blacks from most skilled trades positions in TVA. Apprenticeship training programs that in practice accepted only whites into the 1960s remained a major obstacle in TVA. Another legacy was the continued wariness of the black communities within the valley with regard to TVA's promises of employment. By the 1960s the memory of TVA's 1930s efforts to upgrade its janitorial staff by using black college students may have faded. Yet its insistence on hiring only overqualified blacks for messenger and clerical work continued to rankle. In 1974 black messengers, many of whom had college degrees, complained to the NAACP that they had been denied promotions and opportunities to compete for jobs outside the mailroom and messenger areas.[15]

It is important for historians to place occurrences of discrimination and oppression within a historical context. Certainly in the case of blacks in TVA during the New Deal, TVA officials planned for a future for blacks that resembled the racial status quo in its maintenance of the constraints of politics, economic forces, and racial prejudice and bigotry. In doing so, Arthur Morgan, Harcourt Morgan, David Lilienthal, and Gordon Clapp, among others, also inadvertently laid the groundwork for a long-range program of racial discrimination, the vestiges of which remained in place at least forty years later.

NOTES

INTRODUCTION

1. Revisionist historians have since the 1960s become increasingly critical of New Dealers and their failure to address fundamental social and economic ills. Harvard Sitkoff in *A New Deal for Blacks* (New York: Oxford University Press, 1978) describes the emergence of a racially liberal consensus in the Department of the Interior, the Farm Security Administration (FSA), and the Works Progress Administration (WPA). Critical of the National Recovery Administration (NRA) and the Agricultural Adjustment Administration (AAA), he acknowledges that even the improvements in the "best" departments and agencies were significant primarily for establishing new policies upon which later administrations could build. Raymond Wolters in *Negroes and the Great Depression* (Westport, Conn.: Greenwood Press, 1970) notes the failure of the AAA and NRA to address the needs of black workers and farmers. He characterizes the New Deal as a brokered state, in which the best-organized special interests got the most attention and made the greatest gains. Blacks were weak and poorly organized, and this situation, combined with racism within the administration, guaranteed that blacks would not receive their fair share. Nancy Weiss in *Farewell to the Party of Lincoln: Black Politics in the Age of FDR* (Princeton: Princeton University Press, 1983) asks why blacks voted for Roosevelt despite the shortcomings of the New Deal's racial policies. She concludes that they voted Democratic in gratitude for the economic benefits, however limited, that came their way.

2. For a discussion of the treatment of blacks during the presidency of Theodore Roosevelt, see Thomas Dyer, *Theodore Roosevelt and the Idea of Race* (Baton Rouge: Louisiana State University Press, 1980). For the racial attitudes of Woodrow Wilson, see Morton Sosna, "The South in the Saddle: Racial Politics During the Wilson Years," *Wisconsin Magazine of History* 54 (1970): 30–49.

3. For a discussion of the early years of the NAACP, see B. Joyce Ross, *J. E. Spingarn and the Rise of the NAACP, 1911–1935* (New York: Atheneum, 1972), and Charles F. Kellogg, *The NAACP* (Baltimore: Johns Hopkins University Press, 1967).

4. William Harris, *The Harder We Run* (New York: Oxford University Press, 1982), pp. 95–106; Philip S. Foner and Ronald L. Lewis, eds., *The Black Worker from the Founding of the CIO to the AFL-CIO Merger, 1936–1955* (Philadelphia: Temple University Press, 1983), p. 266.

5. Samuel Roseman, ed., *The Public Papers and Addresses of Franklin Roosevelt*, 2: 11–15, quoted in William Leuchtenburg, *Franklin D. Roosevelt and the New Deal 1932–1940* (New York: Harper & Row, 1963), p. 41.

6. For an overview of the New Deal, the best book remains Leuchtenburg, *Roosevelt and the New Deal*. Also see Paul Conkin, *The New Deal* (New York: Crowell, 1967).

7. Leuchtenburg, *Roosevelt and the New Deal*, p. 347.

8. Paul Burstein, *Discrimination, Jobs, and Politics: The Struggle for Equal Employment Opportunity in the United States Since the New Deal* (Chicago: University of Chicago Press, 1985), pp. 16–17.

9. Susan Hartmann, *The Home Front and Beyond: American Women in the 1940s* (Boston: Twayne, 1982), pp. 3–5.

10. Ibid., p. 21.

11. Leslie Fishel, Jr., "The Negro in the New Deal Era," in *The Negro in the Depression and War*, edited by Bernard Sternsher (Chicago: Quadrangle Books, 1969), p. 8. Also see Weiss, *Farewell to the Party of Lincoln*.

12. *Chicago Defender*, 7 October 1933; *New York Age*, 7 July 1935; Joseph P. Lash, *Eleanor and Franklin* (New York: Norton, 1971), pp. 668–70.

13. James Patterson, *Congressional Conservatism and the New Deal: The Growth of the Conservative Coalition in Congress 1933–1939* (Lexington: University of Kentucky Press, 1967), pp. 5–6, 132–33.

14. Harris, *The Harder We Run*, pp. 104, 105; Fishel, "Negro in the New Deal Era," p. 10.

15. George Haynes, "The Negro and National Recovery," unpublished report for the Joint Committee on National Recovery, 1934, p. 21, NAACP Papers, Library of Congress, Washington, D.C.

16. Harris, *The Harder We Run*, pp. 205, 96–101; Wolters, *Negroes and the Great Depression*, pp. x–xii.

17. Harris, *The Harder We Run*, pp. 101–2. Also see John A. Salmond, "The Civilian Conservation Corps and the Negro," *Journal of American History* 52 (1965): 78.

18. John Kirby, *Black Americans in the Roosevelt Era* (Knoxville: University of Tennessee Press, 1980), pp. 34–35; Wolters, *Negroes and the Great Depression*, p. 71. Also see Sidney Baldwin, *Poverty and Politics: The Rise and Decline of the Farm Security Administration* (Chapel Hill: University of North Carolina Press, 1968). Kirby attributes the FSA's failure to Alexander's limited vision of racial justice and equality and his unwillingness to make a direct attack on the fundamental southern principle of segregation.

19. Kirby, *Black Americans in the Roosevelt Era*, pp. 34–35. Kirby also criticizes Ickes for his unwillingness to identify any special needs or problems of blacks that could be remedied through government intervention.

20. Foner and Lewis, *Black Worker*, pp. 266–72.

21. Mary Francis Berry and John Blassingame, *Long Memory* (New York: Oxford University Press, 1982), pp. 198–99; Harris, *The Harder We Run*, pp. 116–17.

22. For a detailed discussion of the FEPC, see Herbert Hill, *Black Labor and the American Legal System* (Madison: University of Wisconsin Press, 1984); Louis Ruchames, *Race, Jobs, and Politics* (New York: Columbia University Press, 1953); and Louis Kesselman, *The Social Politics of FEPC* (Chapel Hill: University of North Carolina Press, 1948).

23. Harris, *The Harder We Run*, p. 122; Hartmann, *Home Front*, p. 80.

24. Leuchtenburg, *Roosevelt and the New Deal*, pp. 54–55.

25. Thomas McCraw, *Morgan vs. Lilienthal: The Feud Within the TVA* (Chicago: Loyola University Press, 1970), pp. 15–48.

26. George Galloway, *Planning for America* (New York: Columbia University Press, 1941), pp. 3–5.

27. Julian Huxley, *TVA: Adventure in Planning* (London: Architectural Press, 1943), p. 7.

28. John Friedmann, *Planning in the Public Domain: From Knowledge to Action* (Princeton: Princeton University Press, 1987), pp. 78–81; Albert Lepawsky, "The Progressives and the Planners," *Public Administration Review* 31 (1971): 297–303.

29. Lepawsky, "Progressives and Planners," pp. 297–302; Otis Graham, *Toward a Planned Society* (New York: Oxford University Press, 1976), pp. 14–19.

30. For more information on southern regional planning, see Howard Odum, *Southern Regions of the United States* (Chapel Hill: University of North Carolina Press, 1936); Rupert Vance, *Human Geography of the South* (Chapel Hill: University of North Carolina Press, 1932); John Van Sickle, *Planning for the South: An Inquiry Into the Economics of Regionalism* (Nashville: Vanderbilt University Press, 1943); Graham, *Toward a Planned Society*, chap. 1.

31. Huxley, *Adventure in Planning*, p. 9.

32. For an excellent analysis of TVA and its impact on the white population living near Norris, Tennessee, see Michael McDonald and John Muldowny, *TVA and the Dispossessed* (Knoxville: University of Tennessee Press, 1983).

33. Lester Lamon, *Blacks in Tennessee 1791–1970* (Knoxville: University of Tennessee Press, 1981), pp. 89–92; John Stanfield, "The Sociohistorical Roots of White/Black Inequality in Urban Appalachia," in *Blacks in Appalachia*, edited by William H. Turner and Edward J. Cabbell (Lexington: University of Kentucky Press, 1985), pp. 133–35.

34. See McDonald and Muldowny, *TVA and the Dispossessed*.

35. The major anti-TVA suits were *Ashwander* v. *TVA*, 297 U.S. 288 (1936), and *Tennessee Electric Power* v. *TVA*, 306 U.S. 118 (1939). For the firing of Arthur Morgan, see McCraw, *Morgan vs. Lilienthal*, pp. 90–104.

36. Robert Anthony, "Closing the Loop Between Planning and Performance," *Public Administration Review* 31 (1971): 300.

37. Quoted in T. Harry Williams, "Huey, Lyndon, Southern Radicalism," *Journal of Southern History* 40 (1973): 272. For a discussion of southern liberalism during the New Deal, see Morton Sosna, *In Search of the Silent South: Southern Liberals and the Race Issue* (New York: Columbia University Press, 1977); Michael

O'Brien, *The Idea of the American South* (Baltimore: Johns Hopkins University Press, 1979); Daniel Joseph Singal, *The War Within: From Victorian to Modernist Thought in the South, 1919–1945* (Chapel Hill: University of North Carolina Press, 1982); John T. Kneebone, *Southern Liberal Journalists and the Issue of Race, 1920–1944* (Chapel Hill: University of North Carolina Press, 1985).

CHAPTER I

1. Franklin Roosevelt, *The Public Papers and Addresses of Franklin Roosevelt*, vol. 1 (New York: Random House, 1937), pp. 888–89.

2. Franklin Roosevelt, *The Public Papers and Addresses of Franklin Roosevelt*, vol. 2 (New York: Random House, 1938), p. 122.

3. Clarence Hodge, *The Tennessee Valley Authority* (Washington, D.C.: American University Press, 1938), p. 33; Franklin Roosevelt, Message to Congress on Muscle Shoals Development, House Doc. 15, 73rd Cong., 1st sess., 10 April 1933, p. 7.

4. Roosevelt, Message, House Doc. 15, p. 7.

5. Roosevelt, *Public Papers*, 2: 122. Roosevelt in later remarks noted that cities had become weary of "growing up like Topsy." In this 1933 message, however, he abbreviated the phrase to "just grown," expurgating the allusion to the slave in Harriet Beecher Stowe's *Uncle Tom's Cabin*.

6. See Herman Pritchett, *The Tennessee Valley Authority: A Study in Public Administration* (Chapel Hill: University of North Carolina Press, 1943), p. 29.

7. *Congressional Record*, vol. 35 (3 Dec. 1901), pp. 85–86. Also see John Kyle, *The Building of TVA: An Illustrated History* (Baton Rouge: Louisiana State University Press, 1958), p. 7.

8. *Congressional Record*, vol. 36 (4 March 1903), p. 3071. Also see Kyle, *Building of TVA*, p. 8.

9. Preston J. Hubbard, *Origins of the TVA* (Nashville: Vanderbilt University Press, 1961), pp. 27–28.

10. Virginia Vander Veer Hamilton, *Lister Hill* (Chapel Hill: University of North Carolina Press, 1987), p. 52.

11. Ibid.; Hubbard, *Origins of the TVA*, p. 140.

12. Hubbard, *Origins of the TVA*, pp. 292–93; Pritchett, *The TVA*, pp. 16–17; Herbert Hoover, Veto Message Relating to the Disposition of Muscle Shoals, Senate Doc. 321, 71st Cong., 3rd sess., 3 March 1931, pp. 1–8. Samuel Insull's vast utility network, based in Chicago, produced one-eighth of America's electrical power and operated in thirty-nine states. Intertwined companies bought stock from one another. Insull held thirty-five chairmanships and eighty-five directorships. The network began unraveling in 1931 and collapsed in 1932. Insull fled to Europe to escape arrest for fraud. (He was later tried and acquitted.) Insull's private utility empire aroused misgivings among the public in the 1930s and helped fuel support for TVA and other government efforts in the utility field.

13. *Congressional Record*, vol. 77, pt. 2 (22 April 1933), 73rd Cong., 1st sess., p. 2176.

14. Ibid.

15. Executive Order 6161, 8 June 1933; Hodge, *TVA*, pp. 48–49.

16. Paul Conkin, *The New Deal* (New York: Crowell, 1967), pp. 48–49; William Leuchtenburg, *Franklin D. Roosevelt and the New Deal 1932–1940* (New York: Harper & Row, 1963), pp. 54–55.

17. Conkin, *The New Deal*, p. 49. For further discussion of regional planners' thoughts on TVA, see Donald Davidson, "Where Regionalism and Sectionalism Meet," *Social Forces* 13 (1934): 25–31; Howard Odum, "A Case for Regional–National Social Planning," *Social Forces* 13 (1934): 17–21; Rupert Vance, "What of Submarginal Areas in Regional Planning?" *Social Forces* 12 (1934): 315–29; T. J. Woofter, "The Tennessee Valley Regional Plan," *Social Forces* 12 (1934): 329–38.

18. Pritchett, *The TVA*, pp. 27–29; Woofter, "The Tennessee Valley Regional Plan," pp. 330–31.

19. Pritchett, *The TVA*, pp. 3–5.

20. U.S. Congress, House Committee on Military Affairs, Report 48, 73rd Cong., 1st sess., 20 April 1933, pp. 17–18; Hodge, *TVA*, p. 34.

21. "Arthur Morgan Plans," *New York Times*, 6 August 1933; Arthur Morgan, "New Horizons in the Tennessee Valley," *New York Times*, 19 November 1934, Sunday supplement, p. 2.

22. Arthur Morgan, "Social Planning in the TVA," *New York Times*, 25 March 1933. Clippings of the Morgan article, along with many pro- and anti-TVA newspaper articles, have been compiled into a collection entitled "Pamphlets and Articles on the TVA," TVA Files, Knoxville, Tennessee.

23. "Social Planning in Mussolini's Italy," *New York Times*, 25 March 1933.

24. *New York Times*, 11 May 1934, 19 November 1934, 19 April 1936.

25. R. L. Duffus, "A Dream Takes Form on the Tennessee," *New York Times*, 19 April 1936.

26. *Chattanooga Times*, 11 August 1934.

27. *Americus Times Recorder*, 25 September 1934.

28. Criticism of TVA appeared in the newspapers of Oil City, Pennsylvania; Elkins, West Virginia; Pittsburgh, Pennsylvania; Vicksburg, Mississippi; and Wheeling, West Virginia, as well as the *Wall Street Journal, Hartford Courant, New York Sun, Washington Post, Christian Science Monitor*, and *Chicago Tribune*.

29. *Akron* (Ohio) *Beacon Journal*, 16 October 1934.

30. *New York Times*, 11 May 1934, 19 November 1934, 19 April 1936.

31. *Knoxville Journal*, 11 March 1933, 19 April 1933, 2 May 1933; *Knoxville News-Sentinel*, 18 April 1933, 11 April 1933.

32. *Knoxville News-Sentinel*, 7 May 1934.

33. James Hodges, "George Fort Milton," *Tennessee Historical Quarterly* (1977): 405; George Fort Milton, "A Consumer's View of the TVA," *Atlantic Monthly* 160 (1937): 656.

34. A series of surveys and reports done by the Regional Planning Department provided important statistical information. See "Economic and Social Characteristics of Six Tennessee Valley Reservoir Areas," 5 April 1940, TVA Files; David D. Lee, "Rural Democrats, Eastern Republicans, and Trade-Offs in Tennessee, 1922–1932," *East Tennessee Historical Society Publications*, no. 48 (1976), pp. 104–6; Daniel Schaffer, "TVA and Environment: Toward a Regional Plan for the Tennessee Valley," in *Tennessee Historical Quarterly* 43 (1984): 339. Also see Henry Shapiro, *Appalachia on Our Mind: The Southern Mountains and Mountaineers in the American Consciousness 1870–1920* (Chapel Hill: University of North Carolina Press, 1977).

35. Schaffer, "TVA and Environment," p. 339.

36. Ibid., pp. 340–41.

37. Ibid., p. 341.

38. Roosevelt, *Presidential Addresses*, 2: 459.

39. Lester Lamon, *Black Tennesseans 1900–1930* (Knoxville: University of Tennessee Press, 1977), p. 113. Also see John Stanfield, "The Sociohistorical Roots of White/Black Inequality in Urban Appalachia: Knoxville and East Tennessee," in *Blacks in Appalachia*, edited by William H. Turner and Edward J. Cabbell (Lexington: University of Kentucky Press, 1985), pp. 133–42.

40. Stanfield, "White/Black Inequality in Urban Appalachia," pp. 133–34; Edward J. Cabbell, "Black Invisibility and Racism in Appalachia: An Informal Survey," in Turner and Cabbell, *Blacks in Appalachia*, pp. 3–5.

41. Lamon, *Black Tennesseans*, pp. 38–40.

42. Burton G. Wilson, *The Knoxville Negro* (Knoxville: Thrent Printing Co., 1929), pp. 2–30; Joseph Cartwright, *The Triumph of Jim Crow* (Knoxville: University of Tennessee Press, 1976), pp. 223–53.

43. Lamon, *Black Tennesseans*, pp. 244–46; charter for the Knoxville branch of the NAACP, 1918, NAACP Papers, Library of Congress, Washington, D.C.

44. J. Herman Daves, "A Social Study of the Colored Population of Knoxville, Tennessee," Knoxville, 1926, pp. 1–26; Pickens quoted in Lamon, *Black Tennesseans*, pp. 257–60, 269, 272; Stanfield, "White/Black Inequality in Urban Appalachia," p. 138.

45. Gilbert Govan, *The Chattanooga County 1540–1976* (Knoxville: University of Tennessee Press, 1977), pp. 405–9; interview with George Key, president, Chattanooga branch of the NAACP, 20 August 1982.

46. National Urban League, "A Study of Economic and Cultural Activities of the Negro Population of Chattanooga," 1947, pp. 44–47, Chattanooga Public Library, Special Collections; interview with George Key; Mattie McMahon to Robert Baynall, 26 February 1923, NAACP Papers.

CHAPTER II

1. In the seven states of the Tennessee valley, laws passed in the 1880s and 1890s required separate schools for black and white children. Indeed, Tennessee in 1875 adopted the first "Jim Crow" law, and the rest of the South rapidly fell in line. In most areas of the South public accommodations and transportation were segregated according to race. Segregation was so absolute that separate Bibles were provided for blacks who appeared as witnesses in courts of law. As in life, so in death: there were even black and white cemeteries. See C. Vann Woodward, *The Strange Career of Jim Crow* (New York: Oxford University Press, 1974), pp. 67–109; John Hope Franklin, *From Slavery to Freedom* (New York: Knopf, 1967), passim.

2. Tennessee Valley Authority, *Employee Relationship Policy* (Knoxville: Tennessee Valley Authority, 1940) p. 4. The policy was amended in 1940 in some areas, but the 1934 wording on the issue of nondiscrimination was retained.

3. Leslie Fishel, Jr., "The Negro in the New Deal Era," in *The Negro in the Depression and War*, edited by Bernard Sternsher (Chicago: Quadrangle Books, 1969), p. 10. Also see Raymond Wolters, *Negroes and the Great Depression* (Westport, Conn.: Greenwood Press, 1970), pp. 46–57.

4. Gordon Clapp, "Comments on Statements in the National Emergency Council Report on Economic Conditions in the South," TVA Files, Knoxville, Tennessee, pp. 1, 2, 7; TVA, "Annual Report, 1933–1934," TVA Files, p. 48; TVA, "TVA's Employment of Negroes, 1933–1964," staff report, pp. 10–11, appendix A, tables 1, 2, TVA Files.

5. For a detailed discussion of discriminatory hiring practices, see Chapter III.

6. Gordon Clapp to Marguerite Owen, memorandum, 3 August 1939, TVA Files.

7. Ibid.

8. *New York Times*, 6 August 1938, 30 August 1938, 2 September 1938.

9. Clapp to Owen memorandum, 3 August 1939, TVA Files; interview with J. Max Bond, Washington, D.C., 29 May 1975; interview with J. Herman Daves, Knoxville, Tennessee, 4 February 1975, 21 March 1975; interview with Walter Goldston, Muscle Shoals, Alabama, 10 March 1975. All three men were employed in TVA during the 1930s. Bond (1933–1938) and Daves (1938–1963) were the highest-paid blacks in the Authority. Goldston was a labor relations counselor. All three felt excluded from policy decisions and were sensitive to their powerless position. John P. Davis, "Report of the Chief Social and Economic Problems of Negroes in the TVA," August 1935, p. 5, TVA Files.

10. Clapp, "Comments on Emergency Report," TVA Files.

11. Ibid.

12. Philip Selznick, *TVA and the Grass Roots* (New York: Harper & Row, 1966), pp. 69, 70.

13. Clarence Hodge, *The Tennessee Valley Authority* (Washington, D.C.: American University Press, 1938), p. 47.

14. Selznick, *Grass Roots*, p. 6; TVA, "Annual Report, 1933–1934," p. 16; Herman Pritchett, *The Tennessee Valley Authority: A Study in Public Administration* (Chapel Hill: University of North Carolina Press, 1943), p. 122.

15. Hodge, *TVA*, p. 96; Selznick, *Grass Roots*, pp. 195–96; interview with A. J. Grey, Knoxville, Tennessee, 6 March 1975. Mr. Grey was hired by TVA on 18 February 1935 as an assistant geographer in the Land Planning Division, and became the head of the Regional Planning Division. TVA organization charts: Chart No. 1, 6 October 1933; Chart No. 3, 18 September 1934; Chart No. 5, 1 September 1937; Chart No. 7, 1 November 1939, TVA Files; Pritchett, *The TVA*, pp. 170–74, 181–82.

16. Norman Wengert, "TVA, Symbol and Reality," *Journal of Politics* 13 (1951): 383, 378; also see William Leuchtenburg, *Franklin D. Roosevelt and the New Deal 1932–1940* (New York: Harper & Row, 1963), pp. 164–65; Earl S. Draper, "In TVA House," *Journal of Home Economics* 27 (1935): 632.

17. Thomas McCraw, *TVA and the Power Fight 1933–1939* (Philadelphia: J. B. Lippincott, 1971), pp. 111–21; Thomas McCraw, *Morgan vs. Lilienthal: The Feud Within the TVA* (Chicago: Loyola University Press, 1970), pp. 97–99, 92–93.

18. Roy Talbert, *Arthur Morgan of the TVA* (Jackson: University of Mississippi Press, 1987), pp. 37–38; Arthur Morgan, *The Making of the TVA* (Buffalo, N.Y.: Prometheus Books, 1974), pp. 80–84.

19. U.S. Congress, *Investigation of the TVA*, parts 1 and 2 (Washington, D.C.: Government Printing Office, 1939). For a detailed analysis of the NAACP's complaint before the TVA committee, see Chapter V.

20. Bachman to A. Morgan, 19 October 1933, TVA Files, quoted in Talbert, *Arthur Morgan*, p. 152.

21. Quoted in Pritchett, *The TVA*, p. 122. For a complete discussion of TVA and the problem of democratic planning, see Selznick, *Grass Roots*, pp. 3–16, 64–74.

22. Selznick, *Grass Roots*, pp. 134–37.

23. R. Brooks Taylor, chief of the Agricultural Processing Research Division, to John Farris, director of the Commerce Department, 27 July 1939, TVA Files; interview with J. Herman Daves, 4 February 1975; interview with J. Max Bond; TVA, "TVA's Employment of Negroes, 1933–1964," pp. 24–25, TVA Files; Selznick, *Grass Roots*, pp. 113ff. The first cooperative project involved testing paint at Tuskegee in 1939. An unsuccessful attempt was also made to establish cooperation with George Washington Carver's department at Tuskegee. The first cooperative effort on the scale of the white college projects was not begun until after 1960.

24. "Comments by Gordon Clapp to the Joint Congressional Committee on the Brief Filed by Mr. Charles H. Houston Concerning TVA and the Negro, 7/38," TVA Files; Floyd Reeves to Marguerite Owen, memorandum, 1 June 1934, TVA Files.

25. Interview with A. J. Grey; Al Snell, "Report of Reservoir Family Removal Activities," 28 August 1936, TVA Files. TVA was not alone in making direct payment to owners: the AAA also did so. Selznick, *Grass Roots*, pp. 138–41.

26. Virginia Vander Veer Hamilton, *Lister Hill* (Chapel Hill: University of North Carolina Press, 1987), pp. 211–23.

27. John Rankin to David Lilienthal, 29 May 1943, TVA Files. On 24 May 1943 the Mobile shipyard promoted twelve blacks to jobs as welders because of pressure from the Fair Employment Practices Committee. The next day white workers rioted, and more than twenty people were injured before an Army detachment restored order. There were similar though less violent reactions in other cities to the promotion of blacks. John Rankin led the protest against the FEPC, proclaiming that "this is the beginning of a communist dictatorship." See George Tindall, *The Emergence of the New South 1913–1945* (Baton Rouge: Louisiana State University Press, 1967), p. 715.

28. John Sparkman to David Lilienthal, 8 April 1943, TVA Files.

29. Rankin to Lilienthal, 29 May 1943, TVA Files.

30. David Lilienthal to John Sparkman, 23 April 1943, TVA Files. Black police officers were frequently used in all-black neighborhoods. Custom prevented them from arresting whites.

31. David Lilienthal to John Rankin, 19 May 1943, TVA Files.

32. David Lilienthal, *The Journals of David Lilienthal*, vol. 1: *The TVA Years, 1939–1945* (New York: Harper & Row, 1964), p. 629; TVA, "TVA's Employment of Negroes, 1933–1964," appendix list B; interview with Alton Flagg, Knoxville, Tennessee, 4 March 1975.

33. John P. Davis and Charles Houston conducted a month-long investigation in 1934 and published the results in *Crisis* magazine. The second NAACP-sponsored investigation was conducted in 1935 by John P. Davis and resulted in a report on the chief social and economic problems of Negroes in the TVA. The final investigation was conducted in 1938 to gather information to present before the Joint Committee on the Investigation of the Tennessee Valley Authority. In addition, Robert Weaver's investigation of TVA was sponsored by the Authority's board of directors.

34. Robert Weaver to Arthur Morgan, 13 November 1935, pp. 1–6, TVA Files; J. Max Bond, "Report on Negro Intern Training Plan," October 1936, TVA Files; Lloyd Huntington to Gordon Clapp, 4 October 1937, "Employment of Negroes at Hiwassee Dam," TVA Files.

35. TVA, "TVA's Employment of Negroes, 1933–1964," p. 14; Lloyd Huntington to Gordon Clapp, 4 October 1937, TVA Files; Lloyd Huntington to Gordon Clapp, 5 January 1938, TVA Files.

36. NAACP, *Annual Report* 28 (1938): 13–14.

37. Daisy Lampkin to Roy Wilkins, 21 February 1942, NAACP Papers, Library of Congress, Washington, D.C.

38. Pritchett, *The TVA*, pp. 147–48.

39. Ibid., pp. 153, 155–56.

40. Ibid., p. 151; Hodge, *TVA*, pp. 43–44; Selznick, *Grass Roots*, p. 92.

41. Selznick, *Grass Roots*, p. 30.

42. Pritchett, *The TVA*, p. 165.

43. Ibid., pp. 160–65; Gordon Clapp, *The TVA: An Approach to the Develop-*

ment of a Region (Chicago: University of Chicago Press, 1955), pp. viii, ix.

44. Harcourt A. Morgan, "TVA Policy as Philosophy," in Harcourt A. Morgan Papers, University of Tennessee, Knoxville.

45. Selznick, *Grass Roots*, pp. 92–94; interview, L. Frank and J. Davis with H. A. Morgan, 11, 13, 14 October 1944, in Knoxville, Tennessee, Rockefeller Foundation Archives, Pocantico Hills, N.Y.

46. John P. Davis to Arthur Morgan, 2 May 1935, TVA Files; Arthur Morgan to John P. Davis, 31 May 1935, TVA Files. No blacks lived in Norris during the period of TVA control, which lasted until 1948.

47. Arthur Morgan to Harold Ickes, 10 October 1935, TVA Files; Robert Weaver to Arthur Morgan, 12 November 1935, TVA Files.

48. U.S. Congress, Joint Committee on the Investigation of the Tennessee Valley Authority, *Hearings Before the Joint Committee on the Investigation of the Tennessee Valley Authority*, 75th Cong., 3rd sess., 1938, part 4, pp. 6169–73.

49. Talbert, *Arthur Morgan*, pp. 60–61. Talbert maintains that although this attitude is plainly racist, it was not out of line with the thinking of Morgan's contemporaries. Many social scientists and agency heads—including Will Alexander, Franz Boas, and Howard Odum—had changed their thinking by the 1930s.

50. Arthur Morgan, "On the Future of the Colored Race," address, Knoxville College, 12 June 1934, p. 4, TVA Files.

51. Ibid.

52. See for example Arthur Morgan to John P. Davis, 31 May 1935, TVA Files.

53. Arthur Morgan, "Bench Marks in the Tennessee Valley," *Survey Graphic* 13 (1934): 551.

54. Morgan, *Making of the TVA*, pp. 74–76.

55. For a more detailed analysis of Howard Odum's racial views in the 1920s and 1930s, see Nancy Grant, "Howard Odum: Region and Racism," *Research in Social Policy* (1989).

56. Ibid.

57. Harcourt A. Morgan, "Notes," 9 October 1941, H. A. Morgan Papers.

58. Harcourt A. Morgan, "Considerations to Be Given in Carrying Out Objectives of TVA," 20 April 1939, H. A. Morgan Papers. Odum wrote in 1910 that there were such fundamental differences between the races in traits, behavior patterns, and learning capabilities that segregation and an inferior status for blacks must be permanent. See Howard Odum, *Social and Mental Traits of the Negro* (New York: Columbia University Press, 1910), p. 47. Odum reversed himself on inherent differences by 1936, noting that social scientists had made an error in assuming that "races were inherently different rather than group products of differentials due to the cumulative power of regional and cultural conditioning." See Howard Odum, *Southern Regions of the United States* (Chapel Hill: University of North Carolina Press, 1936), pp. 479–83, 486–87.

59. Pritchett, *The TVA*, pp. 150–51.

60. David Lilienthal to Archibald MacLeish, director, Office of Facts and Fig-

ures, 19 May 1942, TVA Files; Gordon Clapp to George Gant, memorandum, 21 May 1942, TVA Files; David Lilienthal to George Johnson, assistant executive secretary, FEPC, 11 May 1942, TVA Files.

61. Lilienthal to Johnson, 11 May 1942, TVA Files.

62. David Lilienthal, *TVA: Democracy on the March* (New York: Harper & Row, 1944), p. 5.

63. Lilienthal, *The TVA Years*, pp. 446–47.

64. Ibid., p. 516.

65. Ibid.

66. Gordon Clapp to W. J. Hayes, Board–Staff Conference on Negro Problems, memorandum, 4 October 1938, TVA Files; John Blandford, general manager, to board of directors, memorandum, 15 May 1939, TVA Files.

67. Clapp to Hayes, 4 October 1938, TVA Files.

CHAPTER III

1. David Lilienthal, *TVA: Democracy on the March* (New York: Harper & Row, 1944), pp. 62–65.

2. For a glowing if folksy description of the benefits of TVA, see R. L. Duffus, *The Valley and Its People* (New York: Knopf, 1944), pp. 125–36. Also see Gordon Clapp, *The TVA: An Approach to the Development of a Region* (Chicago: University of Chicago Press, 1955), passim. For critical accounts see Michael McDonald and John Muldowny, *TVA and the Dispossessed* (Knoxville: University of Tennessee Press, 1982) and William U. Chandler, *The Myth of TVA: Conservation and Development in the Tennessee Valley, 1933–1983* (Cambridge, Mass.: Ballinger, 1984), pp. 43–63.

3. Lilienthal, *Democracy on the March*, pp. 62–65.

4. Harry Case, "Personnel Administration," in *TVA: The First Twenty Years*, edited by Roscoe C. Martin (Knoxville: University of Tennessee Press and University of Alabama Press, 1956), pp. 55–56. The TVA was exempt from civil service rules and could run its personnel department on an independent basis.

5. Case, "Personnel Administration," pp. 55–56; interview with A. J. Waldrep, former general foreman, Wheeler Dam, Knoxville, Tennessee, 20 February 1975; interview with Walter Goldston, Muscle Shoals, Alabama, 10 March 1975; interviews with J. Herman Daves, Knoxville, Tennessee, 4 February and 21 March 1975; Herman Pritchett, *The Tennessee Valley Authority: A Study in Public Administration* (Chapel Hill: University of North Carolina Press, 1943), pp. 294–96.

6. Charles Houston, "Proposed Testimony Before Joint Committee, August 17, 1938," abstract, TVA Files, Knoxville, Tennessee; interview with Alton Flagg, Knoxville, Tennessee, 4 March 1975.

7. Tennessee Valley Authority, *Employee Relationship Policy* (Knoxville, Tennessee Valley Authority, 1940), par. 16, p. 7; interview with Walter Goldston.

8. Testimony of Wallace Butler and James Lee Hawkins Before the TVA

Chickamauga Investigating Committee, 7 September 1938, pp. 7–75, NAACP Papers, Library of Congress, Washington, D.C.; also in TVA Files, Knoxville.

9. Gordon Clapp, "Report on the Hearings at Chickamauga Dam Site, Supplementary General Conclusions," 17 October 1938, pp. 27–28, TVA Files.

10. Ibid.; "Fair Employment in TVA," supervisory training report, 1957, TVA Files; interviews with J. Herman Daves, 4 February and 21 March 1975; interview with J. Max Bond, Washington, D.C., 29 May 1975.

11. John P. Davis, "Report of the Chief Social and Economic Problems of Negroes in the TVA," 1935, TVA Files; Gordon Clapp, "Analysis of the Report of the Chief Social and Economic Problems of Negroes in the TVA by John P. Davis," n.d., section on employment, TVA Files. In the margins of the analysis Clapp wrote: "Davis misinterpreting of conversation with TVA officials. . . . Do not know whether Mr. Neely is quoted correctly." In an interview with Davis, Johnson denied advising TVA to exclude blacks from Norris for any reason.

12. Ibid.

13. G. L. Jensen, personnel representative for Norris Dam, to C. K. Rickey, General Personnel Department, Knoxville, Memorandum, 11 July 1936, TVA Files.

14. Ibid.

15. Pritchett, *The TVA*, pp. 35–36.

16. Clapp, "Analysis," p. 1, TVA Files.

17. Ibid.

18. Ibid., section on employment.

19. Ibid., sections on employment and analysis.

20. Ibid. Clapp contended that a few whites were classified as flagmen and paid 60 cents an hour.

21. Anonymous manuscript, n.d., p. 19, TVA Files. This document was clearly written by a black TVA employee (working in the personnel division) very much disturbed by the evidence of racial discrimination.

22. TVA, "TVA's Employment of Negroes, 1933–1964," staff report, p. 12, TVA Files.

23. Clapp, "Analysis," section on employment.

24. The percentage of blacks dropped from 16.6 percent on 15 June 1935 to 6.4 percent on 15 October 1935.

25. Davis, "Report," 1935.

26. Anonymous manuscript, p. 20; interview with Walter Goldston.

27. Anonymous manuscript, p. 20.

28. Birdius Browne and W. M. Tyler, report, October 1935, TVA Files.

29. Ibid.

30. Robert Weaver to Arthur Morgan, 12 November 1935, pp. 1–5, TVA Files; interview with J. Max Bond. According to Bond, the railroad tracks were used with enough frequency to present danger to children playing near the tracks. The fact that the houses had been on even swampier ground offered little consolation to the group and only hastened the deterioration of the housing.

31. Ibid.

32. Davis, "Report"; Clapp, "Analysis," section on housing; interview with J. Max Bond.

33. Russell Parker, "The Black Community in a Company Town: Alcoa, Tennessee, 1919–1939," *Tennessee Historical Quarterly* 37 (1978): 204–7.

34. Quoted in Charles Johnson and Charles Jackson, *City Behind a Fence: Oak Ridge, Tennessee, 1942–1948* (Knoxville: University of Tennessee Press, 1981), pp. 112–17.

35. J. N. Allen, assistant coordinator, to John Blandford, general manager, memorandum, 19 January 1937, p. 7, TVA Files.

36. Ibid.

37. Gordon Clapp to C. A. Bock, assistant chief engineer, memorandum, 28 November 1936, TVA Files.

38. J. Max Bond to Gordon Clapp, 10 November 1936, TVA Files; Clapp to Bock, 28 November 1936, TVA Files.

39. Clapp to Bock, 28 November 1936. The higher mortality from tuberculosis among blacks was due to environmental rather than biological factors.

40. Gordon Clapp to John Blandford, memorandum, 4 March 1937, TVA Files.

41. Gordon Clapp to John Blandford, memorandum, 5 May 1938, TVA Files.

42. George K. Leonard to T. B. Parker, chief engineer, memorandum, 20 June 1942, TVA Files.

43. Lloyd Huntington to Gordon Clapp, memorandum, 4 October 1937, TVA Files.

44. Ibid.

45. U. S. Congress, Joint Committee on the Investigation of the Tennessee Valley Authority, *Hearings Before the Joint Committee on the Investigation of the Tennessee Valley Authority*, 75th Cong., 3rd sess., 1938, part 6: Testimony of Charles Houston, legal counsel, NAACP, pp. 2360–67; interview with A. J. Waldrep; interview with Joseph C. Neergard, Knoxville, Tennessee, 20 February 1975.

46. W. L. McDavid, black personnel officer, "Camp Conditions for Negroes," TVA Files; R. H. Boyd to C. K. Rickey, memorandum, 27 October 1936, TVA Files.

47. J. Herman Daves, supervisor of Negro training, "Data on Negro Employment, Chickamauga Dam," 31 December 1938, TVA Files. The report was criticized by TVA officials as incomplete and misleading because the percentage of labor turnover and the payroll percentage were not given. These factors tended to offset the higher percentage of blacks in the workforce.

48. For more detail concerning the role of the NAACP and the Joint Committee, see Chapter V.

49. Testimony of Wallace Butler and James Simpson Before the TVA Chickamauga Investigating Committee, 7 September 1938, NAACP Papers and TVA Files.

50. Testimony of George Granville and Winee Bond, ibid.

51. Clapp, "Report on Hearings at Chickamauga Dam"; interview with Ralph Martin, former personnel officer, Knoxville, Tennessee, 14 February 1975.

52. Gordon Clapp to Charles Houston, 20 January 1939, TVA Files.

53. E. B. Schultz to George Gant, acting general manager, memorandum, 16 August 1938, TVA Files; George Gant to Herbert Hudson, 18 August 1938, TVA Files.

54. Interview with Walter Goldston. Mr. Goldston contends that although there were racial incidents at Kentucky, blacks were treated better than at previous projects.

55. George Gant to Lloyd Huntington, 9 February 1942, TVA Files.

56. T. L. Brown to George K. Leonard, memorandum, 19 June 1942, TVA Files; George Gant to Lawrence Cramer, 8 May 1942, TVA Files.

57. Interview with Ralph Martin. Mr. Martin was the black recreational officer at Fontana Dam during the racial difficulties.

58. Gordon Clapp to T. B. Parker, memorandum, 14 July 1942, TVA Files.

59. Malcolm Little to Ed Campbell, 12 June 1943, TVA Files; W. N. Rogers to George Slover, 17 July 1942, TVA Files; interview with Ralph Martin; interview with J. Herman Daves, 21 March 1975.

60. Interview with Ralph Martin; interview with Henry Cain, Muscle Shoals, Alabama, 10 March 1975.

61. George Slover to George Gant, 27 September 1943, TVA Files. In addition, TVA experienced competition from Kaiser Shipyards near Chattanooga, which offered more pay and more agreeable working and living conditions.

62. "Number White and Negro Employed by Pay Status," statistical table I, 31 July 1939, TVA Files.

63. Interview with Walter Goldston; E. B. Schultz to George Slover, memorandum, 19 May 1936, TVA Files.

64. Louis McDade to George Benjamin, 17 February 1936, TVA Files.

65. Anonymous TVA employee (personnel officer) to Roy Wilkins, 1942, NAACP Files.

66. Anonymous manuscript, pp. 12–16.

67. Jack Comer, president of AFGE Lodge 136, to Harcourt A. Morgan, 24 August 1939, TVA Files.

68. John Blandford, general manager, to Mary Pirtle, secretary, AFGE Lodge 136, 20 September 1939, TVA Files.

69. Interview with B. A. Ward, Knoxville, Tennessee, 6 March 1975. Mr. Ward worked for many years as a supervisor of the mail and messenger service. Interview with Alton Flagg. Mr. Flagg was one of the first black clerks hired by TVA. He later worked as a grievance officer in the Equal Employment Opportunity Office.

70. General Program Committee, Mail and Messenger Unit, to Gordon Clapp, 16 June 1942, TVA Files; interview with B. A. Ward.

71. J. Herman Daves to Arthur S. Jandrey, director of personnel, memoran-

dum, 14 February 1941, TVA Files; interview with Alton Flagg; interview with B. A. Ward.

72. Nancy Grant, "Equal Employment Opportunity in TVA 1955–1974," 1975, TVA Files. The system-wide desegregation of TVA buildings did not take place until 1957.

73. Lloyd Huntington, chairman of the Race Relations Committee of TVA, to Arthur S. Jandrey, memorandum, 27 October 1939, TVA Files.

74. "Negro Employment in the TVA," staff memorandum, 23 January 1941, TVA Files.

75. Ibid.

76. "Availability of Negro Skilled Workers," 28 May 1942, TVA Files. The seven cities were Memphis, Atlanta, Knoxville, Nashville, Birmingham, Louisville, and Chattanooga.

77. "Negro Skilled Workers," staff memorandum, 10 November 1941, TVA Files.

78. Summary of Personnel Department meeting, 26 June 1942, TVA Files.

79. Lloyd Huntington to Arthur S. Jandrey, memorandum, 24 October 1940, TVA Files.

80. Rollins Winslow to "J. M.," memorandum, n.d. [1936], NAACP Papers.

81. TVA, "TVA's Employment of Negroes, 1933–1964," p. 9.

82. B. B. Evans, Knoxville College, to Roy Wilkins, 14 April 1942, NAACP Papers.

83. B. B. Evans to Roy Wilkins, 12 May 1942, NAACP Papers.

84. George Slover to George Gant, memorandum, 27 September 1943, TVA Files.

85. Michael L. Brookshire and Michael D. Rodgers, *Collective Bargaining in Public Employment* (Lexington, Mass.: Lexington Books, 1977), p. 23; "Agreement Between Tennessee Valley Trades and Labor Council and the Tennessee Valley Authority," effective 6 August 1940, pp. 2–11, TVA Files. The agreement was subsequently revised in 1951 and 1964 to include nondiscrimination provisions.

86. Brookshire and Rodgers, *Collective Bargaining*, p. 23.

87. A. Philip Randolph, "The Trade Union Movement and the Negro," *Journal of Negro Education* 5 (1936): 54–58.

88. George Gant to Lawrence Cramer, 5 December 1941, p. 5, TVA Files.

89. A. R. Graves, NAACP Tri-Cities Branch, to Arthur Miller, Department of Chemical Engineering, 8 June 1939, NAACP Files; Arthur Miller to A. R. Graves, n.d., NAACP Papers.

90. Malcolm Little to George Gant, memorandum, 9 February 1943, TVA Files.

91. Arthur S. Jandrey to S. E. Roper, president of the Tennessee Valley Trades and Labor Council, 18 August 1941, TVA Files; J. Herman Daves to Malcolm Little, memorandum, 8 May 1942, TVA Files.

92. Comer to Harcourt Morgan, 24 August 1939.

93. George Jackson, International Brotherhood of Electrical Workers, Local 558, to Gordon Clapp, 11 September 1939, TVA Files; Gordon Clapp to George Jackson, 20 September 1939, TVA Files.

94. Anonymous manuscript, p. 11.

95. O. Lowery, business agent, Brotherhood of Carpenters and Joiners, to TVA, 2 October 1941, TVA Files.

96. James Hampton, vice-president, Alabama State Federation of Labor, to Arthur S. Jandrey, 27 March 1941, TVA Files; George Gant to James Hampton, 12 April 1941, TVA Files. The Hod Carriers Union was the official representative of all unionized black craft employees on the Tennessee Valley Trades and Labor Council.

97. Hod Carriers Local 929, "Conference on Interracial Relations Within the TVA," 15 October 1937, NAACP Papers; D. W. Trice, International Hod Carriers Union, to J. Max Bond, n.d., TVA Files; John Turner, International Hod Carriers Union, to C. N. Freedman, Tennessee Valley Trades and Labor Council, 20 June 1938, TVA Files; interview with Walter Goldston.

98. Harry Case, *Personnel Policy in a Public Agency* (New York: Harper & Row, 1955), p. 21; interviews with J. Max Bond and J. Herman Daves; interview with A. J. Grey, Knoxville, Tennessee, 6 March 1975. Of the women employed by the federal government during 1939, 73 percent were clerical workers, 14 percent were in subprofessional jobs (such as nurses and home-management agents), 12 percent were in custodial or mechanical work, and only 1.5 percent were professionals (mostly home economists or librarians). The highest-ranked woman in TVA during the 1940s, 1950s, and 1960s was Marguerite Owen, director of TVA's Washington office and the agency's chief lobbyist. The Civil Service allowed sex-specific requests for job openings. See U.S. Department of Labor, Women's Bureau, "Employment of Women in the Federal Government 1923–1939," *Bulletin of the Women's Bureau*, no. 182 (1941): 19, 30–32. Before the FEPC discouraged the practice, the Civil Service allowed racially specific requests.

99. The only black professional in TVA between 1938 and 1945 was J. Herman Daves, supervisor of Negro training. The first black professional hired for a position unrelated to race was a research chemist hired in 1945.

CHAPTER IV

1. Franklin D. Roosevelt, Message to Congress on Muscle Shoals Development, House Doc. 15, 73rd Cong., 1st sess., 1933; *Congressional Record*, vol. 77, pt. 2, 73rd Cong., 1st sess., 1933.

2. Herman Pritchett, *The Tennessee Valley Authority: A Study in Public Administration* (Chapel Hill: University of North Carolina Press, 1943), pp. 170–73; "Annual Report of the TVA, 1935," TVA Files, Knoxville, Tennessee, pp. 34–43.

3. Pritchett, *The TVA*, pp. 181–84; Clarence Hodge, *The Tennessee Valley Authority* (Washington, D.C.: American University Press, 1938), pp. 81–109, 132–33.

4. Ibid.; David Lilienthal, *The Journals of David Lilienthal*, vol. 1: *The TVA Years* (New York: Harper & Row, 1964), pp. 359–61, 493; also see Michael McDonald and John Muldowny, *TVA and the Dispossessed* (Knoxville: University of Tennessee Press, 1982), pp. 184–87. Ickes, for his part, claimed partial credit for TVA successes, "and while the main credit must gratefully go to that fine elder statesman, George W. Norris, the records will show that it was PWA encouragement—encouragement in the form of the coin of the realm—that gave it not only the means but the opportunity to expand into the vitally important project that it is." Harold Ickes, *Autobiography of a Curmudgeon* (New York: Reynal and Hitchcock, 1943), p. 293.

5. R. Carnahan to L. N. Allen, "Request for Official Consideration of Population Adjustment Problems," memorandum, 11 August 1937, TVA Files.

6. Ibid.

7. Ibid.

8. Ibid.

9. Al Snell, "Report of Reservoir Family Removal Activities," 28 August 1936, TVA Files.

10. McDonald and Muldowny, *TVA and the Dispossessed*, pp. 170–72; this work contains a detailed and critical analysis of the reservoir removal project at Norris, Tennessee.

11. Birdius Browne transferred from the training staff to the relocation section on 30 October 1935. He stayed with relocation until 1937.

12. Department of Psychology, University of Alabama, "A Comprehensive Survey of the Behavior Patterns of the People of a Single Rural Community," 11 May 1934, sponsored by the Civil Works Administration (CWA) and TVA, TVA Files.

13. Ibid. The average pay in the CWA was fifteen dollars a week. William Leuchtenburg, *Franklin D. Roosevelt and the New Deal 1932–1940* (New York: Harper & Row, 1963), p. 124.

14. O. E. Graves to C. A. Towne, 19 October 1935, TVA Files; Tracy Augur to C. A. Towne, 1935, TVA Files.

15. Walter Arrants, Reservoir Property Management, to Dr. [n.a.] Evan, administrative assistant, Farm Security Administration, 21 October 1938, TVA Files.

16. W. M. Chenault to Tracy Augur, 25 June 1934, TVA Files. For further information on the career of George Bridgeforth at Tuskegee Institute and his stormy relationship with George Washington Carver, see Linda O. McMurry, *George Washington Carver* (New York: Oxford University Press, 1981), pp. 58–63.

17. George Bridgeforth to Tracy Augur, 12 May 1934, TVA Files.

18. W. M. Chenault to Tracy Augur, 25 June 1934, TVA Files; Tracy Augur to W. M. Chenault, 30 June 1934, TVA Files; George Bridgeforth to Harcourt A. Morgan, 7 June 1933, TVA Files; George Bridgeforth to Tracy Augur, 17 July 1934, TVA Files; Tracy Augur to George Bridgeforth, 21 July 1934, TVA Files.

19. Nord David to Tracy Augur, report, 21 August 1934, p. 9, TVA Files.

20. Ibid.

21. John Williams, assistant superintendent, Reservoir Clearance, to Isaac

Bridgeforth, September 1934, TVA Files; R. S. Alfrod, Reservoir Clearance, to Isaac Bridgeforth, 29 March 1934, TVA Files; Pat Miller to George Bridgeforth, 10 August 1934, TVA Files.

22. George Bridgeforth to H. A. Powers, TVA agronomist, 26 February 1935, TVA Files; H. A. Powers to George Bridgeforth, 15 March 1935, TVA Files.

23. George Bridgeforth to Pat Miller, 3 August 1935, TVA files; Pat Miller to George Bridgeforth, 27 August 1935, TVA Files.

24. Arthur Morgan to Stephen Early, assistant secretary to the president, 3 July 1935, TVA Files.

25. [N.a.] Olson to R. Carnahan, 11 September 1936, TVA Files.

26. John Snyder, director, Land Acquisition, to John Sparkman, 1936, TVA Files. One regional planner recommended that George Bridgeforth not receive any more replies from TVA, since they would only encourage him to create more problems.

27. John Neely to L. N. Allen, memorandum, 30 August 1937, TVA Files.

28. R. Carnahan, Reservoir Family Renewal Section, to Al Snell, memorandum, 16 June 1936, TVA Files.

29. Ibid.; R. Carnahan to Al Snell, report, 23 June 1936, TVA Files. One planner in the report stated, "The only question in my mind that is really a serious question is the attitude of the white people near this location, and the likelihood of their misinterpreting a lot of noise and hilarity for undesirable behavior."

30. Dorothy Barber to Al Snell, 2 June 1938, TVA Files.

31. Interview with A. J. Grey, Knoxville, Tennessee, 6 March 1975.

32. Ibid. The black communities corresponded with TVA over the following periods: Orrsville, 1936; Riverton, 1936–1937; Kirbytown, 1938; Beulah, 1933–1939; see McDonald and Muldowny, *TVA and the Dispossessed*, pp. 155–94.

33. "Proposed Ordinance for the Zoning of the City of Guntersville," 12 December 1938, TVA Files.

34. There were several versions of the ordinance. The most complete was passed on 12 December 1938.

35. D. A. Johnson to C. A. Towne, memorandum, 9 September 1938, TVA Files; H. L. Menhinick to C. A. Towne, 2 September 1938, TVA Files.

36. D. A. Johnson to A. L. Thomas and Charles Edwards, 1 March 1939, TVA Files.

37. Charles Edwards to D. A. Johnson, 1 March 1939, TVA Files.

38. Lawrence Durish, memorandum, n.d. [1939], TVA Files.

39. James Laurence Fly, TVA counsel, to Earl S. Draper, memorandum, 16 December 1938, TVA Files.

40. Charles Edwards to David Gee, TVA engineer, 17 March 1939, TVA Files.

41. John Blandford, general manager, to Charles Houston, NAACP legal counsel, 7 July 1938, TVA Files.

42. L. N. Allen to N. A. Henderson, chairman, Knoxville Civic Committee, 17 January 1939, TVA Files.

43. Earl S. Draper, director, Department of Regional Planning Studies, report, 20 January 1938, p. 3, TVA Files.

44. Ibid.

45. Earl S. Draper to John Blandford, n.d., p. 4, TVA Files.

46. Gordon Clapp to Charles Houston, first draft of a letter, 5 July 1940, TVA Files; Lloyd Huntington to Gordon Clapp, 8 August 1938, TVA Files; Robert Hines to C. A. Towne, 5 July 1940, TVA Files.

47. TVA contributed $3,000; the National Park Service, $315,000; the state of Tennessee, $20,000.

48. C. C. Crossman to H. L. Menhinick, memorandum, 3 October 1939, TVA Files; National Urban League, "A Study of Economic and Cultural Activities of the Negro Population of Chattanooga," 1947, pp. 55–57, Chattanooga Public Library, Special Collections.

49. H. H. Wilderson to H. L. Menhinick, memorandum, 14 March 1940, TVA Files; Department of Regional Studies, "The Proposed North Alabama State Park for Negroes," 26 August 1940, appendix D, p. 3, TVA Files.

50. Department of Regional Studies, "Recreational Uses and Development of TVA Property," 3 January 1940, pp. 45–48, TVA Files.

51. Lloyd Huntington to Gordon Clapp, 8 August 1938, p. 5, TVA Files.

52. Anonymous, "The School of Norris, Tennessee," *The School Executive* (October 1935), p. 55.

53. Ibid.

54. J. W. Bradmer, town manager of Norris, to Maurice Seay, 14 July 1936, TVA Files; Ira N. Chiles to W. J. McGlothlin, memorandum, 1 November 1943, TVA Files; Mildred Kranock to John Jennings, Tennessee House of Representatives, 21 February 1946, TVA Files; Clapp to Jennings, 3 April 1946, TVA Files.

55. "Notice to Residents of Villages," 1, 2, 19 February 1941, TVA Files; Frank Grove, Alabama Education Association, to Virginia James, principal of Wilson School, 8 April 1941, TVA Files; Arthur S. Jandrey to Gordon Clapp, memorandum, 27 January 1941, TVA Files.

56. Mattie L. Gilchrist, "A Description of School for Negroes at Joe Wheeler Dam," July 1936, pp. 3–6, TVA Files.

57. Ibid. In 1905, two Frenchmen, Alfred Binet and Theophile Simon, developed the first "intelligence test" in order to detect mentally deficient children in the French public schools. The test was subsequently used to test black and white children in the American public schools and to screen out "feeble-minded" immigrants arriving in the United States. In 1916, the test was revised and standardized for American society by Lewis Terman of Stanford University. This Stanford-Binet test was the popular and accepted measure of intelligence during the 1930s and 1940s. TVA's use of the older French test reveals either a lack of knowledge or acceptance of the newer, though still questionable, American test. For further discussion of intelligence testing see Vincent Franklin, "Black Social Scientists and the Mental Testing Movement, 1920–1940," *Journal of Black Psychology* (1980);

Clarence Karier, ed., *Shaping the American Educational State, 1900 to the Present* (New York: Free Press, 1975).

58. *The Kentucky Project* (Washington: Government Printing Office, 1950), pp. 279–81.

59. McGlothlin to Campbell, memorandum, 4 October 1943, TVA Files.

60. Contract, Board of Education of Rhea County, Tennessee, and TVA, 28 August 1943, TVA Files; contract, City Board of Education of Benton, Kentucky, and TVA, 5 July 1941, TVA Files; contract, City Board of Education, Sheffield, Alabama, and TVA, 21 September 1942, TVA Files.

61. L. N. Allen to John Blandford, general manager, memorandum, 19 January 1937, p. 7, TVA Files; Gordon Clapp, director of personnel, to C. A. Bock, memorandum, 28 November 1936, TVA Files.

62. Contracts, Benton–TVA, Rhea County–TVA, Sheffield–TVA, TVA Files; McGlothlin to Campbell, memorandum, 4 October 1943, TVA Files; Clapp to Jennings, 3 April 1946, TVA Files.

63. "Present Status of Employee Training for Negroes," 1942, pp. 1–3, TVA Files. Whites had classes in chemistry, foreman leadership training, and higher mathematics, as well as all the skilled trades.

64. Malcolm Little to Ed Campbell, 4 February 1942, TVA Files; J. Max Bond to [n.a.] Drake, president, Alabama A&M, 14 January 1935, TVA Files; quotation from J. Max Bond, "The Educational Programs for Negroes in the TVA," *Journal of Negro Education* 6 (1937): 151, 147; interview with J. Max Bond, Washington, D.C., 29 May 1975.

65. J. Max Bond, "Educational Programs," p. 151; interview with J. Max Bond.

66. *Chattanooga Times*, 15 March 1938; "People's College," pamphlet, n.p., pp. 7–9, Chattanooga Public Library Special Collections.

67. See for example C. L. Rahey, director of employment, to Dr. W. J. Hale, president, Tennessee A&I College, Nashville, 11 June 1934, TVA Files.

68. J. Max Bond to G. L. Washington, director of mechanical industries, Tuskegee Institute, 19 February 1935, TVA Files.

69. Tennessee Valley Authority, announcement, 23 October 1934, TVA Files; Ralph Martin to Charles Johnson, 27 April 1938, TVA Files.

70. Malcolm Little to Charles Johnson, 8 November 1937, TVA Files.

71. Floyd Reeves to Harold Smith, director of summer quarter, Fisk University, 7 June 1934, TVA Files.

72. Harvey Vaughn to Arthur Jackson, memorandum, 5 April 1934, TVA Files; Al Snell to M. Slayden, memorandum, 12 March 1936, TVA Files; M. Slayden to R. Carnahan, memorandum, 11 May 1937, TVA Files.

73. R. Brooks Taylor, chief of the Agricultural Processing Research Division, to John P. Ferris, director of the Commerce Department, TVA, memorandum, 27 July 1939, TVA Files.

74. L. Campbell, executive secretary to Arthur Morgan, to Ernest Seeman, Duke University, 12 February 1934, TVA Files.

75. Ernest Seeman to L. Campbell, 27 March 1934, TVA Files; Ernest Seeman to L. Campbell, 31 March 1934, TVA Files. Considerable controversy surrounds the scientific contribution of George Washington Carver. One writer maintains that Carver's reputation "depended less on [his] supposed achievements than on his psychological and social utility to both whites and blacks," and that Carver produced no original work and refused to keep proper records of his experiments so that future researchers could attempt to replicate them. This writer does not mention the possible reasons for Carver's refusal to document experiments—for example, the legitimate fear of losing credit for discoveries—nor does he question the possibly biased assessments of Carver's work by his white contemporaries. See Barry Mackintosh, "George Washington Carver: The Making of a Myth," *Journal of Southern History* 42 (1976): 509–28. For a more balanced account of the legend and the man, see McMurry, *Carver*, pp. 256–89.

76. Contract, Tuskegee Institute and the Tennessee Valley Authority, October 1939, TVA Files.

77. Contract, Tuskegee Institute and the Tennessee Valley Authority, July 1940, TVA Files. Control over inventions and research is not an unusual condition in cooperative research projects with government agencies.

78. TVA, "TVA's Employment of Negroes 1933–1964," staff report, p. 24, TVA Files.

79. J. R. Otis, Tuskegee Institute, to Department of Agriculture, 12 November 1935, TVA Files; George Rommel to M. J. Funchese, director, Alabama Experimental Station, 12 November 1935, TVA Files; H. A. Powers, farm management supervisor, to J. R. Otis, December 1935, TVA Files. TVA was criticized for its decision to use phosphate fertilizer instead of the less expensive and easier-to-use nitrates. In addition, poor farmers could only use nitrates, because phosphates required sophisticated farming methods involving crop rotation and nitrogen mixing. Philip Selznick, *TVA and the Grass Roots* (New York: Harper & Row, 1966), pp. 98–99.

80. Selznick, *Grass Roots*, pp. 110–13.

81. Barton Morgan and G. A. Works, *The Land Grant Colleges: Staff Study No. 10, Advisory Committee on Education* (Washington, D.C.: Government Printing Office, 1939), p. 101, cited by Selznick, *Grass Roots*, pp. 112–13.

82. The debate over the extent to which TVA contributed to the economic growth of the Tennessee Valley region has been a long and strident one. A relatively recent study maintains that per capita income growth in surrounding non-TVA areas equaled or exceeded that in the TVA region, although incomes were equal in 1933. See William U. Chandler, *The Myth of TVA: Conservation and Development in the Tennessee Valley, 1933–1983* (Cambridge, Mass.: Ballinger, 1984), pp. 6–8, 43–63.

83. Robert Howes to C. A. Towne, 23 July 1940, TVA Files.

1. TVA, "TVA's Employment of Negroes, 1933–1964," staff report, p. 14, TVA Files, Knoxville, Tennessee.

2. Will Alexander to Floyd Reeves, 20 June 1934, TVA Files; interview with J. Max Bond, Washington, D.C., 29 May 1975.

3. Interview with J. Max Bond; J. Max Bond, memorandum, November 1935, TVA Files.

4. J. Max Bond to Floyd Reeves, Gordon Clapp, and Maurice Seay, report, November 1935, TVA Files.

5. J. Max Bond to Floyd Reeves, memorandum, 15 November 1934, NAACP Papers, Library of Congress, Washington, D.C.

6. J. Max Bond to Gordon Clapp, report, 2 June 1937, TVA Files; Lloyd Huntington to Gordon Clapp, memorandum, 8 August 1938, TVA Files.

7. J. Max Bond to Rufus Clement, Louisville Municipal College, 25 February 1935, NAACP Papers; J. Max Bond to Walter White, 4 June 1935, NAACP Papers.

8. Bond to Clement, 25 February 1935, NAACP Papers.

9. J. Max Bond to Walter White, August 1935, NAACP Papers.

10. Bond to Clement, 25 February 1935, p. 2, NAACP Papers; interview with J. Max Bond.

11. O. W. Wheeler to J. Max Bond, 29 March 1935, TVA Files.

12. J. Max Bond to Charles Cowan, n.d. [1938], NAACP Papers; Charles Cowan to J. Max Bond, n.d. [1938], NAACP Papers; interview with J. Max Bond.

13. Rollins Winslow, "An Alley in the Valley," *Crisis* 44 (1937): 12–13; Rollins Winslow to J. Max Bond, January 1937, TVA Files; J. Max Bond to Rollins Winslow, 12 January 1937, TVA Files.

14. J. Max Bond to Gordon Clapp, 21 June 1937, NAACP Papers; TVA, "TVA's Employment of Negroes, 1933–1964," staff report, p. 49.

15. Interview with J. Max Bond. Bond stated forty years later that he had already decided to leave TVA because he felt that he was not utilized. The investigation of TVA was a convenient excuse to leave. Arthur Morgan was also told not to remove personal papers from his office after he was forced to resign as chairman in 1938. Morgan ignored the order and removed his papers to his farm in Ohio.

16. Charles Cowan to NAACP, n.d. [1938], NAACP Papers; Gordon Clapp to Charles Houston, 29 September 1938, NAACP Papers. As in most job searches, there were accusations that some candidates were being given unfair advantages. A newspaper editor, Webster Porter, was accused of trying to "sell his race out" to get the job. Interview between J. Herman Daves and Dr. Charles Crawford, 13 February 1971, transcript, pp. 1–3, Oral History Research Office, Memphis State University, Memphis, Tennessee.

17. Memorandum, n.d. [November 1938], NAACP Papers; interview with J. Max Bond; interview with Walter Goldston, Muscle Shoals, Alabama, 10 March 1975.

18. Interview with J. Herman Daves, Knoxville, Tennessee, 4 February 1975; J. Herman Daves, "TVA and Negro Employment," *Journal of Negro Education* 24 (1955): 87–90.

19. J. Herman Daves to Malcolm Little, 13 April 1943, TVA Files; J. Herman Daves to George Gant, "Report on the Conference on Full Utilization of Negro Manpower in the War Effort," 30 December 1942, TVA Files.

20. Charles Cowan to NAACP, n.d. [1938], NAACP Papers; interview with J. Max Bond; interview with J. Herman Daves, 4 February 1975; interview with Walter Goldston; interview with B. A. Ward, Knoxville, Tennessee, 6 March 1975.

21. W. M. Tyler, W. L. McDavid, A. I. Thomas, Birdius Browne, J. D. Moore, and F. A. DeCosta, "Labor Relations in TVA," 15 October 1935, TVA Files; Negro Training Staff, report, 1 October 1935, TVA Files; anonymous report (member of Negro Training Staff), n.d. [1938], pp. 1–22, TVA Files.

22. Committee on Negro Training, "Special Considerations in Negro Training," 30 June 1938, TVA Files.

23. TVA, "TVA's Employment of Negroes, 1933–1964," staff report, pp. 14–15; Gordon Clapp to Floyd Reeves, 21 October 1935, TVA Files.

24. Interview with J. Max Bond.

25. J. Max Bond to Emily Clay, chairman of the executive committee, Interracial Cooperation Commission, 20 September 1937, TVA Files; interview with J. Max Bond.

26. Lloyd Huntington to Gordon Clapp, 18 March 1938, TVA Files; Interracial Committee, "Study of Conditions Involved in the Placement of Negroes at Hiwassee Dam and Guntersville Dam," n.d. [1938], TVA Files; Lloyd Huntington to Arthur S. Jandrey, 27 October 1939, TVA Files; Lloyd Huntington to Arthur S. Jandrey, 24 October 1940, TVA Files; George Gant to Lloyd Huntington, 7 July 1941, TVA Files.

27. Nancy Grant, "Equal Employment Opportunity in TVA 1955–1974," 1975, pp. 1–9, 20–24, TVA Files.

28. "Revision of Responsibilities for Negro Relations," 10 November 1942, p. 1, TVA Files; Malcolm Little, chief, Training Division, to W. J. McGlothlin, 7 July 1942, TVA Files.

29. Cranston Clayton, "The Negro in the TVA," *Opportunity* 12 (1934): 111–12.

30. Ibid.

31. Will Alexander to Howard Odum, 15 February 1934; Will Alexander to Howard Odum, 13 October 1934, Howard Odum Papers, Southern Historical Collection, University of North Carolina, Chapel Hill, N.C.

32. William Cole, "Appraisal of the Work of the Commission on Interracial Cooperation," 1942, pp. 1–31, ICC Papers, Trevor Arnett Library, Atlanta University, Atlanta, Ga. In 1935 TVA contributed $3,000 to the University of North Carolina so that it could conduct a survey of the needs of individuals living in the Catawba River Valley area of North Carolina. Members of the university faculty, in-

cluding associates of Odum, were hired by TVA as consultants on regional planning during the 1930s.

33. Will Alexander to Gordon Clapp, 9 October 1940, TVA Files.

34. Gordon Clapp to Will Alexander, 29 October 1940, TVA Files.

35. John P. Davis and Charles Houston, "Lily-White Reconstruction," *Crisis* 41 (1934): 290–291, 311.

36. Charles Houston and John P. Davis to NAACP, memorandum, 4 June 1935, NAACP Papers.

37. John P. Davis to Arthur Morgan, 2 May 1935, TVA Files; Arthur Morgan to John P. Davis, 31 May 1935, TVA Files.

38. Gordon Clapp to Floyd Reeves, 24 June 1935, TVA Files. Some in the NAACP had questioned the wisdom of sending Davis to TVA for a second visit. "The TVA authorities have great bitterness against Mr. Davis because of his article [in *Crisis*] which might mitigate against his securing full and frank statements from TVA officials." Rufus Clement to Walter White, 26 February 1935, NAACP Papers.

39. Clapp to Reeves, 24 June 1935, TVA Files.

40. Clement to White, 26 February 1935, NAACP Papers.

41. Clapp to Reeves, 24 June 1935, TVA Files.

42. Ibid.

43. Arthur Morgan to Harold Ickes, 19 July 1935, TVA Files.

44. Robert Weaver to Arthur Morgan, 12 November 1935, pp. 1–5, TVA Files.

45. Ibid. For a positive account of Ickes's role in the PWA and the impact of quotas on the hiring of black construction workers for that agency, see John B. Kirby, *Black Americans in the Roosevelt Era* (Knoxville: University of Tennessee Press, 1980), pp. 22–23. The PWA and the Resettlement Administration did not escape allegations of discrimination. Also see Leslie Fishel, Jr., "The Negro in the New Deal Era," in *The Negro in the Depression and War*, edited by Bernard Sternsher (Chicago: Quadrangle Books, 1969).

46. John P. Davis, "Worksheet on the Negro and the TVA," 30 August 1943, NAACP Papers.

47. "Davis Report," NAACP Press Release, 16 September 1935, NAACP Papers.

48. John P. Davis, "The Plight of the Negro in the TVA," *Crisis* 42 (1935): 294–95, 314–15. Davis' conception of a new society, though not stated in detail, appeared to involve a socialist economy based on the government ownership of industry and the elimination of private ownership and competition. In 1935 he espoused change through evolutionary rather than revolutionary means.

49. Ibid.

50. Ibid., p. 314.

51. Ralph Bunche, "New Deal Social Planning as It Affects the Negro: A Critique," *Journal of Negro Education* 5 (1936): 59.

52. Davis, "The Plight," p. 314.

53. NAACP, *Annual Report* 25 (1935): 6; Raymond Wolters, *Negroes and the Great Depression* (Westport, Conn.: Greenwood Press, 1970), p. 336; Charles Houston to Walter White, 29 June 1935, NAACP Papers; Walter White to Charles Houston, 7 July 1935, NAACP Papers.

54. Gordon Clapp, "Analysis of the Report of the Chief Social and Economic Problems of Negroes in the TVA by John P. Davis," n.d., section on employment, pp. 2, 4, 16, TVA Files.

55. See for example L. N. Allen, "Analysis by Personnel Division of Report by John P. Davis," 29 May 1936, TVA Files.

56. Will Alexander to Floyd Reeves, 1935, TVA Files.

57. W. C. Sturdevant, director of Information Division, to Arthur Morgan, Harcourt A. Morgan, David Lilienthal, 5 July 1935.

58. For a detailed discussion of the Morgan-Lilienthal fight, see Thomas K. McCraw, *Morgan vs. Lilienthal: The Feud Within the TVA* (Chicago: Loyola University Press, 1970).

59. NAACP to H. Styles Bridges, Maury Maverick, Texas, Bertrand Snell, New York, and Vic Donahey, Ohio, press release, 4 March 1938, NAACP Papers; NAACP to Senator Vic Donahey, telegram, July 1938, NAACP Papers; Charles Houston, memorandum, 10 June 1938, NAACP Papers.

60. Charles Houston to NAACP Branches, memorandum, 6 April 1938.

61. Walter White to Henry Hunt, 28 March 1938, NAACP Papers; Burton Zien to Charles Houston, n.d. [1938], NAACP Papers; Charles Houston to NAACP, memorandum, 27 July 1938, NAACP Papers.

62. Charles Houston to NAACP, memorandum, 8 August 1938, NAACP Papers.

63. James Mead to Roy Wilkins, n.d. [1938], NAACP Papers; Roy Wilkins to Charles Houston, memorandum, n.d. [1938], NAACP Papers.

64. Charles Houston to NAACP, memorandum, 10 August 1938, NAACP Papers; Charles Houston to NAACP, memorandum, 13 August 1938, NAACP Papers.

65. Charles Houston to NAACP, memorandum, 16 August 1938, NAACP Papers.

66. U.S. Congress, Joint Committee on the Investigation of the Tennessee Valley Authority, *Hearings Before the Joint Committee on the Investigation of the Tennessee Valley Authority*, 75th Cong., 3rd sess., 1938, pt. vi, pp. 2348–84; Charles Houston, "Proposed Testimony Before Joint Committee, 17 August 1938," abstract, TVA Files.

67. *New York Times*, 31 August 1938.

68. Charles Houston to NAACP, memorandum, 18 August 1938, NAACP Papers.

69. "TVA Calls Negroes to Tell of Treatment," *Chattanooga News*, 7 September 1938; testimony of Wallace Butler and James Lee Hawkins Before the TVA Chickamauga Investigating Committee, 7 September 1938, pp. 7–75, TVA Files,

also in NAACP Papers; Gordon Clapp, "Report on the Hearings at Chickamauga Dam Site," 17 October 1938, pp. 27–28, TVA Files.

70. NAACP to *Pittsburgh Courier, Baltimore Afro-American, Chicago Defender*, telegrams, 9–11 August 1938, NAACP Papers; Charles Houston to NAACP, memorandum, 18 August 1938, NAACP Papers.

71. [Walter White] to George Fort Milton, 13 September 1938, NAACP Papers.

72. NAACP press release, New York, 7 April 1939, NAACP Papers.

73. Charles Cowan to Charles Houston, 1 September 1938, NAACP Papers; B. B. Evans to William Pickens, 1934, NAACP Papers. Very few copies remain of the three black newspapers of the 1930s: the *East Tennessee News*, the *Flashlight Herald*, and the *Public Guide*.

74. Norman T. Thomas to Roy Wilkins, president of the Tri-Cities Branch, NAACP, 10 June 1939, NAACP Papers. Although most of the members were women, the president was a non-TVA-affiliated male. The Knoxville TVA employee experienced no pressure against joining the NAACP. Interview with J. Max Bond.

75. C. C. Spaulding to John Blandford, general manager, 12 November 1937, TVA Files; John Blandford to C. C. Spaulding, 6 December 1937, TVA Files; J. A. Thomas, executive secretary, Louisville Urban League, to John Blandford, 17 August 1938, TVA Files; John Blandford to J. A. Thomas, 12 September 1938, TVA Files.

76. Charles Cowan to Charles Houston, 25 May 1937, TVA Files. The members of the Knoxville committee were N. A. Henderson, M.D., chairman; H. M. Green, M.D.; Charles Cowan, attorney; Louis McDade, TVA employee; J. Herman Daves, Knoxville college professor; and C. W. Cunsler, TVA employee.

77. Ibid.

78. J. Max Bond to Malcolm Dill, 22 December 1937, TVA Files; A. B. Reed, Boy Scouts of America, Negro Committee, to John Blandford, 5 July 1938, TVA Files; Mattie Miller, Phyllis Wheatley Branch YWCA, to John Blandford, 22 July 1938, TVA Files; Charles Cowan to Charles Houston, 24 September 1937, NAACP Papers; Charles Cowan to Civic Committee, 15 August 1937, NAACP Papers.

79. Charles Cowan to Charles Houston, 26 November 1937, NAACP Papers.

80. L. N. Allen to N. A. Henderson, 17 June 1939, TVA Files.

81. Charles Cowan to Charles Houston, 24 June 1938, NAACP Papers; Earl S. Draper to N. A. Henderson, n.d., NAACP Papers.

82. Gilbert Govan, *The Chattanooga County 1540–1976* (Knoxville: University of Tennessee Press, 1977), pp. 457–58; National Urban League, "A Study of Economic and Cultural Activities of the Negro Population of Chattanooga" (1947), pp. 182–83; interview with George Key, 20 August 1982.

83. National Urban League, "Study," pp. 56–57; *Chattanooga Free Press*, 3 June 1939; interview with George Key.

84. Interview with J. Max Bond. Bond stated that Lilienthal's secretary was an NAACP supporter.

85. A copy of Clapp's "Analysis" is available in the NAACP Papers, 1938.

86. Gordon Clapp to T. B. Parker, memorandum, 14 July 1942, TVA Files.

87. George Tindall, *The Emergence of the New South 1913–1945* (Baton Rouge: Louisiana State University Press, 1967), pp. 285–317; H. L. Mencken, *Americana —1925* (New York: Knopf, 1925).

88. Donald Davidson, *The Tennessee*, 2 vols. (New York: Rinehart, 1948), 2: 121–24; Donald Davidson, "Political Regionalism and Administrative Regionalism," *Annals of the American Academy of Political and Social Science* 207 (January 1940).

89. James Dahir, *Region Building* (New York: Harper Brothers, 1955), pp. 113–15.

CHAPTER VI

1. "Reaffirming Policy of Full Participation in the Defense Program by All Persons, Regardless of Race, Creed, Color or National Origin and Directing Certain Action in Furtherance of Said Policy," Executive Order 8802, 25 June 1941, TVA Files, Knoxville, Tennessee.

2. "Proposal of Negro March on Washington Committee to President Roosevelt," 18 June 1941, Franklin D. Roosevelt Papers, Franklin Roosevelt Presidential Library, Hyde Park, New York.

3. John A. Davis to Malcolm Ross, "Has the Job Which FEPC Has Done Been Without Sanctions?" 14 March 1945, FEPC Papers, National Archives, Washington, D.C. In July 1948 Harry Truman issued Executive Order 9981, which desegregated the armed forces. Compliance was sporadic and gradual. Segregated units remained throughout the Korean War.

4. A. Philip Randolph, "Why Should We March?" *Survey Graphic* (1942): 488–89. For a history of the March on Washington movement, see Herbert Garfinkel, *When Negroes March: The March on Washington Movement in the Organizational Politics for FEPC* (Glencoe, Ill.: Free Press, 1959).

5. George Marshall, National Federation for Constitutional Liberties, to Sam Rayburn, House of Representatives, 28 December 1943, FDR Papers; Herbert Hill, *Black Labor and the American Legal System* (Madison: University of Wisconsin Press, 1984), pp. 230–32. In 1943 the Smith Committee seized the records of the FEPC. It also heard testimony from railroad companies and unions, which complained that the FEPC had condemned their practices unfairly and did not have jurisdiction over them.

6. Mark Ethridge to Stephen Early, secretary to President Roosevelt, 20 August 1941, FDR Papers; John Owens, Los Angeles Forum, to Franklin Roosevelt, 28 December 1943, FDR Papers. Ethridge stated before a southern business audience that "all the armies of the Allies and all of the armies of the Axis Powers could not make the South accept the Negro socially." Quoted in Louis Ruchames, *Race, Jobs, and Politics* (New York: Columbia University Press, 1953), p. 29.

7. John A. Davis to Malcolm Ross, 13 March 1945, FEPC Papers.

8. Ibid.

9. Dorothy Newman, Nancy Amidei, Barbara Carter, et al., *Protest, Politics, and Prosperity* (New York: Pantheon, 1978), pp. 99–107. Also see William Bradbury, "Racial Discrimination in Federal Employment," n.d., in the files of the President's Committee on Government Employment Policy, National Archives, Washington, D.C.

10. Memorandum, White House, "Employment of Negroes in the Federal Government," 3 September 1941, TVA Files. For a detailed analysis of the function of the fair employment officer in TVA from 1945 to 1975, see Nancy Grant, "Equal Employment Opportunity in TVA 1955–1974," 1975, chap. I, pp. 2–14, TVA Files.

11. Lawrence Cramer to George Gant, October 1941, TVA Files.

12. George Gant to Lawrence Cramer, 5 December 1941, TVA Files.

13. Gant to Cramer, 5 December 1941, TVA Files; Lawrence Cramer to George Gant, 17 April 1942, TVA Files; David Lilienthal to George Johnson, assistant executive secretary, FEPC, 11 May 1942, TVA Files.

14. George Gant to Lawrence Cramer, 8 May 1942, TVA Files.

15. Gant to Cramer, 5 December 1941, TVA Files.

16. Clarence Mitchell to George Johnson, 23 December 1942. Mitchell was promoted to associate director of FEPC in May 1943 and went on to serve as the director of the NAACP Washington bureau from 1950 to 1978.

17. Memorandum, War Department to All Liaison Officers, 10 September 1942, FEPC Papers; Wilfred Leland, "Employment of Special Labor Groups," report, n.d., p. 6, FEPC Papers.

18. FDR to William Knudsen, Office of Production Management, 12 May 1941, FEPC Papers; William Knudsen to FDR, 28 May 1941, FEPC Papers.

19. Eli Cohen, Coordinating Committee of Jewish Organizations, to Lawrence Cramer, 24 June 1943, FEPC Papers; George Gant to Stuart Rae, Bureau of the Budget, 4 September 1943, FEPC Papers; E. B. Schultz to George Gant, 20 April 1945, TVA Files; George Gant to Witherspoon Dodge, regional director, FEPC, 24 April 1945, TVA Files. In 1955 TVA reasoned that arguments for maintaining racial identification were outweighed by the possible negative implications; see Gertrude Ford to Francis Shirley, Personnel Records, "Removal of Race from TVA Application Forms," 17 May 1955, TVA Files.

20. Lawrence Cramer to David Lilienthal, 5 April 1943, TVA Files; FEPC, "The Employment of Negroes in the Federal Government," report, 1943, pp. 2–6, TVA Files.

21. FEPC, "Employment of Negroes," p. 4, TVA Files.

22. Gordon Clapp to T. B. Parker, 14 July 1942, TVA Files.

23. Malcolm Little, chief, Training Division, to W. J. McGlothlin, 7 July 1942, TVA Files.

24. George Slover to George Gant, 20 July 1943, TVA Files; George Gant to Arthur Jandrey, 6 May 1942, TVA Files; TVA, "TVA's Employment of Negroes, 1933–1964," staff report, appendix C, TVA Files.

25. TVA, "TVA's Employment of Negroes, 1933–1964," appendix A, statistical table I. Statistics for employment were unreliable because of the great fluctuations in the size of the workforce during the dam-building period. For example, the FEPC noted that blacks constituted 5.9 percent of the total workforce in 1942, whereas the TVA's figure was 7.8 percent. John P. Davis contended that TVA deliberately inflated the percentage of its black employees. See Davis, "The Plight of the Negro in the TVA," *Crisis* 42 (1935): 294.

26. TVA employee to Roy Wilkins, executive secretary, NAACP, 1942, NAACP Papers, Library of Congress, Washington, D.C. This letter was handwritten on stationery from the Personnel Department. The letter was signed "as always——." The writer also stated that he had not shown it to J. Herman Daves. Other letters from the same person, all highly critical of TVA's racial policies, are in the NAACP Papers.

27. Grant, "Equal Employment Opportunity in TVA 1955–1974," chaps. 2–3.

28. Mark Ethridge to David Lilienthal, 29 June 1942, TVA Files.

29. Ina Sugihara, "Our Stake in a Permanent FEPC," *Crisis* 52 (1945): 14–15, 29; Newman et al., *Protest, Politics, and Prosperity,* pp. 11–13, 51; FEPC, "Final Report," 1946, FEPC Papers.

CHAPTER VII

1. See Paul Norgren and Samuel Hill, *Toward Fair Employment* (New York: Columbia University Press, 1964), pp. 180–92.

2. See Louis G. Kesselman, *The Social Politics of FEPC* (Chapel Hill: University of North Carolina Press, 1948), for an account of the lobbying efforts to create a permanent FEPC.

3. FEPC, "Final Report," 1946, FEPC Papers, National Archives, Washington, D.C.; Dorothy Newman, Nancy Amidei, Barbara Carter, et al., *Protest, Politics, and Prosperity* (New York: Pantheon, 1978), pp. 108–9; Michael Sovern, *Legal Restraints on Racial Discrimination* (New York: Twentieth Century Fund, 1966), pp. 15–17.

4. Newman et al., *Protest, Politics, and Prosperity*, pp. 110–11. Also see Nancy Grant, "Equal Employment Opportunity in TVA 1955–1974," 1975, TVA Files, Knoxville, Tenn.

5. W. I. McGlothlin, chief, Training and Education Relations Branch, to Harry Case, director of personnel, memorandum, 20 July 1948; Case to Gant, general manager, memorandum, 26 October 1948, TVA Files. Also see TVA, "TVA's Employment of Negroes, 1933–1964," staff report, statistical table 3, TVA Files.

6. Harry Case to James Houghteling, chairman, Fair Employment Board, 28 December 1951, TVA Files; J. Herman Daves, "TVA and Negro Employment," *Journal of Negro Education* 24 (1955): 87–90; interview with J. Herman Daves, Knoxville, Tennessee, 21 March 1975; interview with Alton Flagg, Knoxville, Tennessee, 4 March 1975.

7. John Olsen to Senator Paul Douglas, 10 October 1951, TVA Files.

8. Paul Evans, director of information, to Ken Moffet, editor, *Memphis Scimitar*, 1 March 1954, TVA Files. See also Hugh D. Graham, *Crisis in Print: Desegregation and the Press in Tennessee* for an account of the major events in the desegregation story in Tennessee.

9. Knoxville Area Urban League, "Report on Supervisory Training in Minority Employee Relations for TVA, January to April 1971," TVA Files; Lynn Seeber, general manager, memorandum to TVA employees, 9 May 1975, TVA Files; George White, director of EEO, to Lynn Seeber, "Situation Report," 1972, TVA Files. The problems of women were sporadically addressed during the first thirty years of TVA. In 1967 Executive Order 11375 provided for equality of opportunity on the basis of sex as well as race, color, religion, and national origin in government employment. A Federal Women's Program was established in TVA. In 1970 the EEO staff was expanded to include a Federal Women's Program coordinator. Complaints among white women were similar to those expressed by black men and women. Underutilization of skills, the closing of certain occupations to women, lack of promotions, and a generally low representation in the workforce were some of the complaints presented to the coordinator. See T. Graham Wells to John Massey, "Proposals on Federal Women's Programs in TVA," 11 June 1969, TVA Files.

10. Gordon Clapp stepped down from the chairmanship of TVA in 1953. His last official memorandum contained the following exhortation: "In the months and years ahead, don't let little minds or the greedy intimidate or enchant you or divert you from your service to the public interest." Quoted in Gordon Clapp, *The TVA: An Approach to the Development of a Region* (Chicago: University of Chicago Press, 1955).

11. Clapp, *The TVA*, pp. viii–xi.

12. Civil Service Commission, "Evaluation of Personnel Management," 3 October–16 December 1966, pp. 3–8, 20–27, TVA Files.

13. L. J. Van Mol to Hammond Smith, regional director, Civil Service Commission, 2 May 1967, TVA Files; Civil Service Commission Evaluation Report 1968, TVA Files.

14. Alton Flagg, personal files, Knoxville, Tenn.; interview with Alton Flagg; EEO Staff, "Negro Employees in TVA," 1968, TVA Files.

15. Civil Service Commission Evaluation Report 1968; interview with George White, director of EEO, July 1975, Knoxville, Tennessee.

BIBLIOGRAPHY

MANUSCRIPT COLLECTIONS

Atlanta, Georgia. Atlanta University. Trevor Arnett Library. Interracial Cooperation Commission Papers, 1930–1941.

Chapel Hill, North Carolina. University of North Carolina. Papers of the Institute for Research in the Social Sciences.

Chapel Hill, North Carolina. University of North Carolina. Southern Historical Collection. Howard Odum Papers.

Chattanooga, Tennessee. Chattanooga Public Library. Special Collections. National Urban League Papers.

Chicago, Illinois. University of Chicago. Regenstein Library. Special Collections. William F. Ogburn Papers.

Hyde Park, New York. Franklin Roosevelt Presidential Library. Franklin Roosevelt Papers.

Knoxville, Tennessee. Tennessee Valley Authority. TVA Files.

Knoxville, Tennessee. University of Tennessee. Harcourt A. Morgan Papers.

Nashville, Tennessee. Fisk University Library. Special Collections. Charles S. Johnson Papers.

Pocantico Hills, New York. Rockefeller Foundation Archives. Rockefeller Papers.

Washington, D.C. Library of Congress. NAACP Papers.

Washington, D.C. National Archives. Fair Employment Practices Committee Files.

BOOKS

Ames, Jesse Daniel. *The Changing Character of Lynching*. Atlanta: Commission on Interracial Cooperation, 1942.

Baker, Paul. *Negro-White Adjustment*. New York: Association Press, 1934.

Baldwin, Sidney. *Poverty and Politics: The Rise and Decline of the Farm Security Administration*. Chapel Hill: University of North Carolina Press, 1968.

Boas, Franz. *The Mind of Primitive Man*. New York: Macmillan, 1924.

Brooks, Lee M., ed. *Manual for Southern Regions by Howard Odum*. Chapel Hill: University of North Carolina Press, 1937.

Bunche, Ralph. *The Political Status of the Negro in the Age of FDR*. Edited by Dewey W. Grantham. Chicago: University of Chicago Press, 1973.

Burns, James MacGregor. *Roosevelt: The Lion and the Fox*. New York: Harcourt, Brace and World, 1956.

Burstein, Paul. *Discrimination, Jobs, and Politics: The Struggle for Equal Employment Opportunity in the United States Since the New Deal*. Chicago: University of Chicago Press, 1985.

Callahan, North. *TVA*. South Brunswick, N.J.: A. S. Barnes, 1980.

Carter, Jay Franklin. *The Future Is Ours*. New York: Modern Age Books, 1939.

Clapp, Gordon. *The TVA: An Approach to the Development of a Region*. Chicago: University of Chicago Press, 1955.

Conkin, Paul. *The New Deal*. New York: Crowell, 1967.

————. *Tomorrow a New World*. Ithaca, N.Y.: Cornell University Press, 1959.

Dahir, James, *Region Building*. New York: Harper Brothers, 1955.

Davidson, Donald. *The Attack on Leviathan: Regionalism and Nationalism in the United States*. Chapel Hill: University of North Carolina Press, 1938.

————. *The Tennessee*. 2 vols. New York: Rinehart, 1948.

Du Bois, William E. B. *The Autobiography of W. E. B. Du Bois*. New York: International Publishers, 1968.

Finer, Herman. *The T.V.A.* New York: Da Capo Press, 1972.

Franklin, John Hope. *From Slavery to Freedom*. New York: Knopf, 1967.

Friedman, John. *Planning in the Public Domain: From Knowledge to Action*. Princeton: Princeton University Press, 1987.

Garfinkel, Herbert. *When Negroes March: The March on Washington Movement in the Organizational Politics for FEPC*. Glencoe, Ill.: Free Press, 1959.

Hargrove, Edwin, and Conkin, Paul, eds. *TVA: Fifty Years of Grass Roots Bureaucracy*. Urbana: University of Illinois Press, 1983.

Hodge, Clarence. *The Tennessee Valley Authority*. Washington, D.C.: American University Press, 1938.

Hubbard, Preston J. *Origins of the TVA*. Nashville: Vanderbilt Press, 1938.

Huggins, Nathan. *Harlem Renaissance*. New York: Oxford University Press, 1971.

Huxley, Julian. *TVA: Adventure in Planning*. London: Architectural Press, 1943.

Jensen, Merrill, ed. *Regionalism in America*. Madison: University of Wisconsin Press, 1952.

Johnson, Guy. *Folk Culture on St. Helena Island, S.C.* Chapel Hill: University of North Carolina Press, 1930.

————. *John Henry: Tracking Down a Negro Legend*. Chapel Hill: University of North Carolina Press, 1929.

Johnson, Guy, and Odum, Howard. *The Negro and His Songs: A Study of Typical Negro Songs*. Chapel Hill: University of North Carolina Press, 1925.

Karl, Barry. *Charles E. Merriam and the Study of Politics*. Chicago: University of Chicago Press, 1974.

Keun, Odette. *A Foreigner Looks at the TVA*. New York, Toronto: Longmans, Green, 1937.

King, Richard. *A Southern Renaissance*. New York: Oxford University Press, 1980.

Kirby, John. *Black Americans in the Roosevelt Era*. Knoxville: University of Tennessee Press, 1980.

Kneebone, John T. *Southern Liberal Journalists and the Issue of Race, 1920–1944*. Chapel Hill: University of North Carolina Press, 1985.

Kreeger, Thomas. *And Promises to Keep*. Nashville: Vanderbilt University Press, 1967.

Lash, Joseph P. *Eleanor and Franklin*. New York: Norton, 1971.

Lawson, R. Allen. *The Failure of Independent Liberalism 1930–1941*. New York: Putnam, 1971.

Leuchtenburg, William. *Franklin D. Roosevelt and the New Deal 1932–1940*. New York: Harper & Row, 1963.

Lilienthal, David. *The Journals of David Lilienthal*. 4 vols. Vol. 1: *The TVA Years, 1939–1945*. New York: Harper & Row, 1964.

———. *TVA: Democracy on the March*. New York: Harper & Row, 1944.

Logan, Rayford, ed. *What the Negro Wants*. Chapel Hill: University of North Carolina Press, 1944.

McCraw, Thomas K. *Morgan vs. Lilienthal: The Feud Within the TVA*. Chicago: Loyola University Press, 1970.

———. *TVA and the Power Fight 1933–1939*. Philadelphia: J. B. Lippincott, 1971.

McDonald, Michael, and Muldowny, John. *TVA and the Dispossessed*. Knoxville: University of Tennessee Press, 1982.

McNeil, Genna Rae. *Groundwork: Charles Hamilton Houston*. Philadelphia: University of Pennsylvania Press, 1982.

Martin, Roscoe C., ed. *TVA: The First Twenty Years*. Knoxville: University of Tennessee and University of Alabama Press, 1956.

Mencken, H. L. *Americana—1925*. New York: Knopf, 1925.

Mertz, Paul E. *New Deal Policy and Southern Rural Poverty*. Baton Rouge: Louisiana University Press, 1978.

Metzger, L. Paul. *Educating the Disadvantaged*. Edited by Russell C. Doll and Maxine Hawkins. New York: AMS Press, 1971.

Minton, John Dean. *The New Deal in Tennessee 1932–1938*. New York: Garland Press, 1979.

Morgan, Arthur. *The Making of the TVA*. Buffalo, N.Y.: Prometheus Books, 1974.

Myrdal, Gunnar. *An American Dilemma*. 2 vols. New York: Harper & Row, 1944.

Nixon, Herman C. *The Tennessee Valley*. Nashville: Vanderbilt University Press, 1945.

Odum, Howard. *An American Epoch*. New York: Holt, 1930.

———. *Folk, Region, and Society: Selected Papers of Howard Odum*. Edited by Katherine Jocher, Guy Johnson, G. L. Simpson, and Rupert B. Vance. Chapel Hill: University of North Carolina Press, 1964.

———. *Race and Rumors of Race: Challenge to American Crisis*. Chapel Hill: University of North Carolina Press, 1943.

———. *Rainbow 'Round My Shoulder*. Indianapolis: Bobbs-Merrill, 1928.

————. *Social and Mental Traits of the Negro*. Studies in History, Economics and Public Law. New York: Columbia University, 1910.

————. *Southern Regions of the United States*. Chapel Hill: University of North Carolina Press, 1936.

————. *The Way of the South*. New York: Macmillan, 1947.

————. *Wings on My Feet: Black Ulysses at the Wars*. Indianapolis: Bobbs-Merrill, 1929.

Odum, Howard, and Jocher, Katherine. *In Search of the Regional Balance of America*. Chapel Hill: University of North Carolina Press, 1945.

Odum, Howard, and Moore, Harry Estill. *American Regionalism: A Cultural-Historical Approach to National Integration*. New York: Holt, 1938.

Odum, Howard, and Willard, D. W. *Systems of Public Welfare*. Chapel Hill: University of North Carolina Press, 1925.

Owen, Marguerite. *The Tennessee Valley Authority*. New York: Praeger, 1973.

Pritchett, Herman. *The Tennessee Valley Authority: A Study in Public Administration*. Chapel Hill: University of North Carolina Press, 1943.

Ransmeier, Joseph S. *The Tennessee Valley Authority*. Nashville: Vanderbilt Press, 1942.

Raper, Arthur F. *The Tragedy of Lynching*. Chapel Hill: University of North Carolina Press, 1933.

Raper, Arthur, and Reid, Ira D. *Sharecroppers All*. Chapel Hill: University of North Carolina Press, 1940.

Russell, Dean. *The TVA Idea*. Irvington-on-Hudson, N.Y.: Foundation for Economic Education, 1949.

Schlesinger, Arthur, Jr. *The Coming of the New Deal*. Boston: Houghton Mifflin, 1958.

————. *The Politics of Upheaval: The Age of Roosevelt*. Boston: Houghton Mifflin, 1960.

Selznick, Philip. *TVA and the Grass Roots*. New York: Harper & Row, 1966.

Singal, Daniel Joseph. *The War Within: From Victorian to Modernist Thought in the South, 1919–1945*. Chapel Hill: University of North Carolina Press, 1982.

Sitkoff, Harvard. *A New Deal For Blacks*. New York: Oxford University Press, 1978.

————, ed. *Fifty Years Later: The New Deal Evaluated*. New York: Knopf, 1985.

Smith, Frank E. *Politics of Conservation*. New York: Pantheon, 1966.

Sosna, Morton. *In Search of the Silent South: Southern Liberals and the Race Issue*. New York: Columbia University Press, 1977.

Southern Regional Council. *The Southern Regional Council: Its Origin and Purpose*. Atlanta: Southern Regional Council, 1944.

Sternsher, Bernard, ed. *The Negro in the Depression and War*. Chicago: Quadrangle Books, 1961.

Tindall, George. *The Emergence of the New South 1913–1945*. Baton Rouge: Louisiana State University Press, 1967.

Turner, Frederick Jackson. *The Frontier in American History*. New York: Holt, Rinehart and Winston, 1962.

Turner, William H., and Cabbell, Edward J., eds. *Blacks in Appalachia*. Lexington: University of Kentucky Press, 1985.

Twelve Southerners. *I'll Take My Stand: The South and the Agrarian Tradition*. New York: Harper & Row, 1930.

Vance, Rupert. *The Collapse of Cotton Tenancy*. Edited by Charles Johnson, Edwin Embree, and Will Alexander. Chapel Hill: University of North Carolina Press, 1935.

———. *Human Geography of the South*. Chapel Hill: University of North Carolina Press, 1932.

———. *Rural Relief and Recovery*. Chapel Hill: University of North Carolina Press, 1939.

———. *The South's Place in the Nation*. Washington, D.C.: Public Affairs Commission, 1936.

Van Sickle, John V. *Planning for the South: An Inquiry Into the Economics of Regionalism*. Nashville: Vanderbilt University Press, 1943.

Weiss, Nancy. *Farewell to the Party of Lincoln: Black Politics in the Age of FDR*. Princeton: Princeton University Press, 1983.

Wilson, Marshall A. *Tales from the Grass Roots of TVA 1933–1982*. Knoxville: Wilson Press, 1982.

Wolters, Raymond. *Negroes and the Great Depression*. Westport, Conn.: Greenwood Press, 1970.

Woofter, T. J. *The Basis of Racial Adjustment*. Boston: Ginn, 1925.

———. *Negro Problems in the Cities*. New York: Doubleday, 1928.

———. *The Plantation South 1934–1937*. Washington, D.C.: Government Printing Office, 1940.

———. *Southern Population and Social Planning*. Chapel Hill: University of North Carolina Press, 1933.

ARTICLES

Auerbach, Jerold S. "New Deal, Old Deal, or Raw Deal: Some Thoughts on New Left Historiography." *Journal of Southern History* 35 (1969): 18–30.

Barde, Robert E. "Arthur E. Morgan, First Chairman of TVA." *Tennessee Historical Quarterly* 30 (1971): 299–314.

Barth, Ernest, and Noel, Donald. "Conceptual Frameworks for the Analysis of Race Relations: An Evaluation." *Social Forces* 50 (1972): 333–48.

Beard, Charles. Review of *The Frontier in American History*, by Frederick Jackson Turner. *New Republic*, 16 February 1921, pp. 349–50.

Bond, J. Max. "The Educational Programs for Negroes in the TVA." *Journal of Negro Education* 6 (1937): 144–51.

————. "The Training Program of the Tennessee Valley Authority for Negroes." *Journal of Negro Education* 7 (1938): 383–89.

Bossard, James H. S. "Sociological Fashions and Societal Planning." *Social Forces* 14 (1935): 186–93.

Bunche, Ralph. "New Deal Social Planning as It Affects the Negro: A Critique." *Journal of Negro Education* 5 (1936): 56–65.

Carstensen, Vernon. "The Development and Application of Regional-Sectional Concepts, 1900–1950." In *Regionalism in America*, edited by Merrill Jensen, pp. 99–118. Madison: University of Wisconsin Press, 1952.

Case, Harry. "Personnel Administration." In *TVA: The First Twenty Years*. Edited by Roscoe C. Martin. Knoxville: University of Tennessee and University of Alabama Press, 1956.

Clayton, Cranston. "The Negro in the TVA." *Opportunity* 12 (1934): 111–12.

Daves, J. Herman. "TVA and Negro Employment." *Journal of Negro Education* 24 (1955): 87–90.

Davidson, Donald. "Dilemma of Southern Liberals." *American Mercury* 31 (1934): 227–35.

————. "Howard Odum and the Sociological Proteus." *American Review* 8 (1937): 385–417.

————. "A Mirror for Artists." In *I'll Take My Stand: The South and the Agrarian Tradition.* New York: Harper & Row, 1930.

————. "Political Regionalism and Administrative Regionalism." *Annals of the American Academy of Political and Social Science* 207 (January 1940).

————. "Sociologist in Eden." *American Review* 8 (1936): 177–204.

————. "Where Regionalism and Sectionalism Meet." *Social Forces* 13 (1934): 23–31.

Davis, John P. "The Plight of the Negro in the TVA." *Crisis* 42 (1935): 294–95, 314–15.

————. "A Survey of Problems of the Negro Under the New Deal." *Journal of Negro Education* 5 (1936): 3–12.

————. "What Price National Recovery?" *Crisis* 40 (1933): 271–72.

Davis, John P., and Houston, Charles. "Lily-White Reconstruction." *Crisis* 41 (1934): 290–91, 311.

Draper, Earl S. "In TVA House." *Journal of Home Economics* 27 (1935): 632–36.

Du Bois, William E. B. "The Negro in the American Social Order: Where Do We Go from Here?" *Journal of Negro Education* 8 (1939): 551–70.

————. "Social Planning for the Negro, Past and Present." *Journal of Negro Education* 5 (1936): 110–25.

Eubank, Earle Edward. "Errors of Sociology." *Social Forces* 16 (1937): 178–201.

Fishel, Leslie, Jr. "The Negro in the New Deal Era." In *The Negro in the Depression and War*, edited by Bernard Sternsher. Chicago: Quadrangle Books, 1969. Originally published in *Wisconsin Magazine of History* 48 (1964–1965): 111–26.

Gavins, Raymond. "Gordon Blaine Hancock." *Journal of Negro History* 59 (1974): 207–27.

Harrison, Hazel. "The Status of the American Negro in the New Deal." *Crisis* 40 (1933): 256–62.

Heberle, Rudolf. "Regionalism: Some Critical Observations." *Social Forces* 21 (1943): 280–86.

Hertzler, I. O. "Some Sociological Aspects of American Regionalism." *Social Forces* 18 (1939): 17–29.

Hill, T. Arnold. "The Plight of Negro Industrial Workers." *Journal of Negro Education* 5 (1936): 40–47.

Holley, Donald. "The Negro in the New Deal Resettlement Program." *Journal of Agricultural History* 45 (1971): 174–93.

House, Floyd N. "Methods of Studying Race and Culture." *Social Forces* 15 (1936): 1–5.

Johnson, Guy. "Does the South Owe the Negro a New Deal?" *Social Forces* 13 (1934): 100–11.

———. "The Negro and the Depression in North Carolina," *Social Forces* 12 (1933): 103–15.

Kantor, Harvey A. "Howard W. Odum: The Implications of Folk, Planning and Regionalism." *American Journal of Sociology* 79 (1973): 278–95.

Karl, Barry. "Presidential Planning and Social Science Research." *Perspectives in American History* 3 (1969): 338–409.

Kollmorgen, Walter. "Political Regionalism in the United States: Fact or Myth?" *Social Forces* 15 (1936): 111–22.

Lepawsky, Albert. "Governmental Planning in the South." *Journal of Politics* 10 (1948): 536–67.

———. "The Progressives and the Planners." *Public Administration Review* 31 (1971): 297–303.

Leuchtenburg, William. "Roosevelt, Norris and the Seven Little TVA's." *Journal of Politics* 14 (1952): 418–41.

McCarthy, James R. "The New Deal in Tennessee." *Sewanee Review* 42 (1934): 408–14.

Mackintosh, Barry. "George Washington Carver: The Making of a Myth." *Journal of Southern History* 42 (1976): 509–28.

Milton, George Fort. "A Consumer's View of the TVA." *Atlantic Monthly* 160 (1937): 653–58.

Mood, Fulmer. "The Origin, Evolution, and Application of the Sectional Concept, 1750–1900." In *Regionalism in America*, edited by Merrill Jensen, pp. 5–98. Madison: University of Wisconsin Press, 1952.

Morgan, Arthur, "Bench Marks in the Tennessee Valley." *Survey Graphic* 23 (1934): 548–52.

Nixon, Herman C. "Whither Southern Economy?" In *I'll Take My Stand: The South and the Agrarian Tradition*. New York: Harper & Row, 1930.

Odum, Howard. "An Approach to Diagnosis and Direction of the Problem of Negro Segregation in the Public Schools of the South." *Journal of Public Law* 3 (1954): 8–37.

———. "A Case for Regional-National Social Planning." *Social Forces* 13 (1934): 6–23.

———. "Errors of Sociology." *Social Forces* 15 (1936): 327–42.

———. "Negro Children in the Public Schools of Philadelphia." *Annals of the American Academy of Political and Social Science* 49 (1913): 186–208.

———. "The Position of the Negro in the American Social Order in 1950." *Journal of Negro Education* 8 (1939): 587–594.

———. "Regionalism vs. Sectionalism in the South's Place in the National Economy." *Social Forces* 12 (1934): 338–54.

———. "Religious Folk Songs of the Southern Negroes." *American Journal of Religious Psychology and Education* 3 (1909): 265–365.

———. "Standards of Measurement for Race Development." *Journal of Race Development* 5 (1915): 364–83.

Ogburn, William. "Does It Cost More to Live in the South?" *Social Forces* 14 (1935): 211–31.

———. "Regions." *Social Forces* 15 (1936): 6–11.

Parman, Donald. "The Indian and the Civilian Conservation Corps." *Pacific Historical Review* 40 (1971): 39–56.

Randolph, A. Philip. "The Trade Union Movement and the Negro." *Journal of Negro Education* 5 (1936): 54–58.

Raper, Arthur. "Gullies and What They Mean." *Social Forces* 16 (1937): 201–7.

Ray, Joseph. "The Influence of TVA on Government in the South." *American Political Science Review* 43 (1949): 922–32.

Reeves, Floyd. "Rural Education Problems in Relation to New Trends in Population Distribution." *Social Forces* 14 (1935): 7–16.

Salmond, John A. "The Civilian Conservation Corps and the Negro." *Journal of American History* 52 (1965): 75–88.

Satterfield, M. Harry. "The Removal of Families from the TVA Reservoir Areas." *Social Forces* 16 (1937): 258–61.

Shapiro, Edward. "The Southern Agrarians and the TVA." *American Quarterly* 22 (1970): 791–805.

Simkins, Frances Butler. "The South." In *Regionalism in America*, edited by Merrill Jensen, pp. 147–71. Madison: University of Wisconsin Press, 1952.

Thomas, Jesse O. "Will the New Deal Be a Square Deal for the Negro?" *Opportunity* 11 (1933): 308–11.

Tindall, George. "The Significance of Howard Odum to Southern History: A Preliminary Estimate." *Journal of Southern History* 24 (1958): 285–307.

Tugwell, Rexford, and Banfield, E. C. "Grass Roots Democracy." *Public Administration Review* 10 (1950): 47–55.

Vance, Rupert. "Howard Odum's Technic Ways: A Neglected Lead in American Sociology." *Social Forces* 50 (1972): 456–61.

————. "The Regional Concept as a Tool for Social Research." In *Regionalism in America*, edited by Merrill Jensen, pp. 119–23. Madison: University of Wisconsin Press, 1952.

————. "What of Submarginal Areas in Regional Planning?" *Social Forces* 12 (1934): 315–29.

Wengert, Norman. "Antecedent of TVA: The Legislative History of Muscle Shoals." *Journal of Agricultural History* 26 (1952).

————. "TVA, Symbol and Reality." *Journal of Politics* 13 (1951): 369–92.

Wiersema, Harry. "The River Control System." In *TVA: The First Twenty Years*, edited by Roscoe C. Martin, Knoxville: University of Tennessee and University of Alabama Press, 1956.

Winslow, Rollins. "An Alley in the Valley." *Crisis* 44 (1937): 12–13.

Wirth, Louis. "Localism, Regionalism, and Centralization." *Journal of American Sociology* 42 (1937): 493–509.

Woofter, T. J. "Difficulty in Measuring Racial Mental Traits." *Social Forces* 13 (1935): 415–18.

————. "Southern Population and Social Planning." *Social Forces* 14 (1935): 16–22.

————. "The Subregions of the Southeast." *Social Forces* 13 (1934): 43–50.

————. "The Tennessee Valley Regional Plan." *Social Forces* 12 (1934): 329–38.

Wye, Christopher. "The New Deal and the Negro Community." *Journal of American History* 59 (1972): 621–39.

REPORTS AND DOCUMENTS

Institute on Southern Regional Development and the Social Sciences. *Findings of the Committee on Coordination of Work Between Negro and White Institutions, 17–27 June 1936.* Chapel Hill: Institute on Southern Regional Development and the Social Sciences, 1936.

National Association for the Advancement of Colored People. *Annual Report* 25 (1935); 28 (1938).

National Emergency Council. *Report on Economic Conditions of the South.* Washington, D.C.: Government Printing Office, 1938.

National Resources Committee. *Regional Factors in National Planning.* Washington, D.C.: Government Printing Office, 1935.

National Resources Planning Board. *National Resources Development Report, 1943.* Washington, D.C.: Government Printing Office, 1943.

————. *Regional Development Plan Report for 1942.* Washington, D.C.: Government Printing Office, 1942.

————. *Security, Work, and Relief Policies, 1943.* Washington, D.C.: Government Printing Office, 1942.

President's Research Committee Report on Recent Social Trends. By Wesley Mitchell, chairman. New York: McGraw-Hill, 1933.

Franklin D. Roosevelt. Message to Congress on Muscle Shoals Development. House Document 15, 73rd Cong., 1st sess., 10 April 1933.

Tennessee Valley Authority. *Employee Relationship Policy.* Knoxville: Tennessee Valley Authority, 1940. Originally published 1934.

U.S. Congress. Joint Committee on the Investigation of the Tennessee Valley Authority. *Hearings Before the Joint Committee on the Investigation of the Tennessee Valley Authority,* 75th Cong., 3rd sess., 1938.

———. *Congressional Record,* vol. 77, pt. 2, 73rd Cong., 1st sess., 1933.

———. House Committee on Military Affairs. Report 48, 73rd Cong., 1st sess., 20 April 1933.

———. House Report 130, 73rd Cong., 1st sess., 1933.

U.S. Government. Executive Order 6161, 18 June 1933.

———. Executive Order 8802, 25 June 1941.

INTERVIEWS

Bond, J. Max. Washington, D.C., 29 May 1975.

Cain, Henry. Muscle Shoals, Alabama, 10 March 1975.

Copeland, Isaac. Chapel Hill, North Carolina, 11 November 1974.

Daves, J. Herman. Knoxville, Tennessee, 4 February and 21 March 1975.

Durish, Laurence. Knoxville, Tennessee, 19 March 1975.

Flagg, Alton. Knoxville, Tennessee, 4 March 1975.

Goldston, Walter. Muscle Shoals, Alabama, 10 March 1975.

Grey, A. J. Knoxville, Tennessee, 6 March 1975.

Haskins, Burt. Knoxville, Tennessee, 21 February 1975.

Johnson, Guy. Chapel Hill, North Carolina, 13 November 1974.

Johnson, Herndon. Knoxville, Tennessee, 27 February 1975.

Key, George. Chattanooga, Tennessee, 20 August 1982.

Love, Willie. Knoxville, Tennessee, 13 February 1975.

Martin, Ralph. Knoxville, Tennessee, 14 February 1975.

Neergard, Joseph C. Knoxville, Tennessee, 20 February 1975.

Waldrep, A. J. Knoxville, Tennessee, 20 February 1975.

Ward, B. A. Knoxville, Tennessee, 6 March 1975.

Wiersema, Harry. Knoxville, Tennessee, 27 February 1975.

White, George. Knoxville, Tennessee, 19 March 1975.

Interview between J. Herman Daves and Dr. Charles Crawford, 13 February 1971. Transcript, Oral History Research Office, Memphis State University, Memphis, Tennessee.

Bibliography

NEWSPAPERS

Americus (Georgia) *Times Recorder*, 1934.
Chattanooga News, 1936–1938.
Chattanooga Times, 1934–1939.
Chicago Defender, February 1933–December 1938.
Knoxville Journal, January 1933–1939.
Knoxville News-Sentinel, 1933–September 1935.
New York Age, 1932–1937.
New York Times, September 1932–November 1943.
Pittsburgh Courier, 1932–1938

DISSERTATIONS

Benincasa, Frederick A. "An Analysis of the Historical Development of the Tennessee Valley Authority from 1933–1961." Ph.D. dissertation, St. John's University, New York, 1961.

Bennett, James D. "The Tennessee Valley Authority and the New Deal." Ph.D. dissertation, Vanderbilt University, 1961.

Kirby, John Byron. "The New Deal Era and Blacks: A Study of Black and White Race Thought 1933–1945." Ph.D. dissertation, University of Illinois, Urbana, 1971.

Minton, John Dean. "The New Deal in Tennessee 1932–1938." Ph.D. dissertation, Vanderbilt University, 1959.

Satterly, Kenneth R. "Donald Davidson, Southern Regionalism and the TVA." Ph.D. dissertation, Brown University, 1973.

Southern, David W. "*An American Dilemma* Revisited: Myrdal's Study Through a Quarter Century." Ph.D. dissertation, Emory University, 1971.

INDEX